THE **Ibanez**
ELECTRIC
GUITAR
BOOK

Steve Vai with Ibanez Universe guitar, 1990

TONY BACON

THE Ibanez ELECTRIC GUITAR BOOK

A COMPLETE HISTORY OF IBANEZ ELECTRIC GUITARS

THE IBANEZ ELECTRIC GUITAR BOOK
A COMPLETE HISTORY OF IBANEZ ELECTRIC GUITARS
TONY BACON

A BACKBEAT BOOK
First edition 2013
Published by Backbeat Books
An Imprint of Hal Leonard Corporation
7777 West Bluemound Road,
Milwaukee, WI 53213
www.backbeatbooks.com

Devised and produced for Backbeat Books by
Outline Press Ltd
2A Union Court, 20-22 Union Road,
London SW4 6JP, England
www.jawbonepress.com

ISBN: 978-1-61713-453-1

A catalogue record for this book is available from the British Library.

DESIGN: Paul Cooper Design
EDITOR: Siobhan Pascoe

Printed by Everbest Printing Co. Ltd, China

13 14 15 16 17 5 4 3 2 1

Contents

THE IBANEZ ELECTRICS STORY

THE REFERENCE LISTING

"My ideas had merit to them – but I don't make guitars, and Ibanez do. They promised to make something I could be proud of, and I was. And I still am."

GEORGE BENSON, ON HIS IBANEZ SIGNATURE MODELS

THE
Ibanez
Electrics
STORY

ONE DAY IN SUMMER 1987, Steve Vai stepped into a warehouse in Philadelphia. Lined up across the floor, in row after row, were 777 identical guitar cases. Vai caught his breath in disbelief, although he knew exactly what he was there to do. In each case was a limited-edition Ibanez Steve Vai model, the JEM777, a shocking dayglo creation in Loch Ness Green, with yellow knobs and pink pickups, a handle-hole in the body, and pyramid-shaped fingerboard inlays. And now Vai had to sign and number every one. Rich Lasner from Ibanez handed him a fistful of permanent markers, and Vai crouched down to start the job at JEM number one. Lasner looked around and suffered his own moment of disbelief. How on earth were they going to sell all these mad-looking guitars? Would they prompt Ibanez's final plunge into guitar-making oblivion?

banez had experienced several shifts in fortune in the 30 years or so since the name first appeared on electric guitars, but this was a make or break moment. No one knew then that the Japanese parent company Hoshino and its US offshoot would build on the success of the JEM and its derivative, the RG, to steer Ibanez to new levels of international success.

The brand itself was an old Spanish name that went back to classical guitars made by Salvador Ibáñez of Valencia starting in the 1870s. Hoshino was the Japanese importer of those guitars, and later it applied the name to its own instruments. The origins of the Japanese firm go back to the years around 1900, when Matsujirou Hoshino started the family business in Nagoya, about 175 miles west of Tokyo. He opened a store there where he sold books and stationery. In February 1908, he added a section for musical instruments – mostly organs at first – run by his son, Yoshitarou, who later set up Hoshino Gakki Ten, the "Hoshino Musical Instrument Store" company.

The great Spanish classical guitarist Andrés Segovia performed in Japan for the first time in 1929, and his visit inspired many Japanese to take up the instrument. Yoshitarou, who by now had taken over the entire business from his father, began importing Salvador Ibáñez guitars that same year, to meet the demand from budding guitarists. Salvador Ibáñez himself was by now dead, but his sons continued to run the Valencia workshop until it was destroyed in the Spanish Civil War in the late 30s. Hoshino then adopted the name for itself, making acoustic guitars in Japan, at first branded as Ibanez Salvador and soon simply as Ibanez.

In 1939, Hoshino's factory was devastated by fire, and with Japan already involved in World War II in the Pacific, Hoshino soon stopped its musical business. Nagoya was bombed by American aircraft in 1944, and most of Hoshino's buildings, including the store, were destroyed in the attack. Following Japan's military defeat in 1945, it took the firm several years to return to some kind of stability. Sales began to pick up in the 50s as, ironically, military spending on the Korean War helped Japan's recovery. One prominent Japanese financier said that the Korean War provided more stimulus for Japanese economic resurgence than all the occupation efforts after World War II.[1]

Hoshino first began to offer electric guitars around 1957, with one eye on the domestic market, as rockabilly and rock'n'roll infiltrated Japan, and another on the growing demand in Europe and the United States. (This book is about Ibanez's electric guitars, so we won't go into detail about acoustics and bass guitars.) From about 1957 to the late 60s, Hoshino acquired its electric guitars from several sources. Hoshino made some itself, in a new factory set up in 1959, Tama Seisaku Sho. Yoshitarou Hoshino's son Masao Hoshino ran this, and Masao's brother, Junpei, became Hoshino's president in 1963. Hoshino contracted outside factories to make other electrics at this time, primarily Tokyo Sound (better known as Guyatone), Teisco Toyoshina (which also made for Teisco, Firstman, and many others), Kiso Suzuki Violin, and Kuroyanagi Gen Gakki.

Most of Hoshino's customers for electric guitars wanted their own brandnames applied to the instruments. These included Antoria and Star in the UK and Maxitone and Montclair in the USA, among quite a few others, but a number of guitars did have Ibanez on them. Some overseas customers may have bought instruments direct from one of the factories rather than deal through Hoshino – for example the Guyatone-made LG models sold in the USA by Buegeleisen & Jacobson (as Winston) and in the UK by Arbiter (as Guyatone) and J.T. Coppock (as Antoria). One of these Coppock-imported Antoria guitars was played in Britain by a young Hank Marvin, later of The Shadows. Viewed from today, this is a puzzling scene, with a bewildering array of often interrelated factories and sales agents and distributors and brandnames.

The Hoshino electrics of the late 50s and the 60s were a mix of solidbody and hollow models. Some of the solids had design features loosely borrowed from American Fender or British Burns guitars, while the hollows were often an amalgam of Gibson and other styles. They were not exactly copies, because they were not intended to duplicate every detail of an existing model. Instead, they were more like Japanese interpretations of Western designs, with little added twists of Eastern taste. They were basic, quirky, and of their time, and they provided a good number of starting-out players with their first taste of a cheap electric guitar.

In the United States, one of the first to do business with Hoshino was Harry Rosenbloom, who ran a thriving store, Medley Music, in Ardmore, on the north-west outskirts of Philadelphia, Pennsylvania. Rosenbloom not only sold famous-brand instruments, just like every other retailer, but also he had his own Elger-brand acoustic guitars made locally, and he imported musical goods, principally from Japan but also from Europe – for example, he brought in Schaller tuners from Germany. "Most retailers at the time were just that," Rosenbloom recalls, "they were merchants. But I was interested in every phase of it. Making my own guitars and importing goods myself – that was unusual, and that was part of the success of Medley Music."[2] Starting in 1959, not far from the Medley Music store, Rosenbloom had set up a German craftsman, Karl Muller, to build the Elger acoustics. Muller worked in a factory that once had been used to make aircraft propellers. It was a year or so after this that Rosenbloom began dealing with Hoshino, buying drums with Hoshino's Star brand and acoustic guitars with his own Elger brand. He came up with "Elger" by combining the names of his two children, Ellen and Gerson. Hoshino began to recognise an opportunity here to get more closely involved in the wider US instruments market, and soon they were discussing bigger plans – of which more shortly.

By now, pop music was fuelling a dramatically increased popularity for electric guitars. In the West, starting in the late 50s, budding musicians formed groups in the wake of successful role models like Buddy Holly & The Crickets in the USA and The Shadows in the UK. By the time the USA had experienced the so-called British invasion, which began in 1964, Japan enjoyed a US invasion spearheaded by The Ventures. The instrumental group from Washington was a sensation in Japan, playing concerts early in 1965, and a year later The Beatles toured. Local groups such as The Blue Jeans and Sharp Five were successful, too. Just as in the West, it seemed as if every Japanese teenager wanted to be in a group and play an electric guitar.

The electric guitar business in the USA during the early to mid 60s was centred on two big names, Gibson and Fender, along with secondary makers such as Gretsch, Harmony, Rickenbacker, Kay, Epiphone, and Guild. They all lined up to tempt guitarists with new ideas and fresh models. In Britain, real American guitars had only just become available as the 60s started because an import ban had been in place for most of the previous decade.

Some of the European names from that time, like Hofner, Framus, and Hagstrom, still held some sway, but most players wanted the real thing, even though homegrown brands such as Burns and Vox provided some decent competition.

Hoshino, meanwhile, decided to reorganise production at its new factory, presumably figuring that it could best supply the new demand for electric guitars by once more using other factories to produce and supply instruments. Around 1965, Hoshino stopped guitar manufacturing at its Tama factory, which concentrated on drums, and shifted to two main sources: Fujigen Gakki, which had recently set up its first proper guitar factory; and ex-Fujigen manager Tadashi Maruyama's Teisco Toyoshina. Maruyama's firm closed around 1970, and some of the workers from there moved on to Fujigen. Hoshino would never again have its own guitar factory, and technically it would remain a trading company – one which buys and sells products but does not manufacture itself.

Fuji Gen Gakki Seizou Kabushikigaisha – which translates as the Fuji Stringed-Instrument Manufacturing Corporation – was started by Yuuichirou Yokouchi around 1960. He had been a dairy farmer after World War II but set up Fujigen after meeting

Yutaka Mimura, a salesman, and they started the firm in a converted cowshed with five workers. For the first few months they made violins, but Fujigen produced its first guitar, a basic nylon-string acoustic, during 1960. In February 1963, Yokouchi and Mimura added electric guitars, and they began to export, usually applying the buyer's chosen brand to its various products. An early US buyer had Fujigen make Rodeo-brand electric guitars, for example.

The company built a new factory that was operational by 1965, based in Matsumoto, about 100 miles north-east of Hoshino's HQ in Nagoya. This beautiful region, sometimes called the Japanese alps, was home to many furniture makers and guitar builders. Fujigen quickly became a highly proficient guitar-maker and, from about 1970, became the main supplier of guitars to Hoshino. Over the coming years, the Fujigen factory would be a close and valuable partner in the developing story of Ibanez.

There was a change in the style of Hoshino's electric guitars that coincided with the move to Fujigen. They were becoming more like copies rather than guitars that were merely influenced by other makers. In visual style if not always in construction and fine detail, the electrics that Fujigen supplied to Hoshino were much closer to particular US guitar models. It was the start of what's since been called the copy-guitar era. Hoshino was not alone in this – most of the sizeable Japanese manufacturers were actively involved – and copying was hardly a new idea. Copying was everywhere, and always had been. In some Asian countries, in fact, copying was considered a culturally acceptable process, in contrast to the view in the West, where the law valued the ownership of designs through a legal system of patents and trademarks.

Japanese car makers, for example, started out by more or less blatantly copying Western designs. The early copies were hardly exact, and the best that could be said about those first faltering attempts was that they had a style all their own. The same might be said about the early Japanese copy guitars. But as we'll see, they didn't appear out of thin air. They were not made because someone at Fujigen or Hoshino or any of the other factories and sales agents simply decided it might be a nice idea to copy some American guitars. From the Japanese perspective, there were a number of sound business reasons for the move to copy guitars. And it was not a conspiracy from overseas: a lot of the initiative to make and develop the Ibanez copies came from the company's American and British distributors.

The first British distributor to buy Ibanez-brand guitars from Hoshino was Maurice Summerfield, who started doing business with the Japanese firm in 1964. Summerfield, a budding 24-year-old jazz guitarist in Newcastle Upon Tyne, north-east England, got chatting with the owner of Jeavons music store, where he went regularly to buy jazz records. Mr Jeavons was desperate to get hold of some cheap guitars to fill a growing demand from beginners who fancied themselves as the next Beatles. He knew that Summerfield and his family were in business as successful toy distributors and presumed that they had experience with importing from overseas. Japan was the obvious source for cheap goods. Jeavons asked Summerfield if he could help.

Summerfield got hold of a list of 20 or so Japanese music companies and wrote to the most likely candidates, asking for quotes on cheap steel-strung acoustic guitars. Four replied, including Hoshino Gakki Ten, and he ordered 500 guitars from each. Hoshino's invoice to Summerfield, dated September 24 1964, was for 500 pieces of "No. 9000 Ibanez Guitar" at £2/5s/7d each (£2.28, about £38 or $60 in today's money). They arrived on October 20, in plenty of time for Christmas. "We did well," Summerfield recalls with a smile. "We sold the 2,000 guitars very quickly, 500 apiece from those four people. We were selling sixpenny toys in those days, so to sell a £9/19s/6d guitar was quite something. We ordered another load – and the keenest suppliers were Hoshino and Kawai."[3]

Summerfield continued to buy Ibanez acoustics from Hoshino, and in 1970 he received his first electrics. Another UK distributor, J.T. Coppock, was already buying electrics from Hoshino, and Coppock used its own brands, Antoria and Cimar. Coppock had used the Antoria brand since the early 1900s on gramophones, accordions, and other musical gear, but it first turned up on electric guitars around 1959, on LG-style Guyatones, and then from about 1963 on the Hoshino-sourced electrics. Like many own-brand guitars that distributors bought from Hoshino, Antorias were very similar and in some cases identical to various Ibanez models.

Summerfield's first electrics from Hoshino were a trio catalogued in 1970 as Ibanez Model No. 1910 (a Yamaha SA30-like semi with basic vibrato), Model No. 1970 (a Fender Coronado-like semi with large scroll headstock), and Model No. 1453 (a Gibson ES-175-like hollowbody). From about 1973, Summerfield added the CSL brand for electrics alongside Ibanez, and also he added the Sumbro brand as a cheaper line below the Ibanez and CSL guitars.

Meanwhile, Hoshino was talking to Harry Rosenbloom at Elger in Ardmore, Philadelphia, about developing the Japanese company's presence in the USA. It was an obvious move: Hoshino wanted to control its own Ibanez brandname and, by creating its own distribution company, compete alongside other US distributors – while making a little more profit. At first, in 1968, Hoshino planned to set up a marketing and sales base in Texas with distributor C. Bruno in San Antonio. That idea failed, and a hook-up with Elger must have seemed the next logical choice. They knew Rosenbloom well, having worked with him since the early 60s, and his Elger Company was now Hoshino's exclusive US eastern-states distributor for Tama and Elger guitars, Elger banjos, and Star drums.

Looking back today, Rosenbloom recalls a meeting with Hoshino's principals, probably at an American trade show in 1972. "That was when we negotiated a joint venture," Rosenbloom says. "Hoshino was really looking to establish something in the States, and I was doing a lot of general importing at the time, so I had the facilities already there. It was a very inexpensive way for Hoshino to get into the United States. At that time they were just selling to the wholesalers." Hoshino acquired a US trademark for the Ibanez brand in July 1972, and toward the end of that year Hoshino and Elger set up their US partnership. They published their first joint American trade ads for Ibanez-brand guitars early in 1973, announcing "select dealerships available" and prominently featuring both company names: Hoshino Gakki Ten Inc of Higashiku, Nagoya, and Elger Company of Ardmore, PA.

Hoshino needed help finding those new dealers. "We travelled around and I introduced them to a lot of music stores I knew about," Rosenbloom says. "These stores had never seen a really good Japanese guitar, so they'd say oh, I don't know about that. We'd say, well, just take a look. And of course we had set them up beautifully, a lot better than how the first guitars had come through. We established a dealer network, working together. It was very primitive – but it worked." Rosenbloom says that Hoshino sent over from Japan what he describes as "a bunch of great key people to run the company."[4] He was always busy with his music store, so he let them get on with the Elger business.

First to arrive of these great key people were Fumio Katoh and Toshitsugu Tanaka. They were both in their early twenties and very excited to be sent to the USA by Hoshino. Like many Japanese who deal with American firms, they adopted Western forenames, becoming Fritz Katoh and Tom Tanaka. "It was a dream come true for me to go the USA," Katoh remembers today. "Although I did have one problem, because I had married in January 1971. But I travelled to America and I joined the Elger Company that August. Harry's 'warehouse' was in fact a normal house, and my first job was to clean up the basement, where there were many rat carcasses and a big broken bed. Eventually I cleared it so that we could store our acoustic and electric guitars there. Tom Tanaka took care of sales, Allan Silverberg was the bookkeeper, and I took care of the warehouse."[5]

Tom Tanaka had a slightly more circuitous route to Elger. He'd joined Hoshino in 1970 through family ties, and the firm promised to send him to the USA, where – as with all the Japanese "key people" who came over to America – he could absorb US business methods and learn to speak English. At first, in 1971, Hoshino packed Tanaka off to Targ & Dinner, one of its US wholesalers, in Chicago. "I was working in their computer room," he says, "punching in data, and in the evening I studied English conversation at a downtown school. But I had no chance to touch the instruments, because of union rules. So I asked Hoshino if I could work at a music shop, so that I could touch the instruments and meet some consumers. Harry Rosenbloom was so kind to accept me to work at his shop. At last, I had the opportunity to touch and even learn to repair Gibson, Fender, and other real instruments. It was so scary, but thrilling, too."

Tanaka chipped in to help search for stores to sell instruments for the new Hoshino/Elger setup. "I found them by checking the yellow pages," he recalls. "I travelled from the Boston area right down to Virginia and Chicago. I was kicked out from the best music store in Manhattan. Henry Goldrich, owner of Manny's, told me he had

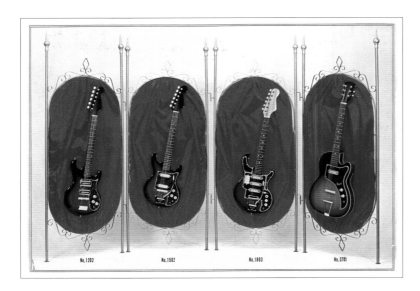

■ The Hoshino company began in Nagoya, Japan, with a **bookstore** (above), adding musical instruments in 1908. In 1929, Hoshino began importing **Salvador Ibáñez** classical guitars from Spain (example once owned by Eric Clapton, right) and later adopted the Ibanez brand for itself. Hoshino became a busy exporter, making some guitars itself and acquiring many others from various Japanese makers, selling instruments (1933 **catalogue cover**, right) to the United States, to Europe, and elsewhere. Electrics were added in the late 50s (**catalogue pages** from 1962, left, and 1960, opposite), including this **model 2103** (below). **Junpei Hoshino** (opposite, below) became president of Hoshino Gakki in 1963.

THE IBANEZ ELECTRIC GUITAR BOOK

Ibanez **PROFESSIONAL GRADE**

No. 3010 Cutaway electric guitar, Finished in similar with No. 2010, Pickguard pickup, 10 ft. cord, double control, standard plug. Carrying case model No. 400 or 450

No. 5070 Ibanez "PACIFIC" Single unit pickup, tone and volume control conveniently mounted for fast action. Artistically desinged and beautifully finished. Carrying case model No. 400 or 450

No. 5100 Ibanez "ATLANTIC" Electric spanish guitar with two unit pickups, Its beautiful appearance is highlighted by decoration accents on mahogany finish. Carrying case model No. 400 or 450

No. 3010   No. 5070   No. 5100

c.1880 Salvador Ibáñez

1964 2103

no intention to carry our guitars at his prestige store – although five years later he helped a lot with our business."[6]

Next to join the Elger operation from Japan was Ryoichi Miyahara, who arrived in October 1973 – and Ryoichi soon became Roy. He had been with Hoshino since 1968 and remembers working from the bottom up. "I knew all the processes and how things were done," he says. "They picked me to go to America and take care of the business, after Fritz Katoh had to come back. By the time I got there, Fritz was already back in Japan, replaced by Hiroshi 'Nero' Ando, and I worked with Tom Tanaka."

When Miyahara arrived, Elger was in the middle of moving across Philadelphia from the tiny basement in Ardmore to a new warehouse about 20 miles east, on the Bridgewater Industrial Park in Bensalem. Elger's press release described the new facilities as including offices, warehouse, showroom, and a repair centre. "It was a nice modern warehouse," Miyahara says. "We had to do everything, from sweeping the floors and doing all the paperwork, to unloading the containers when they arrived from Japan and inspecting and working on the guitars at the checking stations, as well as packing them for despatch."[7]

Rounding out the team was another new recruit, this time an American. Jeff Hasselberger was a budding young guitarist who started doing casual work at Rosenbloom's Medley Music store while still at university. Once he graduated, as an English major, he went to work for an ad agency, copywriting mainly for car companies, and then he left to go freelance. Rosenbloom got in touch again, probably early in 1973. He told Hasselberger about the new deal with Hoshino and asked for some marketing help. "I went to talk to them," Hasselberger remembers, "and I did a little ad for the trade magazines. We sent out some news releases, too, and we started getting the word out that there was this new company and they have this new brand, Ibanez."

At the end of '73, Hasselberger joined Elger full-time. "I decided to go full bore into the guitar thing," he says. "I had a band and I was playing, so I said yeah, what the hell. I still remember the first morning I showed up for work, at the new warehouse in Bensalem. One of the guys actually got up off the floor: I'd woken him up. He was sleeping there."[8]

Wide awake or not, the small team at the new Elger warehouse had their work cut out. And for electric guitars, their work now centred on the line of Ibanez copies that defined the look and style of the guitars offered by the new firm.

Sorting through the evidence from the early 70s and trying to construct a timeline of Ibanez's copy electrics is a frustrating experience today. The catalogues and pricelists that survive are sporadic and often undated, and press ads are rare. Then there are the numerous models that never appeared in any surviving catalogues. What we can say for sure is that Ibanez soon had an impressive line of copies, mostly based on Gibson originals and almost all with a bolt-on neck where the Gibson would have a glued-in (set) neck.

By about 1972, according to some catalogues there were five Les Paul copies: a two-pickup Custom finished in black or gold (model 2350); a Goldtop (2351); a Standard with sunburst finish (2351M; FG-360S in the UK); a Professional (2372); and a first-style Recording (2380). Alongside these were four SG copies: an SG Standard (2354); an SG Pro (2377); an SG Deluxe (2382); and a three-pickup SG Custom with gold-plated hardware (2383). There were three ES copies: a two-pickup ES-175 in sunburst or natural (2355); an ES-345 in cherry (2370); and an ES-335 with small-block markers, in rosewood finish (2374). There was also a Barney Kessel hollowbody electric in sunburst (2356).

Some non-Gibson copies made up the rest of the line by 1972: a Fender Telecaster in white (2352); an Epiphone Caiola in natural rosewood or maple finish (2358); a two-pickup double-cutaway thinline Gretsch-alike in sunburst (2362); a Dan Armstrong See-Through (2364); and a first-style Fender Telecaster Thinline (2368).

Jeff Hasselberger remembers that these early copies were quite well made but had what he calls "a lot of obvious mistakes" on them. For example, the Les Paul copies, beyond the inexactitude of their bolt-on necks, came with the ends of the fingerboards rounded off at the body. "Nobody had showed them that if you're going to copy a guitar, you might as well do it accurately," Hasselberger says. "That's where I got interested in the copies, in the detail area. It was really cool to see them make stuff that was very affordable for people – but with just a couple of fixes, they could be a lot cooler. And it wasn't because they couldn't do things, it was because they just didn't know, or weren't looking close enough, or just a cultural thing."[9] The fingerboard ends were soon squared off properly, and the Elger team set about showing them what else they were missing.

Roy Miyahara noticed some problems, too, with the early Les Paul copies coming in from Fujigen to Elger's HQ in Pennsylvania. "At that time, the most popular item was model 2350," he remembers. "But if a guitarist was used to playing a real Gibson Les Paul Custom, and then they tried this typical Japanese copy, well, it had a very high string action, and the sound didn't have that sustain. It was a cheaper sound. We requested that the factory change the setting of the bolt-on fitting, to sit the neck lower and give easier access to the higher register. I think that was a huge improvement, and some players said later that this was better than the original, even though it still had the bolt-on neck."

The team at Elger did a good deal of work setting up and generally improving the state of the individual guitars that arrived at the warehouse from Japan. Also, they continued to monitor the accuracy and general quality of the copies, comparing them to the real American guitars and noting the reactions of dealers and players. They regularly fed information and suggestions back to Hoshino and on to Fujigen, now firmly established as the main factory manufacturing the Ibanez guitars. At first this was a struggle, Miyahara says, because it was hard to make the factory understand what was needed. "They wanted to change, but they were not really ready with the techniques and

c.1973 2370 ES-345

THE IBANEZ ELECTRIC GUITAR BOOK

c.1973 2350 Les Custom

■ **Hoshino's HQ** remained in Nagoya (pictured in 1970, above), but in 1972 it began a joint venture in the USA with Elger in Philadelphia. Elger's boss **Harry Rosenbloom** is seen in the light suit (opposite) at a trade show with members of the Hoshino family. The **Elger offices** are pictured (alongside) in 1974, and (top) **Fritz Katoh**, **Kit Kitahara**, and **Roy Miyahara** pose outside with a double-neck copy. Katoh would become an important Ibanez designer, and Miyahara was a future Hoshino USA president. Copies of US guitars, and mainly Gibson models, defined the early Ibanez electric lines. Shown here are copies of a **Les Paul Custom**, an **ES-345**, and, on this 1972 **catalogue cover** (right), a **Barney Kessel** model. Catalogues often had logo-less guitars as some Hoshino customers wanted their own brands applied.

equipment they needed in order to change. We demanded so much, saying they had to change the production line because of quality issues – and, of course, at first they didn't want to do that. It was a constant battle. But in the end they always tried, because they agreed with Hoshino's direction of keeping the quality high."[10]

A review of one of Hoshino's Les Paul copies appeared in a British musicians magazine in 1973. Today we take such gear reviews for granted. Magazines have been doing them for years, and the internet provides a forum for anyone with an opinion, no matter how qualified to pass judgement. But back in the early 70s, reviews were almost non-existent. So the short piece in *Beat Instrumental* on a CSL 360S (known as the Ibanez 2386 in the USA at the time) was something of a rarity. "Excellent value for money – that's the verdict," wrote the anonymous reviewer about what he called "the latest and most sophisticated in an ever-increasing line of Japanese guitars".

This guitar was so obviously based on a real Gibson Les Paul that the reviewer said it was impossible not to make comparisons, and he noted differences such as the laminated body, which was thinner and lighter than the real thing, the reversed controls – tones at the front, volumes at the rear – and the bolt-on neck. "Although the pickups are designed on two-pole humbucking lines, they are not precisely balanced to give a smooth sustain," he wrote, highlighting one of the main weaknesses – the pickups – of the early copies.

Then came the inevitable and all-important price comparison: this copy could be yours for £82 "as opposed to around £300 for a good guitar". The body was "immaculately finished" in sunburst, and "though the sound lacks a little top, it's thick and meaty for the most part". The reviewer concluded his little test by calling the CSL 360S "a good rock machine".[11] Summerfield, the British distributor of CSL and Ibanez, must have been delighted. Selmer, the British distributor of Gibson, must have been horrified. *Beat Instrumental* made up for it the following month with a rave review of a real Gibson SG Standard.

Most of these early-70s Ibanez copies took their inspiration from currently available Gibson models of new or relatively recent style. Tom Tanaka says that Ibanez's competitors also tended to copy current models of Gibson and Fender. "But we found that some old and discontinued models of Gibson were played by famous musicians in bands like Led Zeppelin and the Eagles. So we introduced these old-model copies," Tanaka says, "which made Ibanez so popular among young guitarists."[12]

Some players were finding that older guitars seemed somehow better than the new ones made by the leading brands, and from the mid 60s this had led to a new focus on the classic old American electric designs. Eric Clapton was a highly visible and influential example of the trend. Gibson had introduced its solidbody electric Les Paul Model back in 1952, following the popularity of Fender's revolutionary solid Telecaster. In various guises, the Les Paul fared reasonably well for most of the 50s, but after a downturn in sales, Gibson discontinued the original single-cutaway design during 1960. In London in the summer of 1965, Clapton bought one of these discontinued Les Pauls – the now revered sunburst Standard model made between 1958 and 1960 – and soon he used it on the landmark John Mayall album *Blues Breakers*. On the rear of that record's jacket was a small black-and-white photo of Clapton tuning his Les Paul. Even though only part of the back of the instrument was visible, keen-eyed guitar fans knew exactly what it was, and it's arguable that this one picture began the whole old-guitar-is-better fashion.

Another factor was the takeover of several of the best-known American makers by large corporations. The CBS conglomerate, famous for its recording and television businesses, bought Fender in 1965. When Gibson's parent company CMI was taken over by ECL, an Ecuadorian brewing firm, the result was a new owner, Norlin, in 1969. D.H. Baldwin, which made pianos and organs, had bid unsuccessfully for Fender in '65 but managed to acquire the British maker Burns soon afterward, and in 1967, Baldwin also bought Gretsch. There was a growing impression among some players that these new owners were too big and too out of touch with musicians, and that as a result they were doing harm to the quality and integrity of their new charges.

"This new accent on old models became obvious to us," says Hasselberger. "We knew, from the music, if we saw Jimmy Page walk on stage with a Telecaster, or maybe Jeff Beck, we knew that's what we had to do at Ibanez, or if they came out with a Les Paul, then Les Pauls would be hot. I don't think Gibson and Fender were following those things closely or even knew who those people were in a lot of cases. You'd go to the Gibson party at the trade shows and it would be all their jazzer pals: Barney Kessel, Howard Roberts, those kind of guys."[13]

Despite the likes of Clapton, Page, Duane Allman, and others taking up old Les Pauls, Gibson waited until 1968 to reissue the design – and then not the precise models players wanted. Clapton soon became a star with Cream and moved into his subsequent solo work in the late 60s and early 70s, and he did more than any other guitarist to inspire the new interest in older instruments. Soon, dealers were calling them "vintage" guitars, adding a cachet to what used to be known simply as used or secondhand instruments. Original Les Pauls were a notable and visible part of the trend, but many players would happily settle for an old example of any of the classic American electrics, including Fender's Telecasters and Stratocasters, Gibson's ES-335s, Flying Vs, Explorers, and Firebirds, and various other models by Gretsch and Rickenbacker.

Ibanez's move to introduce copies of some of the classic oldies was a smart one, and it happened thanks to on-the-spot reconnaissance from a UK distributor as well as the Elger people in America. Maurice Summerfield in Britain recommended that Hoshino add to the line a copy of the Gibson Flying V, an old model recently given a low-key revival by Gibson. Just as with the original Les Pauls, a number of players had rediscovered the obsolete Vs and found them to be spectacular instruments. "Hoshino were interested and asked me if I could get one, so I bought a Flying V and sent it off to

Musical Merchandise

Hoshino Gakki Ten, Inc.

No. 4, 3-Chome, Shumokucho,
Higashiku, Nagoya, Japan.

c.1973 2377

No. 2351M

No. 2368

No. 2374

c.1973 2387 Rocket Roll

■ Copies continued to dominate the Ibanez lines through the mid 70s, and Gibson remained the main target. Hoshino's UK distributor **Maurice Summerfield** suggested copying a Flying V. The result was the **Rocket Roll** (main guitar), and Summerfield is pictured with one (opposite, top) at a British trade show in 1973. The **rocking V** graphic (opposite) was a feature of Elger notepaper. All Ibanez copies were given four-digit model codes: this **2377** (opposite) imitated a Gibson SG Pro. Two more Gibson copies from a **1974 catalogue** (above) are the **2351M** Les Paul and the **2374** Crest, as well as a **2368** Fender Telecaster Thinline. Swedish jazz guitarist **Rune Gustafsson** (right) appeared with a 2355 ES-175 copy on a **1973 catalogue cover**.

Japan," Summerfield recalls, "and soon they started making a copy. Then one of my salesmen said, well, they've been making such a good job of the Les Paul – have they thought of doing a twin-neck Gibson? So I bought one of those, too, and sent that to Japan. And it worked very well for them and very well for us."[14]

The Flying V copy that Ibanez launched in 1973 was based on the early-70s guitar that Summerfield provided. This differed from Gibson's 50s original, having a mahogany body and neck, a large white pickguard, and three knobs in triangular formation. Ibanez did a reasonable copy, at first with its regular bolt-on neck of the period, adding it to the line as model 2387 and sometimes referring to it as the Rocket-Roll or Rocket Style. The list price was $265, which made it $100 or so cheaper than the recently discontinued Gibson Flying V. A year or so later, the 2387DX appeared with a correct glued-in neck, just like Gibson's.

The V copy was the subject of one of the first Ibanez ads, in print during the second half of 1973. It was headed "Our Newest Oldie" and appeared in two different versions. Each provides some good insight into the way Elger quickly became adept at picking up and exploiting trends. The first ad was aimed at players, and the copy said: "There's something about the feel of a good old electric guitar that makes it special. Pick it up and you can almost hear the million notes it's played. There's something special about the feel of a new Ibanez, like the Rocket-Roll you see here, that makes it special, too. It's got the warmth and feel of an oldie. And there's something else. Most new Ibanez oldies sell for less than the old oldies sold for when they were first introduced. So for a new outlook on oldies, try an Ibanez."[15] It was an approach that played skilfully on the fad for old guitars.

The second version of the Flying V ad was aimed at the trade, and this one said: "If you're a guitar dealer, we don't have to tell you about the demand for oldies. The Ibanez Rocket-Roll here is our newest oldie, but not our only touch of nostalgia. Ibanez 'new oldies' are made to look like, play like, and sound like the models that inspired them. And just to show you that our nostalgia is in the right place, most Ibanez 'new oldies' sell for less than the 'old oldies' did when they were first introduced. So for a new outlook on the business of oldies, see Ibanez."[16] It was another clever piece of copywriting by Jeff Hasselberger, and it showed that Ibanez meant business.

The double-neck that Summerfield suggested first appeared in the Ibanez line early in 1974, produced in a few variants. Gibson had built its SG-style originals only to special order but dropped them altogether in 1968. Now, Ibanez offered three double-neck copies, known in the USA as the Double Axe models and as usual fitted with bolt-on necks (or, as Ibanez liked to call them in its catalogues, "detachable necks"). There was a six-string and twelve-string combo (model 2402, described in Elger's press release as "the most sought-after combination") and a six-string and bass (2404), plus a weird twin six-string (2406) that Gibson had never made and which Ibanez said was good for "open-tuning slide guitar and standard tuning". The list price was $425 in cherry or walnut and

$450 in "custom ivory" (white). Gibson's last pricelist to feature its originals had pitched them between $810 and $875.

In 1974, Harry Rosenbloom sold his share of the US business to Hoshino, which became the sole owner of Elger Company. Rosenbloom was happier developing his store business. "It really was a friendly departure," he says. "It wasn't one of these takeovers. Everybody parted happy, I guess."[17] Yoshitada "Yoshi" Hoshino took over as president at Elger Company. He was the younger brother of Yoshiki "Joe" Hoshino, son of Junpei Hoshino.

Meanwhile, the team at Elger kept their ears to the ground, and one of the old Gibson models they liked was the Explorer. This had been launched alongside the original Flying V back in 1958 to much fanfare, with Gibson grandly calling the duo its Modernistic models. Like the V, the Explorer was certainly a bold creature, mixing angularity and modern straight lines, with a korina body that had a wedge-shaped base and an elongated horn that pushed out beyond the lower cutaway. Also like the original V, it was a failure at the time. But a handful of knowledgeable players and collectors were becoming fascinated by these shortlived but great-playing Gibson oddities.

Roy Miyahara had special responsibility for quality control at Elger, and he would write regularly to Fritz Katoh back at Hoshino in Japan, updating him with his latest plans and concerns. In a letter dated January 21 1975, Miyahara wrote: "We are thinking about a new model, one you already know, the Gibson Explorer guitar. This guitar is played by Eric Clapton and Rick Derringer, and also H.S. Anderson make an Explorer copy, which you can see in the attached photo." H.S. Anderson was a Japanese brand, made by Moridaira. US firms were noticing the Explorer, too: Hamer in Illinois launched its debut model, the Standard, in 1975 as a sort of flame-maple-top Explorer, and a year later Bernie Rico in California would introduce the B.C. Rich Mockingbird, a carved and pointy modern take on the old Gibson.

Miyahara finished his letter to Fritz Katoh by saying he would try to find an original Explorer so he could get some fuller and more accurate specs. "Eric Clapton used an Explorer in concert when he was in Japan, but that guitar has been altered," Miyahara wrote. "On that one, the body shape was a little different from the original and a tremolo bridge had been installed later. The Explorer model that we are planning is totally different from that, so I will send you a more detailed specification later."

Jeff Hasselberger remembers that they sent to Hoshino what little information they could gather, and they reported that Explorers were hot items bringing ridiculously high prices. Fujigen built a sample ready for exhibition at the Elger booth at the summer 1975 NAMM show. This was the annual American business gathering of the National Association of Music Merchants, where manufacturers and distributors showed off and sold their new models to visiting dealers and other trade folk.

"That first Explorer was definitely not exact," Miyahara recalls. "It had the wrong measurements and was the wrong shape." This was confirmed when George Gruhn, a

■ **Jeff Hasselberger** joined Ibanez/Elger in Philadelphia in 1973, creating ads and guitar designs. He's seen in a black T-shirt (opposite) in a **'74 ad** as he fronts a fictional band of Ibanez players. Two more of his ads are shown. The 1973 **Newest Oldie** ad (opposite) features a Rocket Roll Flying V and exploits the vintage-guitar fad, which Ibanez hoped would help sell its well-priced copies. "It's got the warmth and feel of an oldie," claimed

the cheeky blurb. The 1974 **Axe Us Again** ad (right) highlights three copies of Gibson's SG-style double-necks, including a **2402 Double Axe** (below) as well as a white 2406, an unusual twin six-string. Ibanez's copies were pretty good but not always entirely accurate. This **2348 Firebrand** (opposite) has the look of an original Gibson reverse-body Firebird, but it has a later-style non-reverse headstock.

THE IBANEZ ELECTRIC GUITAR BOOK

c.1974 2348 Firebrand

c.1974 2402 Double Axe

vintage-guitar dealer and evangelist, popped by the Elger booth and spotted the Ibanez Flying V. Gruhn told Miyahara that they ought to make an Explorer, too, and was surprised when Miyahara replied that they already did – and then showed him the sample. Gruhn was pleased to see this, but he said it wasn't right. "He happened to have some slides of an original Explorer and handed them to me, so that we could improve things," Miyahara recalls. "That's how we copied it, from his suggestions. We enjoyed trying to get it exact, as close as possible to the original. I remember that Jeff Hasselberger and I almost went crazy with it. We must be exact!"[18]

Maybe Gruhn suggested they try the complete "korina trio" of Gibson's originally planned 1958 Modernistic models. For not only did Elger have Hoshino revise and improve on the Explorer sample, but also they added a new copy of the original 1958-style Flying V and, even more remarkably, a Moderne, the guitar fleetingly devised as a third member of the Modernistic line. It was remarkable because this was a copy not just of a rare guitar, but of one that Gibson had never actually made. Rumours abounded that a prototype or two might have escaped, and a simple patent drawing existed, but the model never went into production. Gruhn had written an article about guitar collectables at the start of 1975, and it was clear this model excited him. "The Moderne is so rare," he wrote, "that we have never even seen one."[19] Hoshino had a sample of the Moderne ready to send to Elger in November, just a few months after that fact-finding NAMM show.

The striking new trio of copies was proudly displayed in Ibanez's 1976 *Golden Oldie Electric Guitars* catalogue. The copy of the Explorer was model 2459, and Ibanez gave it a name, too: The Destroyer. The Moderne copy was numbered 2469 and named The Futura. The new 50s-style V copy was the 2387CT, named the Rocket Roll Sr, and each was listed as having an ash body in "African Korina finish" – a nod to Gibson's korina-wood originals – plus a glued-in maple neck, two gold-plated Super 70 Anti-Hum pickups, and gold-plated hardware. They attracted a good deal of interest, not least from Eddie Van Halen, who played (and modified) a Destroyer, and Sylvain Sylvain of the New York Dolls, who owned a Rocket Roll Sr.

The rest of the copy line was by now even more extensive than it had been in the earlier part of the 70s. An American pricelist from 1976 had a model number for each instrument, as usual, but now also had a name for most of them, as with The Destroyer and The Futura. There were almost two dozen Les Paul variations listed, from the cheapest, the bestselling bolt-neck $260 Les Custom 2350, through the $299.50 Les Deluxe 59'er 2340 in sunburst and the $340 Sunlight Special 2342IV, and up to the most expensive, the set-neck version of the 2350, the $495 2650CS Solid Body DX. That same year, Gibson's regular line of five Les Paul solidbody models ranged from the $599 Les Paul Deluxe to the $739 Les Paul Custom.

Some of the Ibanez guitars had a small and distinctive star logo on the back of each of the tuners, one of several instances where Hoshino products incorporated a star, either figuratively, like this, or in brandnames or model names. There were Star drums, for example, and later guitar series names would include Roadstar and Artstar. The reason was simple: "Hoshino" translates roughly into English as "star field".

Other Gibson copies on the '76 pricelist included the Firebrand 2348 (a reverse-body Firebird V with non-reverse headstock), the L6S 2451 (a copy of one of Gibson's newer and more unusual solids), and the Thinline Stereo 2457 (more or less a 60s-style ES-355TDSV). There were Fender copies, too, mostly Strato 2375 models but also the 2334 Old Style Strat, first shown at summer NAMM 1975, with two-tone sunburst body and maple fingerboard, as well as a Tele or two. But the emphasis remained on Gibson.

Ibanez now had an established reputation for its copies, as an account from the time illustrates. *The Guitars Friend* was a guidebook to all things guitar, published in 1977 by an enterprising mail-order firm in Sandpoint, Idaho. "Ibanez believes there is a place in the world for a good copy," the *Friend* reported, "and they make a copy of every instrument that is now or ever was popular on the American market. Their Flying V copy was so successful that Gibson is now recopying them. Our experience so far: exceptional for the price."[20] It was around 1977 that Hoshino added a distributor for the western US states, Chesbro Music of Idaho Falls, Idaho, to extend the reach of Ibanez sales beyond the territory that Elger was able to cover.

As in earlier years, Hoshino's copies were not all branded Ibanez. Catalogues still often pictured the guitars with nothing at all on the headstocks, presumably so customers who chose to have their own brand on the guitars could easily use this all-purpose sales literature. In Britain, J.T. Coppock continued to import Hoshino's electrics with Coppock's Antoria and Cimar brands on them, and Summerfield was still selling CSL as well as Ibanez electrics. In the States, the Philadelphia Music Co of Limerick, Pennsylvania, was using the Penco brand, and a little further north, Great West in Canada had Hoshino apply the Mann brand. Quite a lot further south, Palings in Australia was importing electrics from Hoshino and selling them with its Jason house brand. European distribution was widespread, through Crafton Musik Ab in Sweden, Levytukku Oy in Finland, Meinl GmbH in Germany, Monzino SpA in Italy, Norsk AS in Norway, and Serlui BV in The Netherlands. Some of those firms are still Ibanez distributors today.

Until the mid 70s, Ibanez guitars had no serial numbers. But Elger wanted to supply a warranty card with each guitar it sold, and so serials became a necessity to identify individual instruments. The first guitars with serial numbers arrived at Elger in October 1975, and the warranty-card system began the following April. The various serial methods for Ibanez electrics are explained in detail at the back of this book, but the system begun in late 1975 had an initial letter plus six digits (and in a very Gibson-like style). The letter indicated the month – from A for January through L for December – and the first two digits were the last two digits of the year. So, for example, a guitar produced in November 1975 might have the number K753621.

c.1976 2459 The Destroyer

c.1975 2387CT Rocket Roll Sr.

No. 2337DX

- Body : Birch top with mahogany body.
- Neck : Laminated maple. Set-In neck.
- Pickups : Twin funky single coil pickups.
- Controls : Two volume and two tone controls.
- Parts : Chrome plated bridge-tailpiece and machine heads.
- Finish : Brown sunburst.

| Full Length : 40" | Width : 17½" × 12½" |
| Body Depth : 1⅝" | Scale : 24½" |

No. 2343

- Body : Selected mahogany body.
- Neck : Selected mahogany. Set-In neck.
- Pickups : One Funky single coil pickup.
- Controls : One volume and one tone controls.
- Parts : Chrome plated bridge-tailpiece and Smooth-Tuner machine heads.
- Finish : Cherry.

| Full Length : 39" | Width : 16" × 13" |
| Body Depth : 1⅝" | Scale : 24½" |

THE IBANEZ ELECTRIC GUITAR BOOK

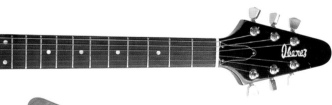

■ Ibanez's move to copy vintage Gibson models reached a high with the "korina trio", three late-50s designs that Gibson called its Modernistic guitars. It showed Ibanez up to speed with the way some players thought that older guitars were somehow better, while Gibson itself seemed out of touch. Shown are the 50s-style **Rocket Roll Sr.** (Flying V), the **Destroyer** (Explorer), and the **Futura** (Gibson's never-actually-issued Moderne), as well as a **1976 ad** (centre). A young **Eddie Van Halen** played a much-modded Destroyer (1978 shot, above) and Sylvain Sylvain of the **New York Dolls** opted for a Rocket Roll ('**76 catalogue**, top). Meanwhile, other Gibson copies continued, like these takes on a **Les Paul Junior** and **Special** (opposite).

c.1976 2469 The Futura

Gibson was not blind to all this copying. It's easy to imagine the scene at the company's plant in Kalamazoo, Michigan, and at parent company Norlin's HQ in Lincolnwood, Illinois, as flustered managers considered what they might do about the problem. At the start of January 1976, Roy Miyahara wrote a letter from his US base at Elger to Fritz Katoh back at Hoshino in Japan. "Mr Yoshihiro Hoshino and Tom Tanaka are here now after visiting Washington DC and New York regarding the problem with Gibson," he wrote, "but it seems they have reached a conclusion and have made a new direction for 1976. I think this decision will be announced when they return to Japan."

Norlin had just got around to trademarking the shape of Gibson's classic headstock. It was the only trademark Gibson had for a "product configuration", in other words a body shape or a headstock shape. Gibson's only other trademark was for its bell-shape truss-rod cover. It was probably the headstock trademark that was at the root of Ibanez's "problem with Gibson" that Miyahara wrote about.

In April 1974, Norlin Music Inc had filed for a trademark for "a design for a pig head profile" (later corrected by erring attorneys to the more suitable "peg head profile"). The basic line-drawing supplied to the trademark office shows that it was for Gibson's venerable "dove-wing" headstock – a nickname that describes the distinctive top shape of the head, where two pronounced wings meet in a central dimple, apparently resembling the outline of a dove's wings. (It's also known as a "moustache" or "open-book" headstock by those who see it more like those shapes.) Norlin's filing suggested that the specific design had been in use by Gibson since 1922, although in fact it dates back to at least 1907.

As usual, it took time for the trademark application to be approved, and Norlin finally received its registration in September 1975. It seems likely that when that registration arrived, Norlin warned Elger and Hoshino to stop using the headstock shape. Ibanez's "new direction for 1976" that Miyahara wrote about may well have been Elger's response to such a warning from Norlin. Elger did not stop making copies, and the guitars in the Ibanez catalogues and pricelists of 1976 did not change much. What they did have was a new headstock design.

Gone was the blatant Gibson dove-wing copy, and in its place was a new design, devised by Jeff Hasselberger and Fritz Katoh, with a smoothly curved central arch and two tiny peaks each side. Hasselberger says the shape was derived from one of the guitars that Ibanez made for the Grateful Dead's Bob Weir around this time. "Enlarging the Gibson headstock looked strange," Hasselberger says, "so I started looking at guitars with big headstocks – like D'Angelicos and other jazz boxes. I originally drew Bob's head shape during one of my visits with him as he coached me with suggestions. It was a good-looking large headstock that shrank down nicely to a regular size."[21]

Time wore on, and Gibson presumably became increasingly irritated by the continued and blatant copying of its designs. The Ibanez models that Elger sold were among the most popular and most numerous, and it seems safe to conclude that they must therefore have been the most annoying. One insider from Elger at the time says that they quite enjoyed taunting Gibson at every opportunity.

Finally, Gibson decided to take legal action. There were rumours during the lead-up to the summer NAMM show in Atlanta, Georgia, in June 1977 that something was about to happen, and on June 9, two days before the show began, Gibson president Chuck Schneider sent a letter to his dealers explaining the situation. "Today, Gibson Inc started legal action in Federal Court to stop the Japanese exporter of Ibanez instruments and its distributor from importing and selling instruments similar in appearance to those manufactured by Gibson," Schneider wrote. "We want you, who have a major stake in the outcome, to know why we are taking this action."

He explained how Gibson had worked for decades to build relationships with musicians by offering what he described as unique instrument designs, and he said that the company was obliged to protect the trademarks and goodwill it had built over those years. "We have previously taken steps to warn various suppliers to stop copying," Schneider wrote, "and, after exhausting our patience, we have begun this legal action. We intend to use every available means to stop others from trading on the valuable assets of Gibson."

Schneider said that Gibson respected competitors who earned their market position by making distinctive products that "compete with Gibson on their own merits". He concluded: "We feel that this legal action is necessary to protect the major investments that Gibson and each of its dealers have made over the years and to preserve an environment of creative competition and progress in our business. We will continue to keep you informed about the progress of this litigation."

Gibson filed its complaint against Elger in Philadelphia's federal court on June 28, claiming infringement of its headstock trademark. A little over a week later, Roy Miyahara wrote another of his letters to Fritz Katoh. "Elger Company has received an official lawsuit letter from Gibson, and we're required to respond to them within 20 days," he reported. "I thought sooner or later we'd have to do business without the copy lines, but I'm surprised that it has come so soon, and it's a good opportunity for Hoshino Gakki."

Elger did not want to go to court. It agreed to stop infringing Gibson's trademarked headstock design – which, as we've seen, it had already done. Elger also stopped using Gibson-like model names in its sales literature, including pricelists. The out-of-court settlement meant Gibson's complaint was closed on February 2 1978.

The whole business shook Elger and Hoshino, who seem to have had little or no taste for fighting any litigation. "We're concerned that we may not be able to keep up the current business without the copy lines, because they are the majority of Elger's sales," Miyahara wrote to Katoh, adding that they might also have to stop copying Fender,

Ibanez's copying – such as the two **Les Paul lookalikes** from the mid 70s shown here – did not go unnoticed at Gibson. At first, Gibson simply complained about the use of its recently-trademarked headstock design. Ibanez took note and made a change to its design. Pictured (opposite, left to right) are the **Gibson head**, the blatantly copying **Ibanez head**, and the **new Ibanez head** introduced in 1976. Otherwise, Ibanez carried on copying, at least for now: there were more Gibson duplications, as on this **1976 catalogue cover** (opposite, top) and the **L5S** (bottom, centre), as well as an unusual **Fender double-neck** (bottom, left) and a **Rickenbacker** copy.

1976 2351M Les Model

1977 2351 Les Std.

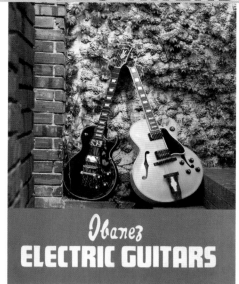

No. 2399

- Body : Carved curly solid maple.
- Neck : Hard laminated maple, Set-In neck.
- Fingerboard : Ebonized rosewood with pearl block inlays.
- Pickup : Two gold plated Super 70 Anti-Hum pickups.
- Parts : Gold plated fancy tailpiece and Smooth-Tuner machine heads.
- Finish : Cherry sunburst.

Full Length 40" Width : 16½"×13¾"
Frets : 22 Scale : 24¾"

No. 2388

- Body : Curly solid maple body.
- Neck : Hard laminated maple. Detachable neck.
- Fingerboard : Rosewood with fancy inlays.
- Pickup : Two single coil pickups.
- Controls : Two tone and two volume controls.
- Parts : Chrome plated tailpiece and machine heads.
- Finish : Cherry Sunburst.

Full Length : 39" Width : 19½"×13½"
Frets : 24 Scale : 24⅜"

Martin, and others, too. "We may have to rely on original models – but that is not enough to generate sufficient volume in business at this point," he concluded.

Elger had indeed for some years been devising and selling Ibanez electrics of relatively original design, alongside the more successful and numerous copies. An early sign of original thinking had come with a quartet of double-cutaway solids, first seen in a 1973 catalogue: models 2611, 2612, 2613, and 2614. On reflection, they look as if someone was deliberately trying to design something that was not a copy. Each had a bound double-cut solid mahogany body, with a black-finish birch top on the 2611 and 2612, a pale natural maple top on the 2613, and a brown natural mahogany top on the 2614. Below the guitars' two humbuckers was a semi-circular plate with four controls, jack, and selector switch (later catalogues showed no control plate and the jack on the body edge).

This line of four models – grouped in catalogues under an early showing for the Artist series name – had six-saddle bridges and separate tailpieces, although the 2611 had a Bigsby-like vibrato, and the pickguard was a curvy, pointy creation. The bolt-on neck of birch or maple had a rosewood fingerboard (maple on the 2613) with unusual star-in-block markers, and the headstock was of the type that became known as the "castle" thanks to the shape of the top, with high sides and central dips, resembling a castle's battlements. It certainly counts as Ibanez's first original headstock design – and this was several years before that battle with Gibson. Ibanez would later move on from this first stab at Artist models to come up with an elegant and important line of guitars.

Another early foray into original designs came with the Custom Series, introduced in 1974, which included a scroll-head Les Paul, the 2405, and another try at a double-cutaway design, the 2662. The scrolled-head guitar was Jeff Hasselberger's idea. He'd seen an odd Les Paul come into Harry Rosenbloom's Medley Music store: it had a scroll-shape headstock that had been fitted when the original broke off. "This recut headstock looked like a Gibson F-style mandolin, and inlaid into it were the words 'Eric Clapton'," Hasselberger recalls. "I looked at it, and it was amusing – but there was also something about it that was kind of cool. An F-style headstock on a Les Paul is actually sort of a neat idea. The Eric Clapton thing put it up for ridicule, but in fact it wasn't bad looking."

He sketched out a design based on the repaired Les Paul and added a scrolly pickguard and fancy inlays to the body and fingerboard. For companions, he drew a bass with an eagle on the pickguard and a few designs for some Strats with carved body and head. "I'd seen a guitar that somebody had taken some wood-carving tools to," Hasselberger says. "Again, I thought that was a pretty cool idea."

He presented his drawings at a meeting with Tom Tanaka and Yoshi Hoshino, and after an interlude of English and Japanese translations back and forth, Tanaka turned to Hasselberger and said simply: "Good ideas – we will do." Hasselberger was somewhat taken aback by this, because in all honesty he had expected that his off-the-wall ideas would be rejected. "And so that was the start of my contribution to product design," he recalls with a smile.

The bass became the Black Eagle 2409B, the carved Strats the three Artwood 2408 variants (Nouveau, Orient, and Eagle), and the mandolin-head Les Paul was the Custom Agent 2405. "The Custom Agent name was a pun on the customs agent, the guy from the government who makes sure you're not importing rhino horns in guitar cases," Hasselberger explains. "I thought it had a bit of a James Bond/secret agent/spy vibe to it."[22]

In 1975, there was an even more striking addition to these early Ibanez original designs. At first it was given model number 2663 and called The Flash, but within about nine months its better-known name was in place: Iceman. The body looked as if someone had given a Gibson Firebird a curved, pointed base and a Rickenbacker-like hooked lower horn, providing a deep easy-access cutaway, and it had a long and pointy headstock. It was resolutely original and unashamedly attention-seeking.

Fritz Katoh, who had established Hoshino's R&D department at the Nagoya HQ in Japan in 1972, was one of those involved in the design of the Iceman, and he says that several firms pooled ideas to come up with the new look. "But it was mostly worked on by the Hoshino team," he says.[23] Hoshino linked up with the Japanese distributor Kanda Shokai, and Kanda had its own brand, Greco – which, like Ibanez, was manufactured principally at the Fujigen factory. Greco's M series of guitars was the Iceman design under a different name. As we've seen, it wasn't unusual for similar Fujigen-made models to turn up with various brandnames, including Ibanez and Greco but running to many others, as determined by each customer.

The original Iceman (or The Flash) came in three versions: the 2663-3P or 2663TC, with one three-coil pickup, two controls, and a four-way tone selector; the 2663, with two pickups and four controls; and the 2663SL, with one sliding three-coil pickup and three controls. The three-coil pickup was another unusual touch, as was the version with the sliding option. "It had two linear potentiometers," Jeff Hasselberger remembers, "like you'd find in a mixing board, and they were screwed into the body cavity underneath, with the pickup mounted to those: that's how it would slide back and forth. It took up a lot of space inside the guitar, so later, although we kept the body shape, we kind of 'normalised' some of that stuff."[24]

The "normalisation" that Hasselberger talks about took a few years to materialise, and in 1978 the Iceman line was revised and expanded to six models. Most of them had two regular pickups, and the models ranged from the bolt-neck chrome-hardware IC100 to the set-neck gold-hardware IC400. The existing models were renamed the IC200 (this was previously the 2663) and the IC210 (this was previously the 2663TC – the one with the static three-coil pickup). The sliding-pickup version of the Iceman had been quietly dropped, but still in full view to all was the Iceman's look-at-me body shape. One

c.1975 Artist 2613

1975 Artist 2662

THE IBANEZ ELECTRIC GUITAR BOOK

c.1975 2405 Custom Agent

■ Gibson's **trademark** for a "pig head" design (below: they meant "peg head") made Ibanez revise its headstock shapes. Gibson's subsequent legal action hurried Ibanez's shift to original designs for whole guitars, which had begun earlier in the 70s with attempts such as the double-cutaway **Artist 2662** (bottom) and the **Custom Agent** (above), an ornate chopped-about Les Paul devised by Jeff Hasselberger. Another transitional move came with Hasselberger's three carved-body Strats, including the dragon-infested **Artwood Orient** (right). A more lasting double-cutaway design began with early models like the **Artist 2613** (main guitar), which has another new headstock for Ibanez, known as the "castle" design.

1975 2408
Artwood Orient

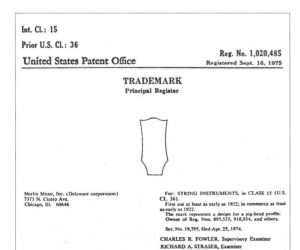

Int. Cl.: 15

Prior U.S. Cl.: 36

United States Patent Office

Reg. No. 1,020,485
Registered Sept. 16, 1975

TRADEMARK
Principal Register

Norlin Music, Inc. (Delaware corporation)
7373 N. Cicero Ave.
Chicago, Ill. 60646

For: STRING INSTRUMENTS, in CLASS 15 (U.S. CL. 36).
First use at least as early as 1922; in commerce at least as early as 1922.
The mark represents a design for a pig-head profile.
Owner of Reg. Nos. 895,535, 918,934, and others.
Ser. No. 19,795, filed Apr. 25, 1974.

CHARLES R. FOWLER, Supervisory Examiner
RICHARD A. STRASER, Examiner

significant musician who noticed it was Paul Stanley, of Kiss, a performer not unfamiliar with the value of flash.

Elger provided Stanley with an Iceman 2663 in April 1977, made a prototype of a personal model in July, and the following year, Ibanez launched the PS10 Paul Stanley Model. It was a smart move. Stanley might not have been a guitarist's guitarist like some other Ibanez endorsers, but his involvement certainly ensured that the brand got noticed. He later had Ibanez make him a custom PS10 with a cracked-mirror front, and from 1979 it provided some spectacular reflections at Kiss's already dazzling live shows. When Stanley had first met the Ibanez people in Japan he was impressed by how accommodating they were and how keen to learn. "And they obviously have the facilities to make anything," he said. "That's a lot more than can be said for [the USA] at the moment. Japan really is the country of the future."[25]

Ibanez signed another artist toward the end of the 70s, one who is still with the company today and whose music could not have been more different to Paul Stanley's. George Benson first heard about Ibanez guitars from his friend Phil Upchurch, who suggested he check them out. Upchurch said the guitars were well made, that Benson was bound to be impressed – and that they were Japanese. "At first I was sceptical," says Benson. "But I happened to be in Seattle, Washington, and I went into a store, saw that name on a guitar, picked it up and played it, and I said wow! I looked at the workmanship – I said this is incredible. But, of course, at that time they were making replicas of American guitars. Knock-offs, I should say, but I won't use that term. They were doing imitations of the world's greatest guitars. Their version of them was pretty impressive, but they were so well made I had to pay attention."[26]

Benson was a bluesy jazzman who could sing well, too, and from his debut album in 1966 onward it was clear he was something special. By the time he visited that Seattle store and tried his first Ibanez, he was a star, thanks to his massive 1976 album *Breezin'* and the top-ten single from it, 'This Masquerade'. Fellow guitarists could tell that his success had not derailed his talent. Benson, meanwhile, was ready for a change of instrument. He'd played all the usual jazz boxes, from Gibsons and Guilds to D'Angelicos and Epiphones, but he found them hard to control in the bigger venues he was now playing. Then he had a chance meeting with one of the Ibanez team.

Jeff Hasselberger knew some of the local musicians who worked on the Mike Douglas television show, broadcast out of Philadelphia, and in August 1976 he got a tip-off that George Benson was due in. Hasselberger turned up at the studio for the rehearsal, and on his way through the building to the stage area, he saw Benson coming toward him down a corridor with his guitar on.

"He was patting his pockets," Hasselberger recalls, "like all guitarists do when we're looking for a pick. He was in a hurry: the band was about to play and he'd just realised he didn't have a pick on him. Being a guitar player, I always carry picks, so I reached in my pocket and pulled out a Fender medium. As he walked toward me, I held it up and went: You looking for one of these? He looked at it, he looked me right in the face, and he said: Hey, thanks man! And he went back and did his rehearsal. It was almost like it couldn't have been more perfect. Later, back in the green room, we started shooting the shit."

Benson said he liked to play with his amp facing him, but he had to crank it up so high in his monitors, and he was having problems with feedback. Hasselberger talked things through and offered to have Ibanez make Benson a guitar – whatever he wanted. Soon they met again, at Benson's house, and Hasselberger took the precaution of bringing a bottle of Courvoisier, which he'd noticed was Benson's tipple. "We sat in his basement family room on a couple of couches, a big coffee table at the front, and we threw paper down and started scrawling out things," Hasselberger remembers.

What emerged was that Benson wanted to stay with an identifiably jazz guitar and that he didn't want a guitar like a Les Paul. Hasselberger said OK, so what about something in between? Exactly, said Benson, I need something between a Johnny Smith and a Les Paul. Hasselberger went away and had samples made of a Johnny Smith and a Les Paul. "I remember going in to the office over the weekend, rolling out some paper onto a conference table, and laying down the Johnny Smith, tracing the body out and making a centre line. Then I laid down the Les Paul on the centre line, and I traced that body out. Then I freehanded in between. I took French curves and kind of smoothed it out – and that was the face-on view of the guitar. I took it over to show George, and he loved it. He said that would be perfect: he really wanted something that was different."

The design they came up with was fourteen-and-a-bit inches wide and just under two-and-a-half inches deep. There were no well-known hollowbody electrics of this modest size. The smallest popular Gibson jazz electric was the ES-175, a touch over sixteen inches wide and nearly three-and-a-half inches deep.

Once the shape and size was established, they filled in the details. Benson wanted a somewhat brighter tone, suitable for concert halls as opposed to clubs. "To be able to project the character of a jazz guitar to a lot of people, that was crux of the challenge," Hasselberger says.[27] To that end, they matched the thinner body to a thicker top and made the internal bass-bar heavier, shifting the natural resonance of the guitar a little higher. The pair of humbuckers were floated from the pickguard rather than bolted to the top. "That way, the body could resonate more uniformly," Benson explains. "If you start breaking up the top, you're losing some vibrations here and there, and you don't get that uniformity."

The tailpiece was a clever design, intended to help balance the low and high strings. Two adjustment-screws increase or decrease the pressure on the three bass or three treble strings – and the look of the two-pronged tailpiece mirrored the look of the headstock inlay, which they'd already completed. Benson points to the logo in that headstock inlay. "For a

1979 Iceman IC210

1979 PS10 Paul Stanley

THE IBANEZ ELECTRIC GUITAR BOOK

■ A great leap forward for Ibanez innovation came with the angular Iceman, launched in 1975 and at first known as The Flash – with some justification. Followers of fashion will spot influences from Gibson's Firebird and from Rickenbacker, but really this was Ibanez's first stab at something wildly original. The first three models were displayed (below) in Ibanez's **1976 catalogue**: the **2663** had relatively conventional pickups and controls, but the **2663SL** had a novel sliding pickup and the **2663TC** had a static three-coil pickup. The TC developed into the later **IC210** (main guitar). All this was enough to attract a keen student of pop ostentation, **Paul Stanley** of Kiss. Ibanez launched a signature model for Stanley in 1978, the **PS10** (below), and the following year Kiss's already dazzling live shows benefitted from Stanley's custom model with **cracked-mirror finish** (right).

year or two, I didn't know what that was. I just thought it looked pretty. Then I noticed there was a 'GB' in there," he laughs. "At first I just thought it was a man's face, and I could live with that: the prince's cowl. They're saying to me that I'm the prince, or king, of guitar! But then, when I realised what they were doing – that they were raising my image and raising me up – I thought, well, they're saying I'm among the best. Wow! It raised my view of Ibanez as a company, because I think they truly respected me as an artist. And that was a great thing to discover."

Beyond the detail and all the effort in designing the guitar, Benson says it came down to a relatively simple set of requirements. "My experience has been in a lot of different fields – R&B, pop, blues – so I needed a guitar that can give me all of that. What I needed was a nice fast neck, a guitar that fit my hands and played well, and something that would hold up on the road. And that guitar did all of those things very well." Alongside the new small-body Ibanez, which became the GB10, he also added what he called a "traditional" jazz guitar, and this became the GB20, with a deeper, 17-inch body and a single floating neck pickup (effectively that copy of a Gibson Johnny Smith, according to Hasseberger).

In January 1977, Fritz Katoh completed a prototype each of the GB10 and GB20 to show to Benson. Once Benson approved them, production of the two new models began, in October, and they were included in a December catalogue. "Ibanez threw a nice thing in my lap," Benson says, "and gave me the chance to express myself and my ideas. They made me look good when they came up with the product. My ideas had merit to them – but I don't make guitars, and they do. They promised to make something I could be proud of, and I was. And I still am."[28]

Benson remains one of Ibanez's longest-standing endorsers, and at the time of writing, a new GB model was introduced, the "Little Georgie Benson" LGB-300 (actually with quite a large body), one of a number of Bensons that have been added to the line over the years. From the start, Benson liked the idea of having different styles of guitar under his signature banner. "That was unusual at the time, save for the various Les Pauls that were pumped out," Hasselberger says. "Most signature models were just that: one model with the artist's name. George thought more expansively than that. He wanted a home with a guitar company where he could develop more instruments along the course of the relationship. It also matched well with what was becoming the Ibanez view of our own place in the world. We would create a line of instruments that could move and change with the music, instead of the other way around. If musicians could change and evolve as artists, so could we as a brand."[29]

Ibanez had started using the Artist series name rather haphazardly in 1973 as a catch-all for some new double-cutaway models, but soon the better-known Artists began to appear, alongside similar guitars with a new series name, Pro or Professional. The first hint that something fresh was on the way came with an entry on a 1974 pricelist, noting the 2402VI Artwood Twin, a "custom built twin-neck, custom order". At $1,500 it was by far the most expensive electric on the list. It certainly looked expensive, too, with its solid double-double-cutaway ash body in natural finish and its overtly fancy appointments.

The Artwood Twin had twelve-string and six-string necks, with a pair of humbuckers and a separate bridge and tailpiece for each, along with a bevy of controls. The ebony fingerboards each had a fancy vine inlay along the length, and a very elaborate pair of headstocks had more vine inlay and scalloped outlines. In fact, it was a copy of an extravagant maple-body double-neck, the Double Rainbow, that Rex Bogue had completed the previous year for John McLaughlin, at Ren Ferguson's workshop in California. Bogue said he was inspired to create the elaborate inlay by the banjos of S.S. Stewart and the art nouveau of Alphonse Mucha.[30] Ibanez adopted Bogue's own term, "tree of life", to describe the inlay.

Apart from its different headstocks, the Bogue guitar provided virtually the entire look of the Artwood Twin, including the triangular tailpiece, which Ibanez later called the Gibraltar. It also had a German-carve body, the distinctive raised "shoulder" running parallel to the edge of the guitar, so named because it was a typical feature of the work of some German guitar-makers. Hasselberger was understandably nervous when he visited Bogue in California, expecting at least a telling-off for using his design. "He was the exact opposite," Hasselberger says, recalling his relief. "He was a real down-to-earth guitar nut with a great sense of humour. He was a generous guy who was actually an Ibanez fan and flattered that we'd even attempt to knock-off his creation. He answered every question I posed and was more co-operative than I could have hoped."[31]

Despite its visual impact, the Twin was, like any double-neck, of limited practical appeal, and Ibanez set about adapting aspects of this interesting design to a number of more mainstream guitars. The first result appeared in a 1975 catalogue, where a lone model number 2617 was shown, showcasing the new Bogue-borrowed style of the Twin in single-neck form. It had the German-carve solid ash body and glued-in neck, a pair of humbuckers, four controls and a selector, and a separate Gibraltar bridge and tailpiece. This time the fingerboard had fancy pearl-and-abalone block markers, and the headstock was the "castle" type used on those earlier Artist models. The whole guitar had the air of something classy and different – but this one was pitched at a more approachable $450. That same year, a Gibson Les Paul Deluxe listed at $580 and a regular Fender Stratocaster was $405.

The Artists and Professionals that followed drew more or less from that template, with some interesting variations along the way. In Ibanez's 1976 sales material, the 2617 was given a name, the Artwood Artist, and it was joined in the revised Artist series by two more new models. The 2618 Artist 24 had a maple/mahogany body and a bound 24-fret ebony fingerboard with dot markers, and the 2619 Artist 22 was a 22-fret version, with the 2617's fancy block markers, and with a two-way mini-switch to combine the pickups in or out of phase (soon changed to two of Ibanez's Tri-Sound three-way switches, which

BENSON BREEZES IN

1976 Artwood Twin 2670

1978 GB10 George Benson

■ Double-necks always seemed an Ibanez speciality, and Elger worker **Dave Humphreys** was the first to order an employee special, caught in this 1976 snap (centre). By far the most ornate double-neck so far was the over-the-top **Artwood Twin** (left) of 1976, based on a similar guitar that Rex Bogue had made for John McLaughlin. In toned-down form, it provided the essence of Ibanez's new Artist and Pro series. A **mid-70s ad** (opposite) for the Twin featured **Marlo Henderson**. In 1976, a lasting partnership began with the jazz-pop guitarist **George Benson** (**1979 ad**, below), and a year or so later, Ibanez issued two signature models: the small-body **GB10** (main guitar) and the larger GB20. Benson remains an Ibanez man to this day. Other f-hole electrics included these two **Artist** models (left) in a **1977 catalogue**.

gave humbucking, single-coil, or parallel-humbucking for each pickup). Also new for 1976 were models for the Grateful Dead's Bob Weir and country sessionman Randy Scruggs, marking Ibanez's first signature guitars and the first entries in the new Professional series. There were also some Les Paul-style Professionals with fancy inlaid bodies and vine-inlaid fingerboards, similar to the earlier Custom Agent.

The connection with Bob Weir came from Jim Fisher, who began working at Elger in 1973 as a guitar inspector and quality controller. "I was a youthful, crazy, opinionated 23-year-old," he says with a laugh, "and I constantly harped about us needing an endorsement from a major guitarist's-guitarist. I also thought that few musicians of that calibre would be interested in playing and endorsing a Japanese copy of an existing American model. Every month we would get the latest experiments and prototypes from our manufacturing plant in Japan, and it was quite evident that we were up to the challenge. This was also an era when Fender and Gibson had frequent problems with quality control."

Fisher told any of his colleagues who would listen that Ibanez ought to have a rock player's signature model. He reasoned that no American company was making such a signature guitar: so far it was all Barney Kessels, Trini Lopezs, Les Pauls, Tal Farlows, and so on. His point was a good one. Fender, for example, would hang around until 1988 to make its first signature models, the Yngwie Malmsteen and Eric Clapton Stratocasters. Gibson, meanwhile, was stuck with its old-jazzers image and would not offer a rock signature model until its Jimmy Page Les Paul of 1995.

Back in the 70s, Fisher's idea was not too popular. Everyone laughed when he said that the guitarists in question should be one from each side of the pond: Bob Weir and Keith Richards. "One Friday lunchtime I asked in front of the crowd if I could take a handful of guitars and, through some contacts I had, show them to the Grateful Dead that weekend," Fisher says. "They reckoned I must be high on something with my insistence that anybody that huge would be interested in our offshore stuff. After the mirth died down, management agreed to my hair-brained scheme and suggested that Roy Miyahara accompany and keep an eye on me."

Fisher remembers the date with Deadhead precision: Sunday August 4 1974. They packed a few guitars into Miyahara's car and drove to the Philadelphia Civic Center for the Dead's soundcheck that afternoon. They met bassist Phil Lesh, Jerry Garcia, and then Bob Weir. "Bob expressed interest in our guitars," Fisher recalls, "especially the Rex Bogue-style double-neck, and he asked if we could make a six-string like it."[32] They were invited to visit again the following night for further discussions.

Back at Elger on Monday morning, Fisher says there was surprise – not only that he and Miyahara had indeed met with the Dead but also that Weir was interested in a collaboration. Fisher reported that Weir wanted to design a guitar from the ground up and didn't want to endorse an existing model. His recollection is that Jeff Hasselberger accompanied him to the meeting that evening and from that point took over the discussions. Hasselberger's recollection is that it was he and Miyahara alone who went to the meetings with Weir. Whatever the detail, Fisher left Elger a few months later, returned to college, and later became a successful chiropractor.

Weir told Hasselberger he wanted a sliding pickup, to help get the sounds he needed to hear. Ibanez built him a guitar with a sliding single-coil between two humbuckers, and then a second guitar, which became the basis for the pair of signature models that appeared in 1976: the 2680 Bob Weir Standard, with dot inlay, and the 2681 Bob Weir Pro, with vine inlay. Although they were part of the Professional series, they were very similar to the new Artist style, derived from the double-neck that had caught Weir's attention, with German-carve ash bodies. "Actually a little bigger than an Artist body," Hasselberger specifies, "with shallower cutaways where the Artist had pointier ones. We started an ongoing relationship on all sorts of gizmos and effects with Bob. He'd use them on stage and in some cases create some truly awful sounds with them. Jerry Garcia was ribbing me about some of the failed attempts, and he said: You're like an evil doctor conducting experiments on our band – the Evil Doctor Hasselberger. And that name stuck."[33]

The other new Professional signature model in 1976 was a single-cutaway version of the Artist style, named for country guitarist Randy Scruggs, son of banjo legend Earl Scruggs. The 2671 Randy Scruggs had the full vine inlay, while the 2671S was a dot version, and both had a chunky, elaborate tailpiece, since nicknamed the harmonica because of its shape. The Scruggs connection was shortlived, and by the '77 pricelist both models were renamed simply Single Cutaway; by the following year, they'd been dropped altogether.

More Artists followed, including a 12-string version of the 2618, a 2622 Artist EQ with three-band equaliser, and the 2629 Artist Semi Acoustic, an f-hole thinline with central body block. Playability was inched forward in 1978 when the glued-in neck of the Artist and Professional models was modified with a new heel-less joint. Other name players took to these new Ibanez models, including Steve Miller, who was high on success from albums like *Fly Like An Eagle* (1976) and *Book Of Dreams* (1977). He first picked up an Iceman, and then in March 1977 Ibanez gave him an Artist 2622, the EQ model, which he described as "just the hottest guitar I've ever seen". After those recent synth-leaning records where he'd played less guitar, he said the Artist turned him on again. "[That guitar] let me control it the way I wanted to," Miller said in '77. "So now I'm back into playing lead a lot."[34]

In 1979, the Artist model names moved to an AR-number scheme for the solids and AS for the hollows (and from 1982 the AM as well as the AS Semi & Full Acoustic series). A few of the existing models continued, such as the 2619, which became the AR300, and a mass of new models would be continually added and others subtracted over the coming

■ The Artist and Pro models provided Ibanez with fine quality and playability in the late 70s. They also attracted several important endorsers, including ex-Poco **Jim Messina** (with Pro **2674** in a **'76 catalogue**, opposite top left), **Steve Miller (1975 ad**, top right) with an **Artist 2622** (below), which had a three-way EQ system on board, and country sessionman **Randy Scruggs** with his signature **2671** (prototype opposite). The Grateful Dead's **Bob Weir** was the biggest rock catch; he had a **custom-built** sliding-pickup guitar (opposite, bottom) and signature models including the **2681 Pro** (above). Ibanez's first single-neck electric 12-string was the **2618/12** (1977 catalogue, right).

ARTIST NO. **2618/12**

1979 Artist 2622

MESSINA, MILLER, SCRUGGS & WEIR

1978 2681 Bob Weir Pro

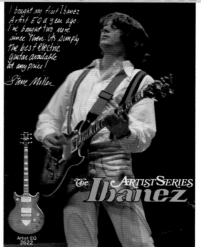

1976 Pro 2671 Randy Scruggs prototype

years, in the process making it one of Ibanez's longest-running series. The most recent Artist at the time of writing is the AR325, introduced in 2012.

Back in the second half of the 70s when these Ibanez solids first appeared, many guitarists saw them as showing off a new confidence and concerted quality from a brand that, if they'd thought about it at all, they probably considered as merely an adept copyist. Al Marinaro started working for Elger in 1976 as a sales representative, and he remembers that his dealers were impressed with Ibanez quality. "They liked the fact that they could take Ibanez guitars out of the box, put them on the wall, and they'd play really well," Marinaro recalls. "Every guitar was set up properly."[35] Despite the accustomed splash of hype, Ibanez put it well in a 1976 ad for the 2618: "The only thing special about the new Ibanez Artist is that it's the best. No frills, no gimmicks – just the finest basic electric guitar we can build." Whichever way you looked at it, the Artists and Professionals marked the start of a new maturity for Ibanez as the 80s rolled into view. The only trouble was, they weren't the type of guitars that many players were looking for.

Some musicians, of course, enjoy rolling against the flow, and that can certainly be said for Andy Partridge of XTC. "I think of myself as probably a songwriter before a guitar player," he apologies. When he went into a music store in summer 1977, he expected to come out with a Gibson Les Paul. Most guitarists would have done exactly that. Instead, he bought an Ibanez Artist 2619. Burning a hole in his pocket was part of the advance his band had just scored from Virgin Records. "I thought yep, I'll know I've made it, because now I can have a Gibson Les Paul." Partridge surveyed the Les Pauls on the walls of his local store, Kempster & Son, in Swindon, south-west England. "But I just fell in love with this Ibanez Artist. It was the feel of it: it felt fantastic under my fingers. Really phenomenally good. It was love at first twang."

Like many guitarists looking for a new instrument, he had little knowledge of who made what and where. He thought Ibanez sounded Spanish and was unaware it was a Japanese guitar. "Most people would rather have bitten off their own limbs at that point than play a Japanese guitar," he suggests. What mattered was how this guitar felt and sounded. "The neck pickup had a sort of deep jazzy tone, and the bridge pickup had a real Gibson cut, but a little bit of Fender bite mixed in. I thought wow, this kind of sounds like both of them … but not."

He also liked the phase switch of his early 2619. "I could get a super-thin 'insect tone' with it. I'd never heard anyone use this insect tone. I thought, I can make that mine – which I never really did, but it came in useful occasionally." And the big block markers helped, too. "Being a rather unsure guitarist, I need huge signposts to tell me you're at such-and-such a fret, so that was a bonus." Once Partridge had his Artist, he used it on every XTC album and tour, insect tone or otherwise. He still owns it today, and while he's had a few other electrics along the way, he considers this one to be *his* guitar. "I guess it is precious," he admits. "I'd feel heartbroken if it was taken away."[36]

Jeff Hasselberger's start-of-year presentation to the Ibanez sales force in 1978 underlined the brand's growing sense of identity and a move forward from the copying of the past. He told the salesmen that when Ibanez's competition was other copy makers, it had the disadvantage of guitar setup costs and advertising – which the other copy makers didn't do. "We've been moving in the direction of original models since the Custom Agent, and now it's complete," Hasselberger told them. "The lawsuit was the catalyst, and now we stand on the merits of our own line."[37] He finished by confirming that delivery of copy models to the Elger warehouse would cease in February 1978.

That year, with the wind in its sails, Ibanez launched three more new-design series: the Concert, the Musician, and the Studio. There were three other new lines, as well, but they were derivative: the Performer and Challenger series, which were quick-fix attempts at less contentious Les Paul and Strat-flavoured styles, and the Jazz Guitar series of SA and FA models, which drew from the well-thumbed guidebook to electric hollowbody design.

The Concert models looked as if a Les Paul-type carved maple top had been married to a bound mahogany Strat-like body shape, topped off with the new-style headstock. This uneasy combination did not hold much appeal, and the handful of CN models lasted barely a year. More interesting were the Musician and Studio lines, essentially two levels of the same overall design. The body shape was broadly Strat-like, but the structure and electronics went far beyond Fender. Instead, they were prompted by a small but increasingly influential Northern California operation known as Alembic.

Alembic had its origins in the Grateful Dead's obsession with recorded and live sound, and it quickly became an umbrella name for a recording studio, a developer of PA systems, and a workshop for guitar repair and modification. Guitar wiz Rick Turner, electronics boffin Ron Wickersham, and recording engineer Bob Matthews formalised Alembic as a corporation in 1970, and the following year they built a bass guitar for Jack Casady of Jefferson Airplane, the first official Alembic-designed instrument. By 1973, Alembic had established itself primarily as a bass maker: the ratio was something like 20 basses to every guitar. The instruments offered a novel and effective combination of high quality multi-laminate neck-through-body construction; attractive exotic woods; heavy tone-enhancing brass hardware; and complex active electronic systems with external power supplies. Alembic's image was distinctly high-end and expensive.

Ibanez's Musician series, new for 1978, took Alembic's key features and popularised them. All the MC models had 24-fret laminated through-necks, a construction style where the neck runs the length of the guitar. Added "wings" completed the body shape, and here these too were laminated, using ash and mahogany or maple. Ibanez claimed that the Musician's pickups alone could provide 15 different tones "and in conjunction with the control available from the EQ Tone System, the possibilities are dizzying". On the top-of-the-line Musician MC400 and MC500, these dizzying possibilities were drawn

1978 Performer PF400

1978 Artist 2617

■ The Artist series typified Ibanez's new confidence as the 80s approached, with this **2617** (above) showing off the double-cutaway carved-top shape and the pleasing attention to player-centric detail. **Andy Partridge** of XTC (left, with Artist 2619) was an early fan. The company's hollow and semi-solid electrics continued with the **FA** and **SA** series (**1977 catalogue**, top),

while two more solidbody series seemed to dither between past and present. The **Performer** guitars (**PF400**, top, and keyed **1978 catalogue** page, right) were newly lawyer-friendly Les Paul copies. The **Concert** models (**1977 catalogue**, far left), meanwhile, seemed like an attempt to marry a Les Paul maple top to a Strat-shaped mahogany body. Both were shortlived.

from an array of controls: two knobs for volume and pre-amp level (and later a third for tone) and three detented cut/boost knobs for bass, mid, and treble; two Tri-Sound switches for pickup coil and phase selection; and a further switch to turn on the battery-powered preamp. The base MC100 and 200 models, meanwhile, had simple conventional controls, and the middling MC300 settled for adding just the Tri-Sound switches. List prices ranged from $445 for the MC100 to $895 for the MC500, at a time when a regular Fender Strat listed at $750 and a Gibson Les Paul Standard at $799.

Sustain-enhancement was flavour of the moment, and the brass hardware on these Musicians was intended to further that cause. What with that and the fancy wood and the circuitry on board, they could be heavy guitars, but they packed a punch for those willing to spend time investigating the possibilities. The Ibanez MCs did much to widen the appeal of the supercharged guitar at a time when some makers were trying to give guitarists a little more electronic scope, now that keyboard players were enjoying the arrival of relatively affordable synthesizers.

The Studio guitars, also introduced in 1978, were like set-neck versions of the Musicians, with a generally simpler and less ornate approach, although the ST300 had a revised version of the EQ system, and there were a couple of double-necks, too. Fashion moved on, however, and the various Studio and Musician models, very much of their time, were gone from the catalogues by 1982.

As usual, Hoshino introduced these new models at the now twice-yearly NAMM trade shows, and for the January 1979 show at Anahiem, California, the western-states Ibanez distributor, Chesbro, organised a jam session at the nearby Knott's Berry Farm theme park. The line-up featured Jeff Hasselberger of Elger on guitar and a stellar host of Ibanez and Tama endorsers: Alphonso Johnson on bass, Bob Weir of the Grateful Dead on guitar, Billy Cobham on drums, and Bobby Cochran, who'd played with Leon Russell and Steppenwolf, also on guitar.

Cochran was a long-standing and important endorser and consultant, based in California. "Rather than have specific ideas for a new guitar design, Bobby had dozens of small suggestions about making the guitars more playable, testing pickups, and advising on fret sizes and other fingerboard tweaks," Hasselberger explains. "After those guys got together at NAMM, they morphed into Bobby & The Midnites, eventually releasing two albums and touring when the Dead was on hiatus."[38]

Meanwhile, the Fujigen factory was in its stride, making some very good electric guitars – and a lot of them were for Ibanez. Fujigen was still the main supplier of electrics to Hoshino, and the collaboration was critical to the growing awareness that a fresh Ibanez style was emerging, built on new ideas and good quality. Fujigen had enjoyed great success in the 60s after its formation around the start of the decade, exporting to the USA and establishing a proper factory around 1965. The factory had made a manufacturing deal with Matsumoto Mokko, which produced wooden parts that

Fujigen assembled, and it started its own brand, Greco, in partnership with the distributor Kanda Shokai.

A downturn in Fujigen's business in 1966 followed the USA's doubling of customs duties on imported electrics, prompting a focus on Greco and the domestic market. By 1969, business was still poor, and one of Fujigen's two founders, Yutaka Mimura, sold out to his partner, Yuuichirou Yokouchi, who steered Fujigen to new success through the 70s, not least by the steadily growing business of making Ibanez guitars for Hoshino.

In 1976, a visitor described the Fujigen site, noting five factories, a finishing plant, and a three-storey office building. The work was divided into several sections, including Materials, Woodwork, Lacquering, Assembly, Special (which meant acoustic guitars), and R&D (which incorporated design, quality control, and production management). "Yoshimochi Kamiyjo, the firm's professional manager, supervises the factory with 193 workers, including 60 females," wrote the visitor. "The plant's production includes about 230 models of electric guitars and 120 models of folk [acoustic] guitars, totalling about 6,000 electric guitars and 3,000 folk guitars [per month], as well as banjos and mandolins."[39] Fujigen outsourced a range of jobs to 25 or so small firms in the area, known in Japan as gaichuus, and these handled painting, sanding, wiring, and so on. The company bought in its pickups from Nisshin Onpa and metal parts from Shin-Etsu.

Makoto "Nick" Sugimoto was a student in 1976, studying law, when his mother – the first of those 60 females to secure a job at Fujigen – pulled some strings to help him visit the USA to learn English and absorb some guitar knowledge. Through Fujigen's contacts, he worked first for Yutaka Trading in Los Angeles, owned by the ex-boss of Fujigen, Yutaka Mimura. There he met Kunio "Kenny" Sugai (more of whom later, as the owner of Performance Guitar). Sugai taught Sugimoto as much as he could about guitars.

Next, Sugimoto moved to Elger in Bensalem and worked there for a few months, learning to repair instruments. One of the guitars he remembers working on was Denny Laine's Ibanez double-neck, a model 2670 that had been supplied to the Wings guitarist in January 1977. "Somebody had fixed the binding on it, a terrible finish, so I cleaned it up," Sugimoto recalls. "But I thought doing repair jobs was like being a doctor, whereas I actually wanted to work making guitars."

With that in mind, he returned to Japan and started in the woodshop at Fujigen in March 1978. Six months later, he moved to the R&D department, where he and his boss Mr Suzuki worked on and made Ibanez prototypes and artist instruments. Sugimoto remembers his first jobs were making a bass for Alphonso Johnson of Weather Report and a production prototype for the new Roadster guitar series. "In my work notes there were 360 guitars waiting to be made: prototypes, guitars for the catalogue, that kind of thing. I remember there were 24 artists named on that list. It was a really busy time for us." One of those artists was Björn Ulvaeus of Abba, for whom Sugimoto made some guitars in 1979, including an Artist 2622 finished in polar white (Abba recorded for Polar

1980 Studio ST3000

THE IBANEZ ELECTRIC GUITAR BOOK

■ The new-for-1978 Musician and Studio series borrowed from Alembic, a West Coast guitar-maker at the Grateful Dead camp and a leader in multi-laminate through-necks, exotic woods, and active electronics. Ibanez popularised the ideas in guitars like the **Musician MC500** (main guitar), and the set-neck **Studio** models (upscale **ST3000**, opposite, double-neck **ST1200**, below, and **1979 ad**, opposite). **Fujigen Gakki** had established itself as Hoshino's prime manufacturing partner in Japan, making all the best Ibanez guitars of the period. The **factory entrance** (opposite) and a shop worker (top left) are pictured in 1976, while **Nick Sugimoto**, who built prototypes and artist instruments, is seen (top) in Fujigen's **R&D** department in 1982. A band of top Ibanez endorsers played at a trade-show event in 1979 (opposite), including **Bob Weir**, Bobby Cochran, and Alphonso Johnson.

1980 Musician MC500

1980 Studio ST1200

Records). "For the name tag at the 24th fret, I had trouble with the first B in Abba, which is flipped," Sugimoto says. "There was no tooling for this. I tried a B upside down, but that looked wrong, with the top smaller than the bottom. I eventually did it by hand – but this was typical of the regular problems we would come up against."[40]

The Roadster models, for which Sugimoto made the prototype, marked the start of Ibanez's introduction of a number of lower-price series, in contrast to the effort spent on the recent higher-end models. There was greatly increased competition in the budget electrics market around this time: Fender launched its Japanese-made Squier brand in 1982, and Gibson had been sourcing Epiphone-brand models from Japan since 1969. The shortlived Ibanez Roadster models, named after the stripped-down hot-rod cars of the same name, were introduced in 1979. They listed around $400 and were strongly Strat influenced – as were the more affordable Blazer guitars that followed in 1980, starting at under $300. Some of the early Blazers were made by the Dyna factory in Japan, but most Ibanez instruments were still made by Fujigen.

Ibanez followed through in 1982 with the revised Roadstar II series – a further use of the Hoshino-related "star" name. By 1984, it offered the basic Strat-flavoured RS130 model at $245 and, moving up through a wide range of models, finally reached the upscale through-neck RS1500, listed at $645. In *Back To The Future*, Michael J. Fox's character Marty McFly plays a Roadstar II RS430 at the start of the movie, when Huey Lewis's teacher character tells him he's "just too darned loud"– and before McFly gets into time travel and ES-345s.

By the end of 1981, Hoshino at last changed the name of its US operation from the now irrelevant Elger Company to the more obvious Hoshino USA. Kimihide "Ken" Hoshino replaced Yoshi Hoshino as president of the US firm. In Japan, the name of the Hoshino Gakki Ten company was changed in 1981 to Hoshino Gakki Co Ltd, and Masao Hoshino became its president. Also in 1981, the company's drum factory changed its name, from Tama Seisaku Sho to Hoshino Gakki Mfg (and in 2009 it was merged into Hoshino Gakki Co Ltd). The distributor Kanda Shokai had started to sell Ibanez guitars to domestic dealers around 1978; before that, there had apparently been little demand at home. In 1982, Tom Tanaka established Hoshino's own domestic sales company, Hoshino Gakki Hanbai, which became the exclusive Japanese distributor five years later. Tanaka was its president until the late 80s.

In 1982, Jeff Hasselberger left the US firm. "That introductory phase of Ibanez history was coming to a close," he recalls. "I could see the fun was over. The next phase was to do it in more of a Japanese way, to organise it – more Japanese-corporate, if you want to call it that. So I decided to leave on a high point. I wanted to do more wacky things, and I could see the possibility of doing that at Ibanez was coming to a close."

Hasselberger left and set up his own advertising and marketing firm. "I feel extremely fortunate to have been in the right place at the right time," he says of his time at Ibanez. "I think we went a long way to change the perception in the USA of guitars that come from across the ocean, and I think I had a great part of creating a tremendous brand. I set out to make some cool guitars and did whatever came to me." He laughs at the memory, and adds: "I remember sitting up late at Jim Messina's place one night and saying: Wouldn't it be great if you didn't have to sleep? Think of all the cool shit you could do."[41]

In May 1981, before Hasselberger left, Ibanez hired a young drummer and ex-art-school student, Bill Reim, as Hasselberger's assistant. At the time of writing, Reim is president of Hoshino USA. Back then, he was a young man who worked for a concert promoter in Philadelphia. One day, he caught a tempting ad in the paper, which read: Musical instrument company seeks art director. "Jeff hired me – and then, probably within about three months, he told me he was leaving to form his own agency," Reim says, recalling the shock. "The Japanese there took on some of Jeff's artist relations stuff themselves, but a lot of it they pushed across to my desk, and I also had to do all the copywriting and so on. The company was small and pretty unstructured at that point." Reim remembers about 65 people in total at the Bensalem HQ when he joined, about half in the office and half in the warehouse.

In fact, he began to get the impression he'd joined a company in decline. In the early 80s, Reim says, Ibanez was in a spiral downward. "They were not linking in to what musicians wanted or needed. They were trying to do things but just didn't have the technical knowhow or a feel for it."[42] There was also the value of the Japanese yen to contend with. For some time, Hoshino had profited from Japanese-made product sold into the USA and other markets around the world at a very competitive price. Now that competitive edge was disappearing as the yen strengthened. At the end of 1975, 1,000 Japanese yen was worth about US $3.20. By 1980, it was closer to $5, and later in the decade it would hit about $8.30. This meant, simply, that Ibanez guitars outside Japan became much more expensive.

Not only that, but as the 80s progressed, the slumbering big two, Fender and Gibson, began to wake up and take notice of the changed world around them. Gibson was in poor health, but matters would improve when Norlin sold out to new owners in 1986, and gradually things began to look brighter for the new leaner and hungrier operation. In 1981, Fender had hired new managers from the American musical-instruments division of Yamaha, the big Japanese company famous for pianos, electronics, and, increasingly, guitars. Fender's owner, CBS, sold the company to a team of those managers four years later, and Fender rapidly regained lost ground.

When Fender looked for a Japanese plant to make a line of vintage reissues as well as some models for a new good-quality budget brand, Squier, it chose Fujigen. Dan Smith headed up the electric guitar team at Fender, and he recalls how impressed he was by the Fujigen operation when he first visited the factory in the early 80s. "There was plenty of

■ Ibanez introduced the **Roadster** models (**RS100**, below) as a new line of Fender-influenced budget guitars, following on three years later with the **Roadstar II**s. Shown opposite are an **RS405** (top) and **505**, and a **Comet**-colours 1984 ad, good examples of the Japanese-made quality that they brought to the lower reaches of the electric guitar market at the time. An RS430 turned up in the hands of Marty McFly in **Back To The Future** (opposite), which must have helped sales. The **Blazer** line (**1980 brochure**, above) was another decent offer for the first-time buyer. Not that Ibanez had ignored the upscale player: Nick Sugimoto at Fujigen made a polar-white Artist 2622 for Björn Ulvaeus of **Abba** (above), and the **Artist** series continued to exude style (Ferocious **1981 ad**, opposite).

ROADSTER OR ROADSTAR?

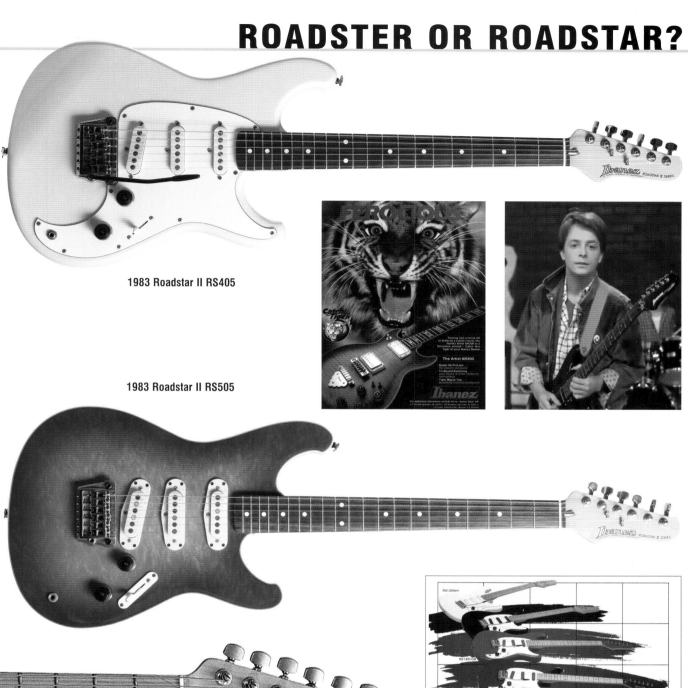

1983 Roadstar II RS405

1983 Roadstar II RS505

1979 Roadster RS100

pride in what they were doing," Smith says. "The factory was very clean, the machinery was all up to snuff, and all the fixtures were well maintained. It was a really good traditional 50s and 60s-style guitar manufacturing facility. It was a real pleasure going there, and the people there were as good as any I've ever known. At the time, our US product was of questionable quality – and the Japanese-made product was of unquestionably better quality."[43]

Aside from Fender's revival, there were newer American names about, too. Kramer was the US brand of the decade, and Jackson and Charvel were making waves, too. Eddie Van Halen was the hottest guitarist on the planet, and the red-and-white striped custom guitar he put together at the Kramer factory in New Jersey was an instantly recognisable icon that helped sell stacks of Kramer's so-called superstrat guitars. "You couldn't give a Les Paul away," Bill Reim recalls. "It was all Strats and superstrats. At Ibanez, we were trying to develop guitars that would compete in that market – but they were pale imitations of what was being put out by some of those other companies that were heavily entrenched in the scene. Kramer was flying on the fuel of Van Halen, a one-man force to be reckoned with. During the 80s it was a Kramer world, and everybody was trying to get a piece of that action."[44]

The superstrat style dominated the design of rock guitars, although to define exactly what constitutes a superstrat and to determine who first made one would fill another book. For our purposes here, we should agree that in the first years of the decade, several American makers developed and adjusted the basic Fender Stratocaster design to suit the needs of extreme-rock players. The makers included Kramer, Dean, Jackson, and Charvel. The new features, in various combinations, included a body with squarer sides, stretched horns, bolder contours, and a slimmer shape, equipped with combinations of powerful single-coils and humbuckers, which quickly resulted in the preferred combination of two single-coils plus a bridge humbucker. All this was partnered by a thinner, flatter neck and a double-locking heavy-duty fine-tuning vibrato system, designed for extreme pitch shifting. Jackson in particular, from about 1984, improved access to the highest of the 24 frets with a through-neck and deeper cutaways, and popularised a drooping "pointy" headstock.

By 1984, Ibanez was offering the Roadstar II RS440 with the newly popular superstrat pickup layout of bridge humbucker and two single-coils (also known as hum-sing-sing or HSS). The influence of the superstrat hovered over every maker's work in the 80s – including Ibanez, of course. For now, in a parallel fad for pointy guitars, Ibanez also leaned on its established allegiance to Gibson's old Flying V and Explorer designs, and it added some upgraded versions to the catalogue.

The Rocket Roll II and Destroyer II models first appeared in 1981, with the high-end versions sporting a Hamer-like combination of pointy body and flame-maple top, while the XV500 of 1983 was an extreme take on the Explorer shape, owing more to B.C. Rich and Jackson. Ibanez followed other 80s trends, too, including the headless fashion, begun by Steinberger, resulting in a couple of shortlived models in the Axstar series, and the guitar-synthesizer fashion, resulting in another shortlived and doubtless expensive mid-decade mistake, the Ibanez IMG2010 MIDI Electronic Guitar and its accompanying IMC1 MIDI Controller box. Guitarists are by and large conservative souls, and they do not want to sling synthesizers around their necks.

A further new American recruit joined Ibanez USA in 1984. Rich Lasner was a guitarist who worked as a repairman and teacher at the 8th Street Music store in Philadelphia. One day, the Ibanez rep told him they were looking for someone who could go out and demonstrate their instruments to potential customers. Lasner sensed an opportunity and went for an audition-cum-interview. Ken Hoshino called out a series of names – Jeff Beck!, Phil Collen!, Steve Lukather! – and Lasner had to play an immediate impersonation for 20 seconds or so. He presumed from the reaction that he'd failed, so he was surprised to pick up a phone message the following day from Ken, who said little more than: You start Monday. "And that," Lasner laughs, "was the auspicious beginning to my beautiful guitar career."

Lasner knew that Ibanez had grown beyond its image as merely a copyist. "They were starting their direction of making things that were more original, in their minds. I'd seen that from things I'd sold in the store. The Artist, for example, really was a beautifully-done guitar." Lasner's own tastes leaned to jazz and fusion, so he was impressed that Ibanez was making George Benson's signature models and that John Scofield and Pat Metheny were in the catalogues as Ibanez artists. "The Benson GB10 changed the image of everyone in the jazz community as to whether or not Ibanez was something you would play," he says. "I got the feeling that, with a little bit of work, we could personify the company with the image of the artist, as they had done with George Benson."

Lasner found himself in a job where the atmosphere was agreeably loose. Ibanez USA did have a business structure, of course, with accountants and stock managers and all the rest that you'd expect to run a sales operation day to day. "But we kind of floated above those groups, and they were never really sure what we were doing," Lasner says. "And by 'we', I mean Bill Reim's team and my guys. We pulled in artist relations, product development, and marketing into one think-tank. We tried to figure out everything from who wants to play this guitar, to what should the guitar be like, to is there an artist we can get for it, and, if so, how do we advertise it." It wouldn't be too long before an ideal combination of those elements came into view.

Meanwhile, Ibanez had introduced a number of vibrato systems in the wake of the popularity of the Floyd Rose double-locking system. The Floyd became the mainstay of many an extreme-rocker's superstrat. Rose and others wanted to improve the standard Fender Stratocaster vibrato, which was notorious for failing to return strings to correct pitch after use. It's necessary only to hear a live Hendrix recording to understand the

1982 Iceman II IC400

■ The impression remained in the mid 80s that Ibanez was unclear about how it could build on the past to create a future. There were a number of remakes of earlier models, including a welcome revival for the **Iceman** shape, with the **IC400** (top) and **RR400** (right)

given hip 80s flame-maple tops. The **DT555** (main guitar) became known as the Phil Collen model when the Def Leppard guitarist played one. Ventures into some of the newer developments in guitar technology were less happy for Ibanez, not least the much hyped

MIDI guitar (**1986 ad**, opposite). Few were shipped and players continued to favour dependable analogue guitars. The **Axstar** series (1985 catalogue, opposite) had smooth-pointy treats as well as a brief fling with another 80s fad, the headless guitar.

'85 AXSTAR ELECTRIC GUITARS

Axstar By Ibanez

1985 Destroyer II DT555

1982 Rocket Roll II RR400

basic problem, but since the 70s, technically adept players had been using ever more extreme techniques, often in the process turning a Strat vibrato into a tuning nightmare. The solution was somehow to try to stop the strings "creeping" at three critical points: across the nut; at the tuner shaft; or at the bridge saddle.

Rose offered his take on the solution, which was to lock the strings behind the nut and also at the bridge saddles. This meant that even the most demonstrative bender could stay in tune. Soon afterward, Rose added fine-tuners at the bridge for any small compensations that might be necessary. "This now made it possible for people to get through entire sets of music or recordings without flipping out of tune," Lasner says. "That was something that was never possible before with a vibrato-equipped guitar. The Floyd locked it at both intonation points, and that was what made his system work."[45]

Floyd Rose first sold his vibratos in the late 70s, but they found a wider audience from 1982, when Kramer began putting them on its instruments and also began acting as manufacturing agent and US distributor. Eddie Van Halen had worked with Rose from the earliest days, and he showed off the Floyd's capabilities … to say the least. An early Kramer ad suggested: "If you don't believe us, ask Edward." Soon it seemed as if every guitarist who played loud, aggressive rock wanted a locking trem.

Ibanez offered its own early take on a new-style vibrato with the Hard Rocker, as seen on some of the Roadstar models from 1982, and three years later, through a series of developments, reached the refined double-locking Edge Tremolo System. Kramer was busily selling licenses for Floyd Rose systems to any brand that could afford them, and offered the same to Ibanez, expecting to sell its regular Floyd system, made by Schaller in Germany. Fritz Katoh, at Hoshino in Japan, was given the task of finding a better way.

Katoh's R&D department at Ibanez had designed some interesting hardware as well as complete guitar models. The Gibraltar bridge was one of the first of these hardware developments. It was intended to help the player make easy height adjustments and then just as easily lock the bridge in place ("rock solid" said Ibanez, to underline the Gibraltar name). Some guitars with the Gibraltar also featured a metal block in the body into which the bridge was fixed for a claimed increase in sustain. The Gibraltar was often teamed with the Quik-Change tailpiece, which had slots to assist rapid string-changing. Jeff Hasselberger's original sketch had the string slots on the bottom, so they would be out of sight, but Katoh came up with the slanted slots on top, which worked better and gave the tailpiece a unique look.

Then there was the Half & Half nut, which exploited the fashion for brass hardware and its alleged enhancement of sustain. It had a half-brass half-bone construction that was said to provide sustain as well as traditional solidity. And the Sure-Grip knobs had ridged rubber rims so that a sweaty-handed guitarist could be sure of getting a grip on his controls. The inspiration came from some Schaller knobs Hasselberger had seen years before, and the material for Ibanez's take on the idea was supplied by Okamoto

Riken, better known in Japan for condoms. Katoh also came up with Ibanez's Velve Tune tuners and the Hard Rocker, Pro Rocker, and Power Rocker vibratos. He was probably more responsible for the detailed look and feel of Ibanez electrics than any other person. Ibanez clearly intended to put copying firmly behind it after the shock of the Gibson action in 1977, and instead it went rushing forward, aiming for originality in all areas and the manufacture of its own hardware and parts. Over the years, this holistic attitude to design and production would become a hallmark of Ibanez's independence. Just as Roy Miyahara had predicted, Ibanez was turning "the Gibson problem" into a good opportunity.

So it was that instead of meekly accepting the existing Floyd Rose vibrato, Katoh partnered with the Gotoh Gut factory in Isesaki, about 60 miles north of Tokyo, to design a Floyd Rose-licensed bridge that suited the Ibanez approach: it would be Ibanez's own, and it would be made in Japan. "The biggest improvement over the original Floyd Rose was the elegant design and the insert-style knife edge," Katoh recalls, "where one side had a rounded shape and the other was straight, so that you could set the correct location with the two studs and get a smooth tremolo action."[46]

The Ibanez Edge featured this and a number of other design improvements, but an important general difference was that it was die-cast, whereas the Floyd was machined. The casting, Lasner says, created hollow spaces inside the Edge and in the process seemed to improve the sound. "As a repairman, I'd put dozens if not hundreds of those original Floyds on people's guitars, and almost to a man they were disappointed over time. Once they'd got past the thrill of it never going out of tune again, they started to hear that it didn't sound like it used to. Whether that was psycho-acoustics or real, we could go on all day, but a lot of people didn't like it." People did like the Ibanez Edge and its later companion, the Lo-Pro Edge. "Floyd's a great guy, and he liked our Edge bridge," Lasner says. "But he felt one of his big mistakes was licensing his stuff to everybody, because some of us were able to make better things – because we had better resources."

Reim and Lasner brought a couple more key people into the think-tank: Bill Cummiskey was hired as Lasner's assistant; and Mace Bailey, who'd started at Elger in 1980 as a guitar checker, was developing his skills as a guitar-maker and feeding ideas into the plans for new models. Meanwhile, a new series for 1985 was the Pro Line, including a Jackson Randy Rhoads-style pointy V and a couple of superstrat-ish models with unusual pushbutton selectors. "Those were essentially just Stratocasters with different colours and a bizarre switching system that I'd rather forget," Lasner says. "And of course we couldn't sell them – because Fender existed. It was becoming obvious to the people that ran the place that they had to be more creative and push a little harder."[47]

The Pro Line series gained a few more similar models before it was dropped a year or two later, but it did at least introduce a new pointy headstock design, one that remains

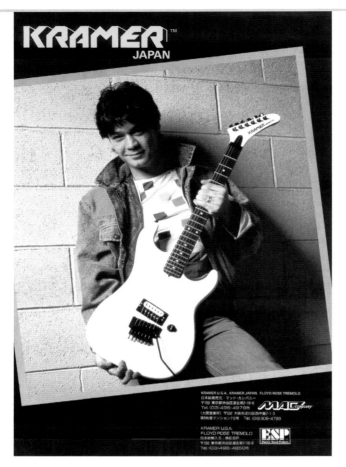

■ Ibanez and every other electric maker were up against the seemingly unbeatable 80s combination of **Kramer** and **Eddie Van Halen** (1986 catalogue cover, left). A good deal of the fuss came from the new idea of a locking vibrato, which kept the otherwise fickle gadget in-tune. Ibanez felt its way with early vibratos such as the **Hard Rocker**, seen in the 1983 "archtop" **Roadstar** ad, opposite. It finally reached the refined double-locking **Edge** system, in a **1986 catalogue** featuring the Pro Line V-shape 2660, right, and on the 2550, below. The **PL2550** had the Pro Line's odd five-switch pickup-preset system, which did not survive. Lasting hardware introductions of the time, pictured below, are the **Half & Half nut** (left), the **Quik-Change tailpiece** (centre), and the **Sure-Grip knob** (right). And the pointiest Ibanez? The **XV500** (far right).

PRO LINE

SPECIFICATIONS	PL1770	PL1880	PL2550	PL2660	PL5050
BODY	ALDER	JUMBO MAPLE/WOODLAMINAT	ALDER	MAPLE THRU NECK-ANGLED	ALDER
NECK	MAPLE 5PC/ANGLED OIL-FINISH	MAPLE 5PC/ANGLED OIL-FINISH	EBONY	EBONY	MAPLE 5PC/ANGLED OIL-FINISH
FINGERBOARD	EBONY	EBONY			EBONY
NO. OF FRET	22	22	22	22	24
BRIDGE	IBANEZ EDGE	IBANEZ EDGE	IBANEZ EDGE	HARD EDGE	ACCU-CAST II-B
STRING LOCK	TOP LOK III	TOP LOK III	TOP LOK III	TOP LOK III	
HARDWARE	BLACK/COP MAT-GOLD	BLACK	BLACK/COP SP-WHITE GOLD	BLACK	BLACK
PICKUP	2 × SUPER 70, 982	2 × SUPER 70, 982	2 × SUPER 70, 982	2 × 16	2 × L20-B
CONTROLS	1V, 1T, 5 WAY	1V, 1T, 3 MINI SWITCHES	1V, 1T, 5 WAY	1V, 1T, 3 WAY	1V, 1 BALANCER, 2 EQ/B
FUNCTION	PU PRE-SET SYSTEM	SOLID SOUND	PU PRE-SET SYSTEM	PU PRE-SET SYSTEM	2-BAND EQUALIZER
FINISH	ROBLAU	MAGNA/BLAU, BIKOKU	BLKBLAU/CHERRY (K2)	BLKBLAU/CHERRY (K2)	CAR/GUN METALLIC/
	CAR/COM METALLIC/	W/CHIN/NATU	CRCGOLD PEARL	PL/PEARL/	PL/PEARL/
	CRCGOLD PEARL/		SPYDER PEARL/		
	SPYDER PEARL/				

1987 Pro Line PL2550

1985 XV500

today as the standard Ibanez head. Meanwhile, the spiral downward continued: business was poor, and Ibanez's direction seemed aimless. "We got to the point where we were shipping maybe only 50 or 60 guitars a month," Reim says of the US operation. "The morale was so crushed. But some of us started noticing a movement out there that we weren't involved in, a whole school of young new players that we should be working with. We couldn't do it, however, with the instruments that were coming to us from Japan."[48]

Gradually, Reim and Lasner and their colleagues, and to some extent Katoh and others in Japan, began to discover how they might be able to get into that movement and develop a fresh kind of Ibanez guitar. They moved beyond the half-hearted Pro Line guitars and felt their way forward. The next new design was the Maxxas ... which at first glance was not obviously an Ibanez product.

Reim had been working on new body designs using sculpted clay models. He was looking for a more ergonomic solidbody, putting aside conventional squared-off shapes and moving to a thinner aerofoil-like design. Lasner, a keen fusion guitarist who used a Gibson ES-335 as his main guitar, began working with Reim. "I'm not a big guy," Lasner says, "so the 335 looked huge on me. And it can be fatiguing if you're standing up for hours playing it. I wondered if I could bring some of that tone, some of the warmth of the semi-hollow, into a guitar about the size of a Strat."[49]

The new design Reim and Lasner worked on was ambitious. "We worked literally elbow to elbow developing the futuristic shape," Reim recalls. "We were in search of something different, and the Maxxas was just that."[50] They aimed for beauty, for sweeping lines, for a look that was different from the pointiness many makers were adopting. They devised a new bolt-on neck joint, which had a smooth, rounded heel and allowed the neck to be positioned further out, with two screws under the neck pickup. It was called the All Access joint, and the Maxxas was the first of several important Ibanez models to feature a similar approach.

They designed the Maxxas's thin body to be made from a hollow front and back joined together over a central core, like a sort of mahogany clamshell. But the peculiarity did not go down well. Lasner says the Japanese were worried that the design was too far-out and might jeopardise attempts to give the Ibanez name a fresh and positive vibe. "They said that we can't put 'Ibanez' on this," he recalls, "that it's going to need another brandname, or we won't put it out. It was pretty much done, so we had to acquiesce."[51]

When the Maxxas finally appeared in 1987, the source of the guitar was mysterious. The large name on the head was Maxxas – but just visible alongside, in smaller type, was "A Division Of Ibanez". Anyone who noticed that may also have wondered about the pickup markings. The humbuckers had an IBZ/USA logo, another new name. In fact, it marked the start of a collaboration between Ibanez and DiMarzio.

Ronald Bienstock was Hoshino USA's general counsel at the time, responsible among other things for working out the legalities of any deals the company made. He was friendly with Larry DiMarzio, who'd started DiMarzio Pickups in Staten Island, New York, in 1975 – the first company devoted to making replacement pickups. Bienstock was urging Joe Hoshino, the longstanding executive director at Hoshino USA, to incorporate US-made products into Ibanez guitars. "I said to him we'd fall behind Kramer, Gibson, Fender, that we had to have American parts. We had to be competitive."

Bienstock eventually got Larry DiMarzio and Joe Hoshino to sit down together at a restaurant table in New York City and discuss a collaboration. It went well, Bienstock says, but the talk stalled on one point: what would Ibanez call pickups made for them and supplied by DiMarzio? "They were nervous about having 'DiMarzio' on the guitars," Bienstock says, "because that would upset Gotoh and other suppliers. So we came up with IBZ/USA, and that worked for both of them. And I think those pickups helped dramatically with the sound of the guitars."[52] The two companies have partnered ever since and Ibanez today still uses many pickups made for them by DiMarzio.

Maxxas, however, did not survive for long, either as a brandname or a guitar, despite an impressive set of innovations, and the MX models were gone from the pricelists by the end of the 80s. Of more lasting importance was a set of designs at first grouped together into the Pro540 series: the P, or Power, the R, or Radius, and the S, or Saber, also launched in 1987. (There was also a weird T model, the 580T Turbot, surely the worst ever guitar name.) They shared DiMarzio IBZ/USA pickups in HSS format, Edge locking vibratos, and simple controls (at first alongside pickup switches, then a regular selector). They also had very thin and fast 22-fret necks: the P and the S marked the first appearance of the Ibanez Wizard neck – just 17mm deep at the first fret, where a Strat, for example, is nearer 20mm – while the R used the slightly chunkier Ultra (19mm at the first fret).

What set the body styles apart from one another were the three quite different profiles. Looking at the cross-section of the bodies, viewed from the base, the P was pretty deep, with angled sides; the R was wedge-shaped, narrowing toward the top, something like a teardrop; and the S was ultra-thin, especially at the edges, and felt like its curving shape was designed almost to hug the player's body. Lasner describes the P in its final pointy form as "a goofy-looking Jackson type of guitar that really never had a reason to live", and it limped on for a few years before falling by the wayside. The R and especially the S, however, found success in different ways in the 90s and later.

The Pro540S – "Saber" was dropped because of prior use by Music Man – provided the foundation for the S line, which is still going strong today as an important fixture in the modern Ibanez catalogue. As with the Maxxas, Reim's experiments with clay models and his search for an aerofoil design, in conjunction with Rich Lasner, produced the S's thin body, which was tapered at the edges and felt wonderfully light, snuggling in to the player. "It was Rich's opinions and insights as a player, plus my own oddball art background, that came together to make what I believe will be a lasting design," Reim says of the S.[53] Mark Wittenberg at Chesbro, Ibanez's west-coast distributor, came up with the 540R's oblong

1989 S540

1989 Maxxas MX3

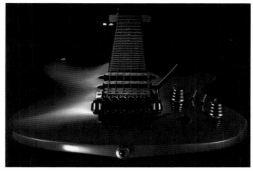

1988 GB30 George Benson

■ In the second half of the 80s, Ibanez set about revolutionising its electric guitar lines. Four designs set the trend, and all aimed their sights at new body forms. Three new recruits at Ibanez USA are pictured working on a clay model of one of those new bodies (left to right: **Bill Reim**, **Bill Cummiskey**, and **Rich Lasner**). Their efforts resulted in the shortlived **Maxxas** (**MX3**, left, and **1987 catalogue** cover with MX2) and the longterm **S style** (**S540**, top). Three of the body profiles are shown above (top to bottom: **P**, or Power, **R**, or Radius, and **S**, or Saber). Meanwhile, George Benson had a new model, the semi-hollow **GB30** (left).

asymmetrical shape, and while the R design enjoyed some success at the time, it would soon provide inspiration for the Joe Satriani signature models – of which more later.

Lasner was still toying with his idea that Ibanez needed personifying. "I laid out on a sheet of paper all the successful guitar companies at the time, and every single one of them, minus ESP, was a person's last name – even if that person didn't exist any more. Gibson, Fender, Jackson, Charvel, Kramer, on and on. They're people." Ibanez, on the other hand, seemed faceless. "I said if we got the proper artist," Lasner continues, "if he could be a spokesperson for the company and also be somebody that immediately attracted everyone's attention, then we could ride the image of the company along that person, and we would all prosper."[54]

But who? Ibanez had already worked with a number of name guitarists to create signature models, and we've seen how this happened with Bob Weir, Paul Stanley, and George Benson. There had been a few more along the way, too: the Lee Ritenour ES-like LR10 (introduced 1981); the Joe Pass hollowbody JP20 (1981); the Steve Lukather Roadstar II RS1010 (1984); and the Allan Holdsworth AH10 and AH20, the first Ibanez guitars with basswood bodies (1985/86). These were all fine guitarists, of course – but not exactly the kind of headline rocker now being sought.

Lasner knew Mike Varney, who ran Shrapnel Records in San Francisco. Shrapnel had arrived with a bang in 1983 when it released Yngwie Malmsteen's debut record, and the label continued to deliver cuts by up-and-coming young guitarists of the high-octane persuasion. One of Varney's sources for these new wunderkinds was his Spotlight column in *Guitar Player* magazine, where he introduced new talent and encouraged submissions. Lasner himself was one of Varney's Spotlight guitarists, featuring in a 1981 column ("it was back when chops meant more than notes," Lasner points out today, "and I must apologise for that").

Lasner called Varney. "I said here's what's going on: we want to personify this company, we need to create a situation where artists will look at Ibanez and think it's a great place to be, and come to us. So, can we partner?" Varney was enthusiastic, and he turned Ibanez on to guitarists like Vinnie Moore, Paul Gilbert, Richie Kotzen, and others. "At the time, these were very young and obscure players, just getting on their feet and starting to move," Lasner says. "But you could see the potential, and Ibanez fully saw that. So we started supporting these guys, seriously supporting them with advertising and clinic tours and guitars of their own."[52]

Ibanez provided personal guitars for them all and issued signature models for Vinnie Moore in 1989 and for Paul Gilbert in 1990. Jim Donahue, who joined Hoshino USA in 1984, starting as a guitar packer and moving into the repair room, remembers the enthusiasm to work with new guitarists. "I was still doing repair in the late 80s, but we kind of shifted into a custom shop," Donahue recalls. "Japan would send us like a hundred necks and a hundred bodies. People would come in every day – Blues Saraceno,

Richie Kotzen, Vinnie Moore, Joey Taffola, Paul Gilbert – and we'd just say: What do you want? And we'd make it. We were trying to get every artist we could get – we wanted the catalogue to be full. Anybody that played guitar that was a shredder, we wanted."[53] It seemed that Ibanez had found its source of new players who needed new kinds of guitars. But a better-known guitarist was also showing up on the radar at Hoshino USA.

Bill Reim remembers a crucial meeting, probably in 1986, called by Joe Hoshino. By now, Mitsuaki "Mike" Shimada was president of the US operation, having taken over in 1986 from Ken Hoshino. Also that year, Yoshihiro Hoshino took over from Masao Hoshino as president of Hoshino Gakki in Japan, and in 1987, Ken Hoshino would become president of the Japanese domestic sales company, Hoshino Gakki Hanbai, replacing Tom Tanaka. Ken would remain in that post until 1995, when Hiroshi "Nero" Ando became president of the sales firm, and in 1988 Tanaka would replace Shimada as president of the US firm, a post he held for ten years.

Anyway, Joe Hoshino called the meeting with Mike Shimada, Rich Lasner, Bill Reim, and a few other key US people, and he told them that they needed an Ibanez equivalent of Eddie Van Halen, and in particular someone to emulate the way Edward had bolstered the image (and the fortunes) of the all-conquering Kramer. "Joe asked if there was anybody out there who could work with us and represent the company and make a big impact on the market," Reim recalls. "We all just looked at each other and said, more or less together, well yes … it has to be Steve Vai."[57]

Joe was impressed with the unanimity and told them to find this Steve Vai, talk with him, and do whatever they had to do to get him to work with Ibanez. By this time, Vai was already a growing force. His break had come in 1980, at age 20, when he'd joined Frank Zappa's elite touring band. His first solo album, *Flex-Able*, appeared in 1984, the same year that Vai replaced Yngwie Malmsteen in Alcatrazz. And toward the end of '85, he hit the big-time, joining ex-Van Halen vocalist David Lee Roth in a new supergroup alongside bassist Billy Sheehan and drummer Gregg Bissonette.

Here was an ambitious, outgoing, talented musician, and, for those with ears and an open mind, a guitarist with enviable musical and technical reserves. Vai served up his remarkable riffs, melodies, and solos using vibrato dives, fast-picking flurries, tapping, noises, feedback, and, of course, a generous touch of showmanship. "He makes everything that Van Halen ever dreamed of and then some," Zappa told *Guitar World*. "He's a good musician and I enjoy playing with him, because he's not just a Mongolian string-bender."[58] It had to be Steve Vai.

Vai learned an important lesson when he played with Zappa. "I realised that I didn't have to be limited to the guitars that people are making and selling in stores," Vai recalls today. Zappa would take a guitar – or any piece of gear – and squeeze it until it screamed for mercy. "Then he'd call the company and say OK, but can you do this to it so I can make it do this, this, and this. He'd do that with any kind of pedal, guitar, musical

THE IBANEZ ELECTRIC GUITAR BOOK

1983 RS1010 Steve Lukather

■ Along with the S style, another new late-80s design was the R, as seen in this **540R** (main guitar). It had a wedge-shape body, superstrat pickups, and a locking vibrato, and it provided the inspiration for Joe Satriani's JS models. The odd-shaped P style (in **1990 catalogue**, opposite, with **Alex Skolnick**) was less successful. More signature models appeared, including the shortlived **Allan Holdsworth** Roadstar derivatives (**1985 ad**, opposite), the 1981 JP20 for jazzman **Joe Pass** (seen with Pass, below), **Steve Lukather**'s **RS1010** (above), and **Vinnie Moore**'s **VM1** (below; like a number of guitars pictured in this book, we have shown it without its vibrato arm).

1989 VM1 Vinnie Moore

1989 540R

notation … anything. Frank was this fountain of creativity in all aspects. And it was always done with a joke, too."

Vai realised it made good sense to poke and change and revise and coax his guitars, to seek the extra fret and the wider bend. He had started in Zappa's band with a trusty natural '76 Strat that had seen him through college, a guitar he loved for its vibrato but hated for its sound. Now he bolted on parametric EQs, different pickups, frequency boosters, all influenced by what was going on in the little workshop under Zappa's studio. There, Zappa's brother-in-law, Arthur "Midget" Sloatman, would lead them in their merry electronic experimentation.

Vai wanted more frets than the Strat had, he wanted one of those new locking vibratos, and he wanted humbuckers. He knew all about what Eddie Van Halen was up to, of course. "I joined Alcatrazz," he recalls of his change of employment in 1984, "so I went down to San Dimas, and Grover Jackson gave me this cool Charvel guitar that was shaped like a Strat but had humbuckers in it. For me it was like glory day. This is what I wanted – but there were still so many things about the guitar that I thought I wanted changed."

This Charvel Strat-style guitar – the Green Meanie as it became known – was Vai's testbed and main working guitar. He wanted this basswood-body guitar to work how he wanted it to work. His addition of a single-coil in the middle of the two humbuckers, for example, wasn't the standard superstrat pickup layout. Vai really liked the sound of a humbucker at the neck and at the bridge, but he also liked the sound of single-coils in the Strat's "in-between" settings. So he had the five-way selector on his guitars arranged to give two in-betweens as well as the three main settings of each pickup alone. "For those two settings," Vai explains, "the coil is split on one of the humbuckers, which turns it into a single-coil pickup, plus you get the middle pickup, which is a single-coil. So you get your Strat in-betweens. Now, obviously, it doesn't sound exactly like a Strat, because a guitar's body has a lot to do with it. But I thought that was an absolutely brilliant idea. I've never wanted anything else or reached for anything else."

Vai needed more from his vibrato system, too. Specifically, he wanted to be able to pull up higher than a regular system would go. "Most Strats weren't set up that way, and if they were, it would only go a little sharp," he recalls. "If a Strat went up a half-step, that was a lot. Then when the Floyd Rose came along, it was a blessing and a curse. The first Floyd didn't have fine-tuners, so it was almost useless. The moment you clamped the string down, it went out of tune. How do you get back? Such a pain in the ass, man. Somebody woke up and put the fine-tuners on it, and it was like a revelation. For me it changed everything. But … I still couldn't pull up on it – they didn't make them so you could get any lift."[59]

Vai considered the design and asked himself what was stopping the Floyd from pulling up. It was the body wood behind the vibrato, he concluded, so that had to be routed out. His guitar tech, Elwood Francis, did the job on the Charvel with a rattail file. "It was the third time I'd done that for him," Francis recalls. "The first was on another Strat; the second on his pink Jackson 'Ike Turner' Soloist."[60] Vai remembers that one of the first of his pieces to benefit from the new vibrato range was 'The Attitude Song', a 1984 solo instrumental piece heard on a *Guitar Player* flexidisc and on *Flex-Able*. "If you listen to that, the melody, the harmonics, it's all over the place – I'm pulling up notes a fifth!"[61]

Vai was the talk of the biz when he joined David Lee Roth's new post-Van Halen outfit at the end of 1985. They spent the early months of 1986 recording a debut album and around June began pre-production rehearsals for live dates, playing their first gigs in August, which started a US tour that ran more or less non-stop until February 1987. Vai took nine guitars on that tour: the Charvel Green Meanie was his main one, but also to hand were four Performance parts guitars, a Tom Anderson Custom, a yellow Jackson Custom Soloist, and two custom guitars made by Vai's friend Joe Despagni, the Flame and the Lightning Bolt.

The Charvel's striking green finish was achieved with SparVar dayglo green over a white primer, with a very light clear coat on top. "I repainted it in hotel bathrooms several times throughout the tour to keep it bright," Francis says. "It obviously was never given a chance to properly dry, so it grimed up fairly quick, giving it the mouldy look."[62] The Performance guitars were put together from parts made by Kunio "Kenny" Sugai at Performance Guitar, whose shop was just down the street from Vai's house in Hollywood. They were quickly assembled by Steve Soest, Gavin Menzies, and Francis after some of Vai's instruments went missing during the pre-production rehearsals at Perkins Palace theatre in Pasadena. One of the Performances, Playboy, was the most-used spare guitar until the Tom Anderson arrived during the tour.

Ibanez first tried to approach Vai probably early in 1986. He was busy recording and rehearsing with the Roth band, but it seems that Ibanez managed at least to get one guitar to him, although no one can now remember exactly what it was. It came to Rich Lasner's attention later in the year when, during September 1986, he saw a cover interview with Vai in *Guitar Player* and noticed a comment about the missing guitars. "Most of my other guitars were ripped off this June from the rehearsal studio in Pasadena," Vai told the magazine. Included among the five lost instruments was what Vai described as "a pukey-green Ibanez that has like a green-black snakeskin front".[63]

Lasner arranged to take another guitar to Vai at one of the band's shows. He and Mike Shimada flew to a Roth gig in Buffalo, New York, at the end of September 1986, bringing with them a prototype Ibanez Maxxas. They thought the oddball Maxxas design might be different enough to interest Vai. But a problem soon became evident when, before the band's soundcheck, Vai plugged the guitar into his amps on the Memorial Auditorium stage. The semi-hollow body of the Maxxas fed back like crazy at

Vai's preferred gigging volume. "So it was like, well, we all know this *looks* cool – but back to the drawing board," Lasner remembers.

Perhaps a solidbody Maxxas might work, they figured. A little later, toward the end of 1986, they had one ready, finished in a similar snakeskin to the lost guitar. Someone had a number for Vai's parents on Long Island, and Lasner made the call. He told them he wanted to get a new guitar to their son. "I said we don't want to impinge on your family," Lasner recalls, "but would it be possible if we sent a guitar wrapped as a Christmas present, and you put it under the tree, and it's just from us?"

Lasner came off the phone with everyone happy. "We had a solidbody Maxxas," he says, "painted it pink, green, and white snakeskin, wrapped it in some really jolly Christmas stuff, and FedEx'd it over to their house."[64] The day after Christmas, Lasner got a call from Vai. OK, he said, you got my attention – what do you want? Lasner said well, we really, really, really want to do a guitar with you. Vai relented. All right, he said, how about we try something?

With the Roth tour finally over in February 1987, Vai considered his road-worn gear. The Charvel had taken a battering. "Green guitar died," he'd noted succinctly and ominously in his diary in October after the vibrato mounting collapsed during soundcheck at a prestigious date at Madison Square Garden in New York City. Steve Blucher of DiMarzio took the guitar away and had it quickly repaired, but tuning problems remained. In November, after another gig, Vai wrote: "Started out incredible, then the guitar went out in 'Elephant Gun'."[65] On the last date of the tour, the Performance Playboy got broken onstage, and Vai – with keen assistance from bassist Billy Sheehan – apparently enjoyed breaking it up some more backstage. "Every time I picked that one up, something happened," Vai recalls. "It was one of those Edsels."[66]

Vai called Ibanez after the end of the tour and said he was interested in their gadget-of-the-moment, the SDR1000 stereo digital delay. Lasner saw this as an opportunity to fly out and take him a couple of SDRs – and talk guitars. "He wasn't totally on with it, but then he had a lightbulb moment," Lasner remembers. "He said he had a bunch of guitars where he loved the body on one, the neck on another, the frets on this one, the pickups on that – and he said he wasn't really a hundred percent happy with anything he had."[67] Lasner suggested that Vai make notes on each of the guitars that had something he absolutely loved, send them to him in Bensalem, and they would build him something that combined all the ideas.

A week later, back at Ibanez HQ, the guitars showed up from Vai. As far as Lasner remembers, there was at least a Tom Anderson, a Charvel, and a Performance. Vai's tech Elwood Francis remembers shipping to Ibanez the Performance guitar known as Spots – it was finished with blue and red spots on a white ground – and that it was "visually close" to what became the JEM, apart from a different body handle and a standard recessed trem rout. "This was the guitar that we did all the tweaks to," Francis recalls. "We'd covered it with skateboarding stickers – it became the 'skate' guitar – and Kuni made an extended 24-fret neck which I installed on the guitar. I had to rout the neck-pickup cavity and move it toward the bridge, and then I shaved the bottom cutaway to get better access to the top frets."[68]

The guitars that Vai sent to Ibanez had his notes stuck on them, as requested, with one saying "This neck feels great", another "This neck joint is good", and so on. Vai liked the neck on the Anderson, Lasner recalls, and the scoop for the left-hand at the cutaway on the Charvel, while the Performance had the body handle he wanted to incorporate. Working from the notes on the guitars and from Lasner's further discussions with Vai, Mace Bailey at Ibanez made prototypes. The body shape was fairly straightforward, Lasner remembers. "Mace and I sat down and literally traced out a Strat and then expanded it," he says, "changing the cutaways and some of the basic volume of it, making it a little thicker and definitely with a squarer edge."

One prototype had a solid maple centre core and hollow outer wings, possibly mahogany. Another was a solidbody, possibly maple or alder, maybe basswood, but it certainly had Vai's requested exploding finish. "I think that took more time than anything else in the design," Lasner says with a smile, recalling this oddity that never made the final production models. "He wanted a brittle green fluorescent finish, done in such a way that if he hit it against something, the paint would shatter. And we did finally get that to work properly."[69] Lasner remembers pink pickups – humbucker, single, humbucker – supplied by DiMarzio, coloured controls, and much larger body-handles than the way they finally turned out.

Vai's recollection is that he sent out specs of his ideal guitar to several companies at this time, and not just Ibanez. "Once I joined Dave Roth, and that *Eat 'Em And Smile* record came out, and the *Crossroads* movie came out – well, as you can imagine, all the guitar companies were very eager for me to use their instruments." He's referring to a Walter Hill movie released in March 1986, loosely based on the Robert Johnson story, where he played Jack Butler, the devil's guitarist, in a remarkable guitar duel – and also to the debut Roth album, which had come out in July, just in time for the big tour. "You can't buy the kind of advertising in a magazine that you can get when a star artist is using your gear," Vai explains. "So they were all calling me."

He remembers that "beside the obvious" there was Yamaha and Kramer in the frame, at least. To some extent he was reticent, because he was well aware of how some players would appear hugging a guitar in an ad and yet never use the instrument, and how often they would flip from one company to the next. "I do have a lot of companies that I work with," he says today, "but the relationships are decades old."

He recalls sending specs and pictures to five or six companies. Back came the guitars – eventually. And they had very little to do with what he had asked for. "It was usually just one of their existing models, slightly tweaked." Kramer, he says, seemed more interested in wining and dining and rides in the limo – but they, too, took ages to send him a guitar that still wasn't what he wanted. "Ibanez took just three weeks and gave me a guitar that was exactly what I wanted," Vai remembers. "In fact, it was better than what I wanted."[70]

Ibanez had its own reasons, beyond natural efficiency, to be so quick. Lasner and Reim had realised that they might be able to launch a signature guitar by Vai at the forthcoming summer NAMM show, just months away. Vai looked as if he might be exactly the personification of the brand that Lasner had in mind, and with business still in the doldrums, Ibanez needed a new and exciting guitar sooner rather than later.

Lasner remembers taking the two Ibanez prototypes to show Vai and sitting down at the guitarist's kitchen table, accompanied by a couple of Japanese colleagues from Ibanez management. Lasner pulled the first prototype out of its case and presented it to Vai. Vai did not play it. Instead, he produced some tools and proceeded to take the guitar apart. Lasner's companions looked horrified. "Steve said relax, I do this to every guitar I have," Lasner recalls. "He explained that he really wanted to know how the guitar worked. He put it back together, and he said: You know, this is a damned good guitar. He said he liked this guitar, it was really well done. He checked out the second guitar and he liked that, too. So we left one with him, and we took one back to the shop. I think he wanted the one with the breakaway paint – that was interesting to him. So, those guitars were essentially 90 percent of what the production guitars became. Most of what was missing was cosmetic."[71]

There were two main cosmetic additions beyond the prototype appointments. Ibanez called the first one the Lion's Claw, which consisted of six scooped furrows behind the Edge vibrato, to assist pull-ups. The second was a set of Disappearing Pyramid fingerboard markers. The prototypes had regular dot markers, but that seemed too ordinary for such an extraordinary guitar. What to do? Bill Reim came to the rescue at the last minute. Reim began with an idea for geometric pyramid shapes, gradually re-drawing and reducing them down into flat two-dimensional images. "Steve and I talked a lot about this pyramid icon," Reim remembers, "and I said how about this disappearing pyramid concept? I said we'll use odd colours that kind of match the body. I rendered it, and Steve thought it looked great and said we should try it. The whole guitar was a real homogenisation of a lot of different ideas that people were putting on the table, but mostly it was Steve. He was very definitive. He knew what he liked and he knew what he didn't like."[72]

Ibanez had its new guitar. And it was not a straightforward guitar to make. Hoshino Japan faxed a hand-drawn spec sheet of the finished design to Fujigen on April 15 1987, which meant that Nick Sugimoto at Fujigen R&D had only two months to make finished samples for the guitar's launch at the all-important NAMM show in June. "We had a big meeting about the 540S and R, and I was told that I should stop those – I should make the artist guitars for Steve Vai, for NAMM," Sugimoto recalls. "So I had only two months to finish them. The project was really confidential: at the factory, and even at Hoshino. Only the vice president and president knew about it, and maybe three or four other people. I said, you know, I'll have to tell the paint-shop guys, and they said well … maybe you could tell them it's for some other maker?"[73]

Sugimoto remembers Rich Lasner and Mace Bailey visiting Fujigen to select the woods and other details for the Vai guitar. Lasner says they went through hundreds if not thousands of blocks of wood, rejecting or approving each one based on weight and the noise it made when they hit it. "We got stared at," he laughs, "these two white guys down on their knees with rubber mallets asking each other if this block sounds any good. I don't think we knew a whole lot about basswood, tonally, when we started using it."[74]

Sugimoto recalls that the trade-show samples he eventually sent to the USA were not completely finished. "They hadn't decided the exact shape of the pickguards, for example. So we made various different-shape pickguards, but I did not assemble the guitars. I just made the neck and body, finished them up, and the fingerboard, and shipped them to Hoshino."[75]

Finally, the sample guitars were ready, just in time for the NAMM show, which took place in Chicago, beginning on June 27 and running for three more days. The Ibanez stand was buzzing with excitement from the start. What was it they were hiding under that big black shroud, prominently displayed on the stand and permanently watched over by a serious-looking security guard? What was Ibanez being so secretive about? At last the moment arrived when all would be revealed. It was the talk of the show, and the stand was absolutely packed.

Rich Lasner was there, of course, and he remembers Steve Blucher from DiMarzio and Bill Reim from Ibanez in front of the big monolith, still covered up. "And you could see all the guys from Kramer," he says, "who had been pretty much kicking our ass for the last couple of years with Van Halen. They were standing there with their arms folded, wondering what on earth's going on. We dropped the black cloth, and there's a giant poster of Steve Vai playing the JEM. Everybody applauds. I look over at the Kramer guys. Their jaws are on the floor, and they're walking away. That to me was a moment of, like, wow! We actually may have done this. You know? We did something here."[76]

The JEM was an instrument with a unique combination of features, and it looked nothing like any other electric guitar. It had a body in one of three striking fluorescent colours, with matching headstock and colourful contrasting pickups and controls. The basswood body itself was a sort of extended Strat shape, with squared sides, pointy horns, and a Monkey Grip handle-hole.

The Monkey Grip name was probably borrowed from horse-riding, where a "monkey" is a handle that clips to the saddle to offer the rider something to hang on to when the going gets rough. Vai used it for some show-off stage antics where he'd whirl his guitar around and hang on to the handle. He also figured it gave the guitar an

■ The big breakthrough for Ibanez came with the **Steve Vai** models, launched in 1987. Vai was a guitarist's guitarist who hit the big-time when he joined ex-Van Halen vocalist David Lee Roth's new band. Vai's main axe at the time was a Charvel known as the **Green Meanie** (seen with Vai in a **Carvin amps ad**, opposite, top), and some elements of that and other Vai guitars made it to his new Ibanez design. **Mace Bailey** at Ibanez USA made prototypes (he's pictured with one, right), and Vai signed a final **spec sheet** (far right) with the prophetic words: "Oh yeah – a hit." The guitar had a very distinctive look: colourful features, "Monkey Grip" body handle, and "Lion's Claw" cutout behind the vibrato to enable pull-ups. The debut **JEM777** model in green (main guitar) was a limited edition of 777, each **signed and numbered** by Vai (top), and an elaborate **1988 ad** was devised (left). The guitar was indeed a hit.

1987 JEM777LG

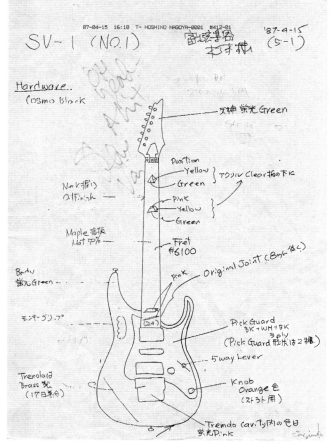

instantly unique look (although a few 60s Guyatones and Teiscos had featured something similar). "I knew no one else would do this, because it was too outrageous," Vai says. "It's a very identifiable feature. How else could you create a really identifiable instrument?"

The Edge locking vibrato system had Lion's Claw furrows behind the bridge – it was a guitar that seemed to have outlandish names for everything – and these added some crucial extra pull-up space. At first, there was a bridge guard on the vibrato, intended to stop the player's palm from pressing down and detuning the system, but a legal claim by Kahler prevented its continued use. The DiMarzio pickups were in humbucker, single-coil, humbucker formation (HSH), probably for the first time on a production guitar, and Vai got his favoured single-coil in-between settings thanks to Steve Blucher at DiMarzio, who tweaked the five-way switching circuit. The maple neck was more or less Ibanez's thin Ultra style, with a little more chunk and a cutaway neck heel.

There was a maple fingerboard featuring the distinctive Disappearing Pyramid inlays, a 25½-inch scale, and 24 frets, scalloped from the 21st upward. According to Vai, the scalloped board was inspired by Billy Sheehan's Yamaha basses and by a guitar Yngwie Malmsteen had showed him. "Yngwie said: With these, you can really grab the note by the balls. Brilliant! Exactly right, because that's what it feels like."

The guitar had a distinctive name, too: the JEM. Vai says it was a nod to Joe Despagni, his childhood friend who became a guitar maker and, as we've seen, had built or modified several instruments for Vai. "Joe might have been the guy that put the first monkey-grip handle on one of my guitars," Vai recalls. "He was a dear friend, and he called his company Jem. I wanted to help him, so I called the Ibanez guitar a JEM to bring light to what he was doing. That's what I was thinking at the time, but now I see how it could have been very … confusing. But it really was a tip of the hat, to help him. And you know what happens: after a while the name doesn't matter, and then the guitar becomes what it is."[77]

The first batch of the new guitars was made at Fujigen in July 1987, when 296 of the limited-edition JEM777LGs were shipped. The JEMs had debuted on Ibanez's June pricelist in three colour variations. That limited-edition JEM777LG in Loch Ness Green listed at $1,590, while the regular JEM777, in Desert Sun Yellow or Shocking Pink, was $1,299. No wonder Lasner wondered if these guitars would sell: not only did they look odd, but also they weren't exactly cheap. A Gibson Les Paul Standard listed a touch over $1,000 in 1987, and a Fender American Standard Stratocaster was $650. The JEMs weren't just distinctive: they had an upscale vibe and a price to make you stop and think.

Lasner says the team at Ibanez balanced the thought that the JEMs might be hard to sell with the idea that the attention they brought was good promotion for the brand. But they needn't have worried. "In fact," he says, "all 777 of the limited-edition model were sold within the month that we allowed them to go out into the world. They were gone immediately."

This was a remarkable turn of events, and Vai himself had a rare shock. When he got his first royalty cheque from the proceeds of the first run, Vai called Lasner and said there'd been a horrible mistake. "He told me he was going to tear up the cheque," Lasner recalls. "I asked what he meant. He said it was made out for an enormous sum of money, just an impossible amount. I told him it was correct. And that's the first time I ever heard Steve stop talking. He was dumbfounded for at least 15 seconds. It was brilliant. I loved that I could make him so happy that he couldn't even talk! The JEM was a wild success from the very first day of sale. Amazing, really."[78]

Andy Brauer wrote an early review of a couple of JEM models in *Guitar Player* magazine. "I really like the way the Ibanez JEM series looks – grade A for innovation and color design," he said. After detailing the visuals and the vibe, Brauer considered playability, admiring the Edge vibrato – "an improvement over the current Floyd Rose design" – and praising the guitar's general "meticulous craftsmanship" and "players-minded functional design". He liked the neck, which for him felt like "a cross between a vintage 1961 Fender Stratocaster and a Charvel/Jackson". Brauer said that once he'd tweaked the setup "the guitar was happy as a clam", and he enjoyed the range and tones he could get from the pickups. "Unique design and functional detail are part of the magic that makes the JEM series stand out," he wrote. "Off-the-wall visuals and good usable tone qualities make [it] a real alternative to purchasing a custom-made guitar. … The overall feel of the JEM series is excellent."[79]

Ibanez had an even better trick up its sleeve. Also released that summer was the new RG550 model. Perhaps it was a little overlooked, what with all the razzmatazz of Steve Vai and the JEM launch, but it would turn out to be an even more important guitar in Ibanez history. The new RG style was almost identical to the JEM – minus the wild colours and fancy inlays, the Monkey Grip handle, and the scalloped frets. If Vai and the JEM were beacons that drew a great deal of attention to Ibanez, then the various RG models would be the lights that burned brightly and consistently, all day and every day.

The RG550 was the first example of the new-style RG and should not be confused with the RGs that Ibanez was already making. The '87 pricelist still included a number of existing Roadstar RG models, from the $299 RG120 to the $599 RG440, but these all had the old-style Strat-like rounded body shape, they had 22 frets, and they had a regular bolt-on-neck heel. The new 550 really was an almost-JEM, with the slim-horned square-edged body, the 24-fret neck, and the hum-sing-hum pickup layout. It had a new neck joint, too, which Ibanez called the tilt neck, a variation on the JEM's cutaway neck heel – both of which were designed for easy, smooth top-fret access. And the RG550's neck was Ibanez's new and very thin Wizard neck, just 17mm deep at the first fret, where a Stratocaster, for example, is nearer 20mm.

Also launched alongside the new RG and the JEM were the semi-hollow Maxxas and the Pro540 P, R, and S models, which we looked at earlier. Together they formed a

At the same time that Ibanez launched the Vai JEM models, it introduced the new-style RG (**RG550**, above, and 1987 launch-year **catalogue**, opposite), in effect a JEM without the flash. Some of the old-style RGs, like this **RG420** (below), continued for a short time, but the new RG was a supreme metal machine that took Ibanez on to big success in the 90s. Ibanez has described the RG with good reason as "the streamlined, no-nonsense all-time favorite of fast players". Meanwhile, along with the new-style RGs, Steve Vai's new JEM models (**777** in yellow, opposite) helped to define Ibanez's developing popularity among players like **Paul Gilbert** of Racer X and Mr Big (in **1988 RG ad**, right), another of Ibanez's new fast-gun endorsers. Gilbert was awarded his own signature models from 1990.

1986 Roadstar II RG420

1987 RG550

1988 JEM777VDY

remarkable and tangible revival for Ibanez, with distinctive designs, thin necks, smooth heels, 24 frets, and superstrat-style pickup layouts. The Maxxas and 540P proved to be shortlived, but the RG, JEM, and S are still going strong today. The new RG550 listed for $659 in '87 – in other words, about half the price of a regular JEM, and it was the RG in particular that provided Ibanez's affordable new-style guitar. In its various guises, the RG would enjoy a wide popularity that transformed the brand's policies and fortunes.

"The RGs sold by the thousands," Lasner says, "and still do. They definitely helped to stabilise the company financially. We were able to do a whole line of those guitars. And Steve was just gracious – there was no deal for him in the RGs at all. He just said yeah, that sounds like a great idea to promote the guitars."[80]

Vai himself is philosophical today when he looks back at the RG and its similarity to the JEM design. "My business arrangements with Ibanez are confidential," he says, "but I can tell you that, as part of the original negotiations, I allowed them to make the RG guitar. How could I be in business with someone for all these years if I thought they stole something from me? They have been very fair, and the JEM and other guitars I designed for and with them have been smashing successes. Actually, overwhelming."[81] The RG has indeed enjoyed great success over the years. "It created a whole new world of Ibanez aficionados," Lasner says.[82]

Vai is aware of the scale of that success. "The RG, as far as the statistics that I've heard, has been the second biggest selling guitar in recent years," he reports, "second only to the Strat. Like the JEM, it's got that playability, it's got those 24-fret necks, it's got the cutaway, it's angular, it looks cool, it looks metal-y." His JEMs do continue to sell, too, Vai notes with satisfaction – 25 years and more since the first models were introduced. "The people who are the fans and stuff, and collectors, and people who like a fine type of guitar, they will still buy the JEM. And I've never wanted to play anything else. Still, to this day, I reach for my JEMs, because nothing else is as comfortable. I like to visit New York now and then, and I like to visit Napa, but there's no place like home."[83]

Ibanez has issued a number of different JEM models over the years since the introduction of the 777 (they're all detailed in the reference section at the back of this book). A further addition to the early line was the JEM77FP, another visually arresting guitar, but this one had to wait to go on sale until the year following the original models. The FP in the model name stood for Floral Pattern finish, describing the vivid printed cloth that was bonded to the guitar's body. At first, says Nick Sugimoto, Ibanez planned to make just one guitar like this, a special instrument custom-made for Vai. Sugimoto, who worked at the Fujigen factory's R&D department, had recently helped Fender develop its paisley-finish Telecaster reissue models, which also employed a bonded-material finish. That proved to be useful experience.

"The fabric for the FP was from curtains that my wife and I had in our living room," Vai says. "I was trying to come up with a unique idea for a look on the guitar, and I always liked this curtain fabric we had. I just wasn't sure if this material could be used for a finish on a guitar, but Ibanez made it happen beautifully. They ordered a ton of this fabric from the manufacturer and figured out how to adhere it to the guitar and put a smooth finish over it. The result is that every guitar is different. It's my feeling that these JEMs are the best sounding ones. The finish you use on an instrument has an effect on the sound, and I suspect that the fabric does something to the resonation."[84]

Sugimoto got to work with an iron and some glue, bonding the fabric to the one-off JEM's body and applying a paint seal over the top. He soon saw it in action – with unforeseen results. "At the end of the '87 NAMM show, there was Steve on stage with this flower-pattern guitar," Sugimoto remembers with a sigh. "And, of course, all the distributors saw this – and they wanted this other new JEM guitar, too! So now we had to work out how to make it as a production model. That meant a lot of work, developing glue sprays, sealing coats, and so on. That's why it took eight months from the NAMM show before we could issue that guitar."[85]

The JEM series has continued to provide surprises as Vai and Ibanez push each other to find yet more outrageous features. There was a 20th anniversary model in 2007 that had a see-through acrylic body with internal LEDs, and the JEM2KDNA, one of Ibanez's special millennium models in 2000, had Vai's DNA incorporated into the fingerboard's vine inlay. "I went to the hospital down the street here, and I had a lot of blood drawn," Vai remembers with a smile. "It's not like there's a tiny drop of my blood on those guitars. There's a lot! I had to eat plenty of bananas after that. A hundred years from now, if they get cloning down, maybe they can take one of these DNA guitars and clone me out of the guitar – and then maybe that guy can get his music on the radio."[86]

The RG series and its derivatives have come even further since that first RG550 in 1987, with a wide selection of feature sets over the years on a slew of models spanning all price points. At its heart, however, a modern RG nearly always harks back to the '87 template, with a slim-horned square-edged body shape, a thin 24-fret neck, and a smooth neck heel. It's Ibanez's "guitar for the world", a concept that had been floating around at Hoshino since at least the 70s Iceman, the idea that Ibanez might have its own Les Paul, its own Stratocaster. Thousands and thousands of budding guitarists have begun and many have prospered using an RG or RG-style model. Ibanez describes it today with understandable pride as "the streamlined, no-nonsense all-time favorite of fast players".[87]

In the late 80s and into the early 90s, following its introduction of the JEMs and the new-style RG guitars, Ibanez found a fresh confidence, buoyed up by this welcome success. Fender was impressed, too, and tried to copy the Ibanez RG style with the Talon model, launched under a new brand, Heartfield, in 1989. "And on top of that," says Jim Donahue, "they went to Fujigen to get it made. So they went to our factory, they used our everything. These were desperate times! Metal was on top of the world."[88] It didn't hurt

ROADSTAR
RG340

New Ideas For Today's Musicians
Ibanez

■ As the new RG series grew in popularity in the late 80s and early 90s, the old-style RG, like the **RG340** (1988 ad, left), was soon gone. Some new-style RGs, like the **RG350 and 360** (**1988 ad**, opposite) did not last, but there was the occasional custom model to make you smile, such as this **RG550** (above) with snake-inlay fingerboard. Metal-friendly sharktooth markers appeared on a number of RGs, for example this **RG760** (right). Steve Vai's **JEM77FP** model (below) was a one-off just for Vai, but when he played it at a trade-show event, demand led to a production model in 1988. It used fabric like Vai's home curtains bonded to a JEM body. Vai is pictured with the model in a **1988 ad** (opposite).

THE IBANEZ ELECTRIC GUITAR BOOK

CURTAIN CALL FOR MISTER VAI

1991 RG550 custom

ROADSTAR
RG350
RG360

New Ideas for Today's Musicians

Ibanez

1992 RG760

1988 JEM77FP

Ibanez's growing success when Kramer, the brand that had dominated the 80s, went bust in spectacular fashion around the end of the decade. There were many reasons for Kramer's lingering death, which dragged on into the early 90s, but one of the contributing factors had been a strike at the Korean factory that made some of the brand's guitars. The first Ibanez electrics made in Korea were the EXs, a line of budget RG-derived models that debuted in 1988 – although the brand's main production remained in Japan, primarily at Fujigen. But it was also in the late 80s that Ibanez began to experiment with producing guitars in the USA.

At first, this happened because Hoshino USA noticed how some American brands were successfully promoting their instruments as custom-made. "We offer you an infinite variety of opportunities to participate in the design of your instrument," read a 1986 Jackson catalogue, for example. Rich Lasner recalls that the US team wanted to find a way to compete with the image that these makers presented. "Even though their guitars were made in a factory and assembled like any others," he says, "the image was that they were handmade in California. So while we didn't have any manufacturing capability at the Bensalem facility, we figured we could create the appearance of a custom shop by putting together instruments from Japanese parts, and the resulting guitars could say assembled in USA."

Beginning around 1988, the US firm began assembling the three 540 models – 540P, 540R, and 540S – from parts supplied by Fujigen in Japan. Each was given an Ibanez neckplate that bore the Bensalem address – 1726 Winchester Road – stressing the US contribution to these guitars, and most had "H&S" stamped in the neck pocket, standing for Heartfield & Starfield.

H&S was a joint venture by Fujigen and Hoshino: Heartfield was a brandname used by Fujigen, and Starfield was a rough English translation of Hoshino. Part of the Bensalem facility had been used for Tama drums, and now some space was put aside for assembling guitars. Fujigen was obviously interested in developing production in North America – in 1987 it had helped Fender start its new Mexican factory with another joint venture, F&F. Fumiaki Yokouchi, the son of Fujigen founder Yuuichirou Yokouchi, came over from Japan to take charge of H&S. "People would order stuff, and we would have these already-made bodies, necks, and electronic harnesses, and from those Japanese parts we would assemble the guitars," Lasner explains.

Next came the USA Custom guitars, starting in 1989. "It was a step up from the parts-assembled guitars we were already selling," Lasner recalls. "Fujigen sent two or three more people over and set up shop with just a couple of pin-routers. We'd use pre-done bodies that weren't routed for pickups yet."[89] Jim Donahue, then in the repair shop at Hoshino USA, remembers Fujigen bringing over the necessary gear to make guitars. "This was good for us," he says, "because we had been using basic tools, and all of a sudden they brought in all this machinery. Also, they brought guys that knew how to build. I learned how to make jigs, the right tools to use for the job, how to make templates – all this stuff that you wouldn't learn in your life unless somebody was to teach you."[90] The prospective customer for a USA Custom guitar could visit an Ibanez dealer and choose from an array of possibilities, including graphic finishes, one of eight IBZ/USA or DiMarzio pickup layouts, a few choices of fingerboard wood and inlay, and a regular or reversed headstock.

The Custom Graphic finishes, for the UCGR models, were painted by artists Pedro Cruz, Dan Lawrence, or Pamelina Hovnatanian. Inspired by the kind of work that Jackson offered, their artworks ranged from the gruesome to the amusing: the illustrations had names such as Alien's Revenge, Grim Reaper, Icy Hand Of Death, Necromancer's Castle, Winged Being, plus about 20 others. There were also several Custom Metal Design models (UCMD), mostly in snakeskin and other textured metallic looks, using bonded fabric in a similar way to the recent JEM Floral Pattern model.

Next, Hoshino wanted a location in Los Angeles so that it could be involved more directly in the music scene there. Mace Bailey had worked at Bensalem since 1980, at first as a guitar-checker, and had developed into a valued member of the team, able to customise guitars and make prototypes. Bailey's first custom job at Bensalem had been for Charlie Burchill of Simple Minds, in 1985, after Bill Reim had met the guitarist at Live Aid's Philadelphia stage. Bailey made Burchill a Roadstar with hollowed-out body and f-hole, pained blue by Leon Reddell, as seen in the band's 'Sanctify Yourself' video.

Ibanez's presence in Los Angeles had so far been limited to Chuck Fukagawa, who worked out of the offices of Chesbro, the western-states distributor. Fukagawa had occasionally used the services of local guitar-maker Mike Lipe, and Bailey was sent out to California at the end of 1989 to join with Lipe and set up an LA shop, along with Chris Kelly to run artist relations. Kelly had worked at Bensalem since 1986 and was formerly with Robin Guitars in Texas.

"We started out in a little garage bay in North Hollywood, on Victory Boulevard," Bailey recalls. "Mike borrowed a spray booth from the car guy two bays down. That went on until Hoshino found some property to rent a few blocks north, at 7101 Case Avenue, which became the LA office, the custom shop, and a warehousing facility for guitars and Tama drums."[91] Kelly found artists – including everyone from Carlos Santana to Kurt Cobain – and Bailey and Lipe made Ibanez guitars for them. They also built instruments for Ibanez's top endorsers such as Steve Vai, Joe Satriani, Paul Gilbert, and others, including some spectacular triple-neck guitars for Vai. "Any model that was artist-driven came from the custom shop at that time," Kelly says.[92] The custom shop continued to flourish, and in 2005 it was relocated a little further north to Sun Valley, where it still operates today.

During 1990, Hoshino decided to move H&S from Bensalem to Los Angeles, as an independent company and located at a separate location from the Case Avenue custom

1989 USA Custom Metal Design Metal Leopard

■ Ibanez wanted to create the impression of US-made guitars, and set up **H&S**, assembling Japanese parts at the Philadelphia HQ (putting together a **540S**, second right). The **USA Custom** models had wild graphic options, such as the horrific **Trick Or Treat** (main guitar, top) by artist Pamelina, as well as (opposite, left to right) **Unzipped**, **Cosmic Swirl**, and **Chop Shop**. There were also the textured Metal Designs, such as this **Metal Leopard** (above). More were featured in a **1991 promo sheet** (right). The US team made custom guitars for artists, too, including an f-holed Roadstar for Charlie Burchill of Simple Minds (opposite). Meanwhile, the EX series were the first Korean-made Ibanez guitars (**EX140**, opposite).

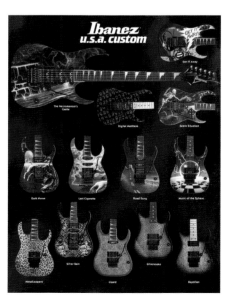

1991 USA Custom Graphic Trick Or Treat

1989 EX140

operation. H&S Guitar Technology Inc was on Saticoy Street, North Hollywood, a mile or two to the west of Case Avenue, across the Hollywood Freeway, and the firm was involved in the production of two series of largely US-made Ibanez guitars.

The American Master MA models were through-neck RG-style guitars, made at first by Roger Gresco, and then later by Tak Hosono in Glendale, California. Hosono remembers that Fukagawa asked him early in 1990 to supply these instruments for H&S. Hosono had been a founder of the ESP company in Japan in 1975, working there for four years, repairing instruments, building custom guitars, and handling factory liaison and quality control. In 1979, he moved to Los Angeles, working with artists such as Frank Zappa, Stephen Stills, and Bob Marley. "In 1987, I started Hosono Guitar Works in Glendale," Hosono says. "I made original-design replacement guitar necks and bodies, which I sold to music shops and mail order customers." He also did OEM work (where an outside maker produces a guitar for a company that puts its own brand on it) for Sadowsky and for Robin – as well as for Hoshino, making the Ibanez American Master instruments and some Starfield-brand guitars.

Hosono worked on the American Master MA1 model, offered with a flamed or quilted maple top, which he describes as an exotic-looking guitar. He made them at his Glendale shop, and then H&S in North Hollywood painted them, put on the hardware, and set them up. "They were very difficult guitars to build," he says, "due to a lot of lamination work, the through-neck construction, and 5A-grade exotic maple tops."[93] Hosono estimates making about 200 to 250 guitars and the same of basses, and he says production stopped by the end of 1991. Hosono would go on to join the Ibanez LA custom shop in 1997, and at the time of writing he still works there.

The second series of guitars devised in conjunction with H&S at its California location were the Exotic Wood models (UCEW), shown in the 1991–92 Ibanez catalogue with impressive figured maple or lacewood-topped mahogany bodies and All Access bolt-on necks. No one today is quite sure who made the bodies of these for H&S (necks were all from Fujigen), although Hosono thinks a small company in Northern California called Wild Wood was involved, but there were problems with quality, and he suspects few were shipped. The UCEWs were gone by the time the 1993 pricelist appeared, and this marked the end of the H&S Ibanez experiments, with H&S closing its doors for good around this time.

Also US-made at this time, back east, were three USA Custom RG models (USRG), built by Dave Bunker of PBC Guitar Technology in Coopersburg, about 35 miles north of the Bensalem office in Pennsylvania. Bunker remembers that Jim Donahue and Tom Tanaka approached PBC. "They liked some of our technology, especially the Tension Free neck, and wanted an American-made high-end guitar and bass line," he says. "The guitars were all their designs – we just made a better, more classy American version and included our patented neck."

The Tension Free neck system used a pivoted rod instead of a conventional truss rod, intended to reduce stress on the neck and maintain tone and sustain. Bunker made the Ibanez USRG10, 20, and 30 from 1993 to 1996. The 10 had a fixed bridge, while the 20 and 30 had vibratos, and each model had an alder body with figured maple top. PBC made the guitars and basses, and Ibanez furnished electronics and hardware. Bunker estimates they built several thousand until one of PBC's owners ended the deal, a move that dismayed him. "At the time," Bunker says, "Ibanez sales on the guitars were heading up at a very steep rate of growth, and they told us that within two more years their needs from us would be around 500 to 700 instruments a month."[94] Bunker went on to design his patented Touch Guitar and later moved part of his Bunker Guitars business to Utah. He continues to build high-end custom guitars and to log and select specialty woods for guitar makers.

Despite all this activity intended to provide Ibanez with either the illusion or the reality of made-in-USA guitars, the regular Japanese and Korean-made lines had hardly been quiet. The 1992–93 catalogue celebrated the 20th anniversary of the American operation. "We began Ibanez USA in 1972 with the idea of bringing high quality, very affordable guitars to American guitarists and bassists," ran the blurb. "First these were inexpensive instruments patterned after popular American guitars and basses of the times; later, we came into our own by creating original designs for guitarists such as George Benson and Bob Weir. And to be honest, we've had our share of odd and sometimes downright weird instruments that raised a few eyebrows, but that's all part of the growing process."

That catalogue detailed signature models for Reb Beach, Frank Gambale, George Benson, and Paul Gilbert; it featured endorsers Alex Skolnick, Larry Mitchell, and Jennifer Batten with their 540s; and it highlighted some new R (Radius) models, the 442 and 542, as well as the already extensive RG line and its budget Korean-made offshoot, the EX line (renamed RX in 1994).

The '92 catalogue also had plenty of interviews with Ibanez artists. One name included among several long-standing endorsers was jazz-fusion guitarist John Scofield – who would have to wait until 2001 for a signature model. He told the story of getting his first Ibanez around 1979. "I was in Japan, my old guitar had broken, and they gave me an instrument that was pretty much a copy of it, an Artist series AS200," Scofield said. "It sounded great to me, and I've been playing it ever since. I'm a one-guitar kind of guy. The AS200 is my favourite realisation of the classic 335 design. They've updated it slightly but retained all the qualities that make the design timeless. I think it's the best guitar that Ibanez makes."[95]

The first spread in that '92 catalogue presented Steve Vai's Universe seven-string guitars, introduced a couple of years earlier. Vai was by now busily winning polls and plaudits as a new guitar hero, playing on the second David Lee Roth album, *Skyscraper*,

1991 USA Custom
Exotic Wood UCEW1

1991 USA Custom
American Master MA1

THE IBANEZ ELECTRIC GUITAR BOOK

Jennifer Batten and Friends
Ibanez 540S

Ibanez moved its H&S operation to California in 1990 and also set up a US custom shop there. More **USA Custom** models appeared, backed by H&S, including this **American Master** (main guitar) built mainly at Hosono Guitar Works in Glendale, and this **Exotic Wood** guitar (top), also made in California. The separate custom shop, meanwhile, made guitars for artists and endorsers, including this **triple-neck**

for **Steve Vai** (above, held by custom shop guitar-maker **Mace Bailey**). **Jennifer Batten** appeared in a 1989 ad for the **540S** (above), and **Reb Beach**'s Voyager featured the All Access Neck joint and an unusual end-cutaway body (right). The last of the USA Customs were the **USRG**s, made back east by PBC in Pennsylvania. This **USRG30** (below) has a figured maple top and PBC's Tension Free neck system.

The acclaimed Ibanez All Access Neck Joint is featured on both the RBM1 and RBM2 models.

The RBM's signature end-cutaway houses an upward facing output jack that holds guitar cables securely during even the most gymnastic performances.

1994 USA Custom RG USRG30

and joining Whitesnake for a while. But it was his impressive 1990 instrumental album *Passion And Warfare*, the most successful guitar-led record since Jeff Beck's *Blow By Blow*, that turned him into a solo star. The track 'Blue Powder' alone was enough to make most guitarists think about giving up and finding a new path.

The seven-string idea came from a casual conversation in a hotel room between Vai and Ibanez's Rich Lasner. "We were talking about guitars, and Rich told me had an eight-string," Vai recalls. "And I'm thinking, well, how do you play that? That's really bizarre. He asked if I wanted Ibanez to make me one. I said no, I didn't think I'd be able to play it – but a seven-string, I could see that. Why don't you guys make me a JEM with an extra string? That was the extent of the conversation. Took about a minute. And it created a whole sub-culture of music. It's not like this brilliant idea. It's right up there with hey, let's put 24 frets on it, a cutaway so we can pull up on the bar … or another string on it."[96]

Guitarists had toyed with adding an extra string before this. Gretsch, for example, had made some seven-string models for guitarist George Van Eps, and a production version remained in its catalogue for a decade from 1968. This time, the idea was to provide an extra low-tuned string so that Vai could, as he describes it, "tune it down and start chugging away". The guitar Ibanez made for him was in effect a JEM with a wider neck and custom-made hardware and pickups. Vai says he used it on most of the Whitesnake *Slip Of The Tongue* record and also on his own *Passion And Warfare*, and he appears with one prominently on that record's jacket. After a legal tussle with Maestro Alex Gregory, who claimed prior rights to the seven-string idea, Ibanez issued a series of production models, starting in 1990 with the Universe UV7, in black, white, or swirl finish. However, the seven-string guitar would not find widespread success until nearer the end of the 90s – more on that later.

The swirl finish was a spectacular painted look devised by Darren Johansen, where each finish has a unique multi-coloured bucket-of-paints effect. It had first come to wider attention on a limited run of Fender Stratocasters and Telecasters in 1983 with a streaky look nicknamed the "marble" or "bowling ball" finish. In 1990, Ibanez had Johansen apply his swirled technique to the Universe UV77MC, and then two years later to some JEM77 six-string models.

That 1992 catalogue opened with the Vai Universe and JEM models, but next up was Joe Satriani, whose JS signature models had first appeared a couple of years earlier. Satriani was flying high as a solo guitarist, having reached many ears with his spectacular instrumental album of 1987, *Surfing With The Alien*. A year later he found popular acclaim when he played guitar with Mick Jagger on the Stones singer's first solo tour, performing in Japan, Australia, Indonesia, New Zealand, and the USA.

Satriani shared with many of his fellow guitarists a frustration over the limitations of existing instruments. Unlike most, however, he would see his experiments and theories result in a set of Ibanez signature models, which continue to be produced today. That frustration had led the young Satriani to bolt humbuckers to Strat-style bitsers and to generally fiddle with his guitars' physical and electronic specs. When in the late 70s he settled in Berkeley, California, he taught guitar at Secondhand Guitars, where he learned a lot from the store's repairwoman, Jane Hunter (mother of jazz guitarist Charlie Hunter). Gradually, he came to some conclusions. He liked the mass of a Strat peghead, the way the tuners were arranged, and he liked the Fender scale-length. For neck profile, he was warming to something between Fender's C and D profile. (Fender's standard 60s neck was the B, with C and D the slightly wider variants.)

It's the first of many examples that show Satriani as a guitarist keen to go his own way – and generally that meant against the prevailing trends. Shredders, he says, were demanding almost flamenco-like wide, flat fingerboards with big frets, but that seemed to him to homogenise their sound. "They sounded like they were all related to each other," he says with a smile. Satriani had grown up listening to what he describes as third-generation electric blues players, the architects of rock'n'roll and rock music. Many of them played old Fenders and Gibsons with necks that had unusual profiles and even some extreme radiuses – and for Satriani, that all meant that you could hear each individual player. "When I played one of those flat necks with the big frets, suddenly I heard more of somebody else than I heard of me. I thought that was really strange – and I figured I had to avoid that at all costs."

He liked humbuckers, too, and in his first band, The Squares ("like Green Day with a little bit of Van Halen thrown in"), he played a Kramer Pacer. He had two rules: no wah-wah; no vibrato bar. Everybody else was doing that. Gradually, however, he learned to love Floyd Rose vibratos, especially when the fine-tuner version appeared. Satriani was slowly making up his mind about what he needed from a guitar – and during the rather long period between the *Surfing* album's completion and its release in 1987, he met up with Ibanez. The introduction came through Steve Vai, who had been one of Satriani's students.

Satriani didn't know much about Ibanez, but through Vai and also Cliff Cultreri at Satriani's label, Relativity, he made contact with Ibanez and met Rich Lasner at the '87 NAMM show. Soon after, Ibanez gave him a 540 Radius (and another model, details since forgotten). Satriani first appeared as an Ibanez endorser in the 1988 *Artist Spirit* catalogue. Then things started going crazy. He got the gig with Jagger. "Suddenly, everybody wanted to get me to play their stuff," Satriani remembers. "It really ramped up. And I wound up on the cover of the guitar magazines, and there was a story in *The Wall Street Journal*, and then it was *Rolling Stone*. By the time we left for Japan, my world was entirely different. It was difficult to say no to some of these manufacturers, because I'd had a wonderful run as what I would call ... a slightly under-utilised and under-paid musician," he laughs. "But I had to put the brakes on all these offers I was getting." He wound up borrowing a bitser Strat from Larry DiMarzio for the Jagger dates – which set

1991 FGM100 Frank Gambale

THE IBANEZ ELECTRIC GUITAR BOOK

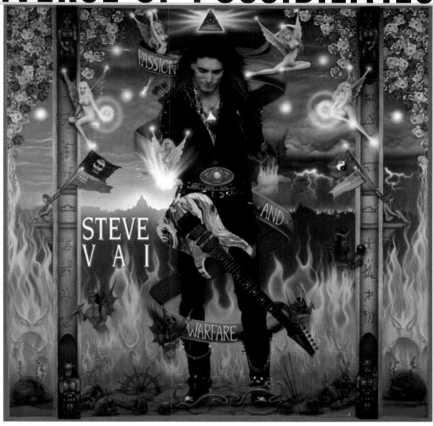

1990 Universe UV77

■ **Steve Vai**'s next Ibanez project was a seven-string guitar, launched in 1990 as the Universe. "It created a whole sub-culture of music," Vai says of the metal seven-string guitar's success in subsequent years. This **UV77** (main guitar, left) is finished in a swirl-paint effect devised by Darren Johansen and later seen on some JEMs, too. Vai is pictured (above) with a swirly Universe on his 1990 album **Passion And Warfare**. Before the seven-string, Vai experimented with longer-scale six-string necks that had extra lower frets, and one of these ended up with Ibanez endorser **Larry Mitchell** (seen opposite with a double-neck: note the **position dots** on the six-string neck). Fusion stylist **Frank Gambale**'s signature FGM model appeared in 1991 (pink **FGM100**, opposite), based on a 540S, while long-term Ibanez player **John Scofield** (pictured in a **1988 catalogue**, centre), waited until 2001 for his **AS200** to become the JSM signature guitar.

Ibanez wondering what was going on. During 1989, Satriani did some solo touring and started work on what became his third album, *Flying In A Blue Dream*. This was when he really started getting into the 540 Radius – and tweaking it like mad, with the help of his San Francisco repairman, Gary Brawer, and also the guys at Ibanez's LA custom shop. They took out the middle single-coil, refinished the body, re-carved it, drilled it – you name it. "I insisted on different fretwire, different fret size, different potentiometers," he says. "I pushed Ibanez to find a different manufacturer for the bridge, because I didn't like the consistency of the metal they were using. This main guitar of mine, which we called Black Dog, had every experimental compound radius on it."

Black Dog, a sort of Frankenstein 540 Radius, gradually turned into the JS model. Satriani and Ibanez worked on clay models of the body – the unusual method devised by Bill Reim that the Ibanez team used to develop work-in-progress body designs. They put more curves in it, extended the top horn, created more of a cutaway for the bottom one, and they sat the two humbuckers right into the wood. They stuck a Roadstar neck on it and experimented with the size of the frets and the radius of the neck. Reim recalls taking a clay body to Satriani in the studio, which the LA shop then copied for the JS prototype. "It really was a meeting of minds," Satriani says. Mostly, and despite all the work, it came down to simplicity. He needed a three-way selector, not a five-way, for example, and he liked as few controls as possible, not separate tones and volumes.

"I wanted something very simple, very plain," Satriani says. "I did not want my name written on it. I didn't want mother-of-pearl snakes or vines, upside-down crosses, any of that. Once again, I was going in the opposite direction of the trend. While Steve was looking for oddities to add to his guitar, I was looking for something that in a way would go unnoticed. Maybe it's because I grew up playing a Telecaster. I just wasn't into using the guitar to be a statement of flamboyance. I wanted something that was as solid as a Tele but as beautiful and effective as the perfect pearl necklace on the most beautiful black dress. I wasn't looking for the feather boa – and there was a lot of that about. I wanted something that was going to look really great 30 years from now."[97]

The JS models first went on sale in 1990. "Three years of comparing ideas, building numerous prototypes, and working on every nuance of guitar design has now produced a contemporary classic," claimed Ibanez.[98] Three Satriani models were announced, all with dot neck, rosewood board, basswood Radius-style body, Edge vibrato, two DiMarzio humbuckers, and those simple controls. The $1199.95 JS1 came in black or white; the $1799.95 JS2 had a stunning chrome finish; and the limited-edition $2299.95 JS3 offered a striking custom graphic, individually painted by Donnie Hunt.

The JS2 was quickly withdrawn as it became clear that the chrome finish was almost impossible to produce with the quality and consistency that everyone wanted. The chrome would lift from the body and form cracks, which was not ideal. "On mine, we had to put some heavy clear tape over the cracks so I wouldn't rip my skin open," Satriani explains. "My main chrome guitar, which I called Chrome Boy, for some reason had more of those problems than my other two – Pearly and Refractor – and I had to retire Chrome Boy a number of years ago."[99] The neck on Chrome Boy was taken as the template for all the JS models, with Satriani's favoured multi-radius shape. Pearly was stolen from Satriani by a bogus roadie at a gig in Florida.

Nick Sugimoto at Fujigen says the factory completed only seven JS2 chrome guitars, including those given to Satriani. At first, he says, they tried plating the body with a traditional method, by dipping it into a solution. That resulted in some spectacular explosions of the finish. Next, Fujigen tried vacuum plating. Sugimoto called about 50 companies, and all but one laughed at the request. "This one company in Osaka said they'd like to try it," he remembers. "But gas inside the wood was forced out by the pressure, and the chrome would change to a nickel colour. Then we'd get incredible electric shocks when we tried to buff the finished bodies."[100] Fujigen had no alternative, and the JS2 was cancelled. Finally, in 1998, Ibanez would issue a production chrome model, the JS10th, that had a chrome-finished plastic body made in Korea.

Donnie Hunt was an artist friend of Satriani's wife, who worked in the fashion industry. "Donnie was one of these artists that painted everything in his life," Satriani says, "so he painted his phone, his walls, his refrigerator. He had a particularly crazy bent that was half Day of the Dead, half African art, and he was from Texas, too, so he had a little bit of a Tex-Mex thing going." At first, Hunt painted some of Satriani's tour outfits with his characteristic skull-and-bones designs.

Then, Bill Reim at Ibanez suggested that Hunt paint some JS guitars. It worked well: Hunt liked to work fast, and Satriani remembers him painting hundreds of the JS3 guitars. When Hunt did one that he thought Satriani might like, he'd give him a call. "I wound up with four or five of these guitars, and they were all different," Satriani recalls. Hunt knew that Satriani liked the ones with larger figures and in certain colours. One in particular, known as Blue Donnie, became a favourite, with blue, white, and grey skulls. "I played that for quite a while, and I think it was my number one guitar up until the point that it, too, was stolen," Satriani says.

In 1992, three new JS models were added to the line: the $2299.95 JS4 with painted body by Joan Satriani; the $2299.95 JS5, painted by Carol Satriani; and the $999.95 JS6, with an oil-finished natural mahogany body and a fixed bridge. Meanwhile, the $1199.95 JS1 added a central single-coil between the two existing humbuckers. Satriani's sisters, Joan and Carol, were both professional artists and seemed like logical additions alongside Donnie Hunt to create more art guitars.

They worked in a different way to Hunt ("less cavalier, let's say, about spreading the artwork around," according to Satriani) and so the plan was for far fewer guitars than Hunt painted and a much longer schedule. Carol's style was representational, and her design was called Rain Forest, a leafy green creation; Joan was more avant-garde, and she

FLYING IN A BLUE DREAM

■ **Joe Satriani**'s signature guitars for Ibanez were based on a 540R model he played and experimented with, known as **Black Dog** (on magazine cover, right). A trio of Satriani guitars were launched in 1990: the **JS1** (white guitar, opposite), the **JS2** (main guitar, below), and the **JS3** (blue guitar, opposite), each of which had a body individually painted by artist Donnie Hunt. This spectacular **1990 ad** (above right) references his Flying In A Blue Dream album. The **chrome finish** of the JS2, seen in an Ibanez **promo shot** with Joe (above left), proved impossible to apply consistently, and the model was quickly dropped. It did at last appear successfully, on a plastic body, for a tenth anniversary model (the **JS10TH**, opposite).

BLACK DOG & BLUE DONNIE

1998 JS10TH

1991 JS1

1990 JS3

1990 JS2

made her design, Electric Rainbow, by layering colours and cellophane and then ripping the cellophane from the surface. It's been estimated that fewer than 50 of Joan and Carol's guitars exist, although the exact number is not recorded.

The line settled down from 1994 with the JS1000 and cheaper JS100, recently adding the 24-fret JS2400, and Satriani continues his relationship with Ibanez today. He describes Ibanez as an artistic partner. Ibanez provides him with instruments and an income outside of the music; he provides Ibanez with innovation based on real experience, which continues to range wide. There's his solo work and Chickenfoot – his band with singer Sammy Hagar, bassist Michael Anthony, and Red Hot Chili Peppers drummer Chad Smith – but also with G3, Satriani's touring project that features him plus two (changing) guest guitarists. Over the years, his G3 comrades have included Steve Vai, Paul Gilbert, Steve Lukather, and many others.

"A guitar company needs feedback," Satriani says, "in the same way that Leo Fender needed to get feedback from those little country swing bands that he would give instruments to. He'd ask them how's it working, what should I do? It's an important part of the formula: we as players say yes, you can call this a Joe Satriani guitar, and I will play it everywhere. Then the guitar company comes back to us and says great – now what do you need, how can we make the instrument feel better and respond better? That relationship is so important."[101]

It's a relationship that Ibanez built on during the 90s, issuing signature models for Reb Beach, Frank Gambale, Paul Gilbert, Pat Metheny, and John Petrucci. Winger's Reb Beach had a series of Voyager models with bodies that had wedge-shaped "end cutaways", simple controls, Edge vibratos, and EMG or IBZ pickups. Jazz-rocker Frank Gambale took the 540S and made it his own: his FGM models featured different pickups, smaller frets, and Ibanez's smooth All Access neck joint. Paul Gilbert of Mr Big went for a fixed bridge and reverse headstock, HSH DiMarzios, and the visual impact of big fake f-holes on his PGM's body. Jazz legend Pat Metheny's PM100 was a double-cutaway neck-pickup jazz box with 17th-fret neck join and 16-inch body, while John Petrucci of Dream Theater endowed his RG-style JPM with a thicker Ultra neck, coil-tap switching, and brash graphics.

Al Marinaro, sales rep in key eastern states for 20 years from 1976, says that a good deal of Ibanez's success has always come from its network of hard-working dealers – a music-industry force not always recognised in the history of guitar brands. "If there were no reps to sell to the dealers and no dealers to sell the instruments, there would be no Ibanez," Marinaro says, justly proud of his place in the chain from maker to player. "Any guitar company must listen to the market and come out with products that the market is looking for. And the only place you can get that information is from the dealers, and from the consumers who come in their stores and say what they want. The dealer tells the rep, and the rep tells the company." Marinaro points to some of the dealers who helped shape Ibanez's success, from the time of the copies of the 70s to the brand's coming of age in the late 80s, and through to the 90s and beyond. "Sam Ash Music did a lot of work promoting Ibanez," he says. "Manny's did, too, and so did Chuck Levin's Washington Music, and Brook Mays. On the West Coast, of course, there was this local chain store called Guitar Center. All these people were active. They enjoyed working with the company and the reps, and they promoted and pushed the devil out of their products. Couple that with a good artist campaign, and it really helped build Ibanez to what they are today."[102]

Ibanez rode through the late 80s and into the early 90s with its successful RG and S models, and it was by now one of the hottest brands around, especially among metal and extreme rock players. But then something upset the balance: musical fashion changed. Hardly unexpected, and certainly not unusual. But an upset, nonetheless.

Rich Lasner had left in 1989 to join Yamaha's guitar development operation over in North Hollywood (and today he runs G-Rok R&D in Novato, California). Bill Reim was still at Hoshino USA, and he takes up the story. "We had just come out with seven-string guitars," Reim says, "steering the Ibanez line in the direction of even higher technicality – but it was completely blown out of the water by all this stuff happening in the grunge scene. We did manage to come up with some designs that would appeal to that market, the Talman and so on, and we aligned ourselves with some players we felt were not quite so mainstream. For instance, we hooked up with Kevin Shields of My Bloody Valentine – one of my favourite bands."[103] Reim's cultivated taste for British bands had also led to Ibanez working with Simple Minds, New Order, Kitchens Of Distinction, and others.

Grunge emerged around the turn into the 90s as an antidote to hair metal and anything else deemed overly technical. As with punk before, the back-to-basics grunge players found relatively cheap instruments appealing, and there was an accent on being seen to *not* play old-school favourites. In particular, this meant that Fender's also-ran models made a good showing among the leading grungemen of the time, including J. Mascis in Dinosaur Jr. with various Jazzmasters, Thurston Moore in Sonic Youth with Jazzmaster, Jaguar, or Mustang, and Kurt Cobain in Nirvana with Jaguar and Mustang. "Everybody wanted used guitars that didn't stay in tune," laughs Jim Donahue. "Nobody wanted pointy headstocks, nobody wanted Floyd Roses, nobody wanted shiny. We became labelled as the pointy-head shiny-guitar company. And, again, we almost died."[104]

There was a rush among guitar makers to try to absorb this pawn-shop mentality into some new (old) designs – and so retro was born, at least as far as guitar design was concerned. The idea was to grab the vibe of classic 50s and 60s styles and morph them into something sort-of new. An early showing came with the revived Charvel brand's Surfcaster model, launched in 1991, with its Fender-ish pearly pickguard, Danelectro-like lipstick pickups, and Rickenbacker-style slash soundhole and triangular fingerboard markers. Suddenly, it seemed, grunge and retro were cool. Metal and modern – the twin

1992 JS4 Electric Rainbow

1992 JS5 Rain Forest

■ Two more JS art guitars appeared in 1992, both painted by Joe's sisters: **Electric Rainbow** (above) was by Joan Satriani and **Rain Forest** (right) by Carol Satriani. Artists lined up for Ibanez axes, and J from **White Zombie** opted for a star-infested **Iceman** (below, and **1994 ad**, opposite). Brash graphics got you noticed: **John Petrucci** of Dream Theater (**1996 catalogue**, opposite) went for a collage on his JPM model, while **Paul Gilbert** of Mr Big (**1991 catalogue**, opposite) preferred painted-on fake f-holes for his PGM guitars. In contrast, jazz legend **Pat Metheny**'s signature Ibanez, the **PM100** (opposite), had a relatively conventional hollow body but with better high fret access.

1998 Iceman ICJ100

THE IBANEZ ELECTRIC GUITAR BOOK

1996 PM100 Pat Metheny

pillars of Ibanez – apparently were not. Ibanez's first response was the RT series of 1992, which seemed like Fender-y RGs: alder body, rounder neck profile, traditional vibrato, some with tortoise guards, but with the RG shape, locking tuners, 24 frets, and HSH pickups. They lasted barely a year.

Next up was the more radical (for Ibanez) Talman series, in two body styles: the TC, lumpy and offset, or the TV, with a pointier lower horn. The designs were created at Ibanez's Los Angeles office. Tatsuhiro "Mick" Suyama had been working for Hoshino since 1987, and he was based at the LA office for six years from 1991. He remembers the communal effort there to come up with the Talmans. "We had two luthiers and an artist relations guy, and we all got together and started drawing shapes," Suyama says. "Finally, we came up with two we liked. The TC was known for its use by Tom Morello of Rage Against The Machine at the time, and the TV became known for Noodles, of Offspring. He has his own signature model today with the original TV shape."[105]

The Talmans were introduced in 1994, with a single TC model, the three-single-coil 530, and two TVs, the HSH-layout 650 and 750. All had simple vibratos, and at first the Talman bodies were made of Resoncast, known elsewhere as MDF, a compressed wood-and-resin material. Various other models were added, including real-wood versions, but many players considered them un-Ibanez, and all were gone from the catalogues by 1998. "We knew we had to move very quickly to address this changing market," Reim says, "but by the time we came out with the Talmans, it was just as the grunge scene hit its peak. It really was a case of too little too late."[106]

Closely related to the retro vibe – which Ibanez called "the classic alternative" – was the idea that by reissuing earlier models, guitar companies could carve out an easy route to some hip old styling. Ibanez described the set-neck Ghostrider models, also new for 1994 and another LA-office creation, as "descendants of the famous Ibanez Artist models of the late 70s", although the bodies were smaller, with pointier horns, and made of alder. They had a short stay in the line, too. A more lasting reissue came with the revival of the angular 70s Iceman design, last seen in the 1982 catalogue. In 1995, Ibanez launched a couple of new Icemen, with or without vibrato, as well as a Paul Stanley version, the PS10, including a signed and numbered limited edition. The Iceman design remains in the line today, an early survivor and a striking reminder of one of Ibanez's first and most endearing attempts at originality.

Rob Nishida in the LA office saw a local band, Korn, playing Steve Vai's Universe seven-strings in a small club. Chris Kelly, then artist relations manager in LA, recalls getting Korn's demo cassettes. "I sent them more seven-strings, and the relationship developed from there," Kelly says.[107] Bill Reim remembers a chance conversation in the Ibanez warehouse one day in the 90s. "This kid working in our guitar-checking staff pulled me to one side and says, dude, you've got to check out this band Korn, they're awesome."[108] Korn were indeed awesome: their debut record appeared in 1994, and four years later they scored their first number-one album, *Follow The Leader*. Their dark, brooding brand of nu-metal popularised down-tuned and multi-stringed guitars, and guitarist James "Munky" Shaffer helped to revive Ibanez's seven-string line, which had been floundering since the introduction of the Universe models in 1990.

"We had just got rid of our last seven-string from the warehouse," Reim says, "and suddenly it turns around and everybody is looking for seven-strings." Ibanez was caught short, and Reim was dismayed to see Schecter, ESP, and others beating them to market for the new demand sparked by Korn, Limp Bizkit, and others. The first post-Universe Ibanez seven finally appeared in 1998, the RG7620 (with vibrato) and 7621 (fixed bridge). Again, Reim praises Vai's equanimity. "With Steve, it's not just about Steve. He thinks about the whole welfare of the company. He feels like he's part of it, and he wants to do what's best for the company. So he gave it his blessing, and we were back in the game again."[109] More sevens at various pricepoints were added to the line, with a model for Korn, the K7, in 2001, superseded by the Apex signature guitar for Munky in 2007. By 2012, there would be 13 various seven-string models in the Ibanez catalogue.

Up at the top of the pricelist, the Prestige name has been attached to some guitars (and often added to the headstock logo) to indicate a higher-end model, although not with any evident consistency. Like many makers, however, Ibanez also tries hard to compete in the budget market, always vigilant for fresh production sources. Around 1998, a sub-brand was created for budget models, GIO, at first to indicate new Indonesian and Chinese manufacturing sources. A "G" in the model-name prefix (and usually "GIO" alongside Ibanez on the headstock) became the sign of a budget model: the affordable version of the RG series was renamed, from RX to GRX and later also GRG; there were budget takes on the S series, the SA and GSA lines; and there was a new cheaper style of the double-cutaway Artist, the GAX series.

Meanwhile, Korean production would stop for Ibanez around 2008, while Japanese production continued, as ever, and mainly for higher-end models. At the time of writing, Ibanez uses two manufacturers in Japan (including the longstanding Fujigen), one in Indonesia, and five in China.

The new Artcore models, introduced in 2002, were mid-priced hollowbody electrics, made in northern China by a producer specialising in this kind of guitar. Jim Donahue, who left Ibanez in 2003 after 19 years with the US company and set up his own Noah James firm, points to an Artcore vibrato as a modern example of Ibanez's insistent independence. "Being Ibanez, we couldn't use a real Bigsby, so we made our own," he says, "which we ended up paying a royalty on anyway. We made three different bridges, and each mould cost something like $30,000. It's a Bigsby-style vibrato bridge – but it's Ibanez. No other company would do that. I remember being sent a sample guitar once that said Ibanez on the bridge seven times: the bridge plate said Ibanez, and every saddle said Ibanez. Both pickups said Ibanez. It said Ibanez on the headstock. There was Ibanez

2011 APEX100 Munky

■ **GIO** was a new sub-brand for Indonesian and Chinese-made models, like this blue **GRX150** (opposite), a budget RG-style model. Retro was hot in the 90s as brands discovered the cool factor of 50s and 60s guitars. Ibanez took a step into this new-old world with the **Talman**, in two shapes: the TV and the TC (**TC530**, top). Ibanez

called them the classic alternative in a **1994 ad** (opposite), which also features the retro **Ghostrider**. **Korn** (seen in a **2000 ad**, Rule of 7, opposite), spread the metallic word on down-tuning and multi-stringed guitars. Following the band's K7 signature seven-string, guitarist **Munky** had his own APEX seven-strings from 2007, including

this recent **APEX100** (main guitar), vividly described by Ibanez as a lowend bone-crusher. **Paul Stanley**'s PS10 model was revived in the 90s, with this **1995 ad** (top) pushing the PS10II as well as a limited edition. **Andy Timmons** was a long-time RT player (on a **1994 album**, opposite), awarded his own signature model in 1999.

118

1994 Talman TC530

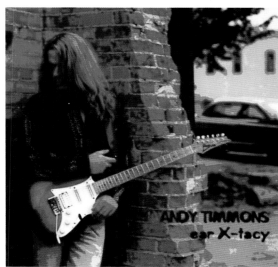

ANDY TIMMONS
ear X-tacy

2012 GIO GRX150

on every machine head. So it said Ibanez at least 17 times. I said this is stupid, this is ridiculous. But that's Ibanez for you."[110]

Fritz Katoh, the designer responsible for many of Ibanez's finest moments, left Hoshino in 1995, setting up his own Fritz International Associates three years later. There were also changes upstairs in Ibanez management. In 1998, the long-serving Hoshino USA vice-president, Roy Miyahara, became president, taking over from Tom Tanaka. Miyahara left in 2002, when Bill Reim became president of the US operation, the first American to hold the post. In Japan, Tom Tanaka became president of the main Hoshino Gakki company in 2005, a position he still holds at the time of writing, while in 2009, Shinichi Kubo took over from Hiroshi Ando as president of Hoshino Gakki Hanbai, the domestic sales firm.

With seven-string guitars established in the line, in 2007 Ibanez introduced an eight-string guitar, the RG2228, with a necessarily ultra-wide neck (about two inches at the nut and three at the body), custom hardware, including a fine-tuning fixed bridge, a 27-inch scale, and a suggested tuning of (low to high) F, A-sharp, D-sharp, G-sharp, C-sharp, F-sharp, A-sharp, D-sharp (perhaps best understood as an extra F-sharp and B below a regular six-string set, and then everything down a half-step). The origins of the eight-string go back further, with Conklin often cited as the pioneering maker, but for Ibanez, the story began in 2003. That's when the LA artist-relations office started to work with the Swedish band Meshuggah, building various custom eight-strings for Fredrik Thordendal and Mårten Hagström. A Meshuggah signature eight-string, the M8M, was added to the line in 2012.

Mick Suyama at Hoshino Japan says that in recent years most new Ibanez guitar designs have been created in Japan and some in Los Angeles. The LA artist-relations office, with accompanying custom shop, has been in operation since 1990, at various locations, moving to its current site in Sun Valley in 2005. The LA shop was responsible for a further retro-flavoured design, the Talman-like Jet King, launched in two slightly different shapes in 2005. These didn't last long, but the style survives in the ORM, the signature model for Omar Rodriguez-Lopez of The Mars Volta, which debuted in 2008.

In 2007, Hoshino established the Ibanez Guitar Design Center in Nagoya, Japan, with two designers and a woodworking specialist. The first model from the new Center was the FR, introduced in 2008, another Talman-like retro guitar, but this time leaning a little more to the style of a two-humbucker Telecaster. The Darkstone DN models followed a year later, also born in the Design Center. "They're more like a Les Paul-type set-neck guitar," says Suyama, "with two humbuckings and a separate bridge and tailpiece, plus a double cutaway body and more of an Iceman-ish body tail."[111] Some ideas still come from Ibanez's international distributors, too, such as the new-for-2012 Roadcore RC320, developed and named with help from Headstock, Ibanez's British distributor since 1996.

Perhaps the most unusual manifestation of old-Ibanez influence came with a guitar that Paul Gilbert asked the LA custom shop to make for him. He'd found some pictures of an Iceman, which had always been one of his favourite pointy guitars, and he fiddled with them in Photoshop, flipping the thing around and upside down to see what might look good. At the time, he'd been revisiting some favourite old players, too, and he remembered Frank Marino's SG with multiple single-coils, so he had DiMarzio make him a new single-coil pickup. Marino had angled one of his pickups: Gilbert tried that, and ended up with all three single-coils angled. His custom guitar was delivered in 2007. And what did he call this opposite-Iceman? A Fireman, of course. The buzz among Gilbert fans encouraged Ibanez to release a couple of Japan-only limited edition models in 2009, the FRM1 and 2, followed by a Chinese-made FRM100 production model in 2011.

In 2006, a signature model appeared for Mick Thomson of Slipknot, the masked nine-piece from Des Moines. The six-string MTM1BR was specifically designed to cater for Thomson's low tuning, down three half-steps from regular and with the low C-sharp dropped to B (low to high: B, F-sharp, B, E, G-sharp, C-sharp). What could be more metal? "Early in the band there wasn't a definitive tuning," Thomson says. "Sometimes it would be C, sometimes it would be, well, hit your open string, *dnggggg*, and whatever it is, we all tune to that. Working in a guitar shop, where I taught for three-and-a-half years, I got to experiment with strings and gauges. I wanted to get the string tension to feel the same as if I was playing 9 to 42 tuned to E, but I'm actually down to C-sharp."

Thomson is a long-time Ibanez fan, even though he took a detour with B.C. Rich in the band's earlier years. His fourth-ever guitar, at age 19, a good few years before Slipknot, was a 540SLTD – it followed a Hohner Tele copy, a Hondo Kramer-ish model, and a Peavey Tracer. He saved up from his job at the post office to buy his green 540, and he absolutely loved it. Within a year, however, dead broke and faced with the age-old choice between somewhere to live or something to play, he sold it for $400. "I've been looking for that guitar for years," he says with a sigh. "If you've got that thing and it's in good shape, I'll give you a grand for it right now."

At first in Slipknot he played RG560s. "You could pick them up for between about $175 and $300 – the best thing in the world. The place where I taught, I did all the repairs, too, so yes, give me that shitty guitar, and I'll do all the tweaking. And if you're into playing fast … oh, my, god. There's nothing on earth better than a used 500-series RG. I'd load it up with EMGs, shim the sustain block, and get that bridge real solid – I never needed the whammy." Once the band obtained some notoriety and the guitar companies started shouting at them, Thomson switched to B.C. Rich, and soon he had a signature model, the Warlock-based M7.

By the early 2000s, he was ready to move, and Ibanez seemed the right place to go. Thomson remembers Mike Taft and Rob Nishida from Ibanez's LA artist-relations office bringing over a few things they'd had built for him, toward the end of 2003, right around

2010 RGA8

2008 Artcore Custom AF125

2007 JEM20TH

**2009 FRM1
Paul Gilbert**

■ The **Jet King** models (**2008 catalogue**, top right) built on the Talman retro style, and the **DN** Darkstone guitars (**2009 catalogue**, left) added a hint of Iceman at the body tail. Paul Gilbert took a more radical look at the Iceman and came up with the **FRM1** (right). As a sort of reversed Iceman, the witty name for this twisted retro creation was the Fireman. Steve Vai and Ibanez pushed hard to offer yet odder takes on the JEM model, and for its 20th anniversary (**JEM20TH**, opposite) they had a see-through plastic body with internal LED lights (aglow in the **2007 ad**, top). **Artcore** was Ibanez's name in 2002 for new Chinese-made hollow and semi-solid models, like this **AF125** (main guitar). Beyond a mere seven, an eight-string model appeared for **Meshuggah** (**2012 ad**, above), and other eights were added, like this **RGA8** (opposite).

the time the band was recording *Vol. 3*. After the usual to and fro, Ibanez perfected what Thomson wanted, and the MTM1 first appeared in the 2006 catalogue, with the MTM2 added a year later. They featured a fine-tuning fixed bridge, something first seen on the Satriani JS2000 four years earlier. "I switched to fixed bridges," Thomson says, "but I always loved the way a Lo-Pro Edge felt, so this was perfect. How is that bridge not in more guitars?"

More recently, the new signature MTM10 and MTM100 models were launched, with a body shape that Thomson describes as "like a Warlock got raped by a Randy Rhoads V". Thomson plays hand-built guitars made at Ibanez's LA custom shop, but he's well aware that not all companies work as hard as Ibanez to make the regular signature models as close as practically possible to his own one-off instruments. "It's got to be as faithful as possible to mine," Thomson says. "I have to be able to grab one from a store and have it sound and feel right. If someone's buying it, I want them to get the same experience that I have. I've played other things where it's obviously a paint job put on something, just to generate some revenue from a fanbase. But there were no fights with Ibanez. They did it right. Even the bolt-ons without active pickups – everything sounds good on them, too, and they play good. The top-line model is as damn close as you can get to the one I play."

Thomson did some guitar clinics for Ibanez a few years ago. For someone used to playing to huge audiences, it was a surprisingly nerve-wracking experience. "I'm not someone who needs a lot of attention," he says. "I wear a mask, and I love that. I don't have to be: hey, everybody look at me! A lot of people who are performers, that's a huge part of their personality. It's not part of mine. I feel really awkward with people looking at me. I play in front of hundreds of thousands of people at festivals – but put me in a room with 300 people, and now it's weird. What I do love is helping people find out how to learn. If some kid wants to talk about the band, I don't want to talk about it. But if you want to talk about guitar … ask away."[112]

Nick Sugimoto, who we met earlier in the book, is a veteran of Ibanez guitar making. He worked at the Fujigen R&D department in Japan from 1978 to 2002, and in more recent years he has made a number of Ibanez's limited editions at his Sugi Guitars workshop in Matsumoto. One notable production was the JEM-EVO of 2012. This was a scratch-by-dent-by-ding re-creation of the guitar that has been Steve Vai's favourite since about 1993, the JEM that he calls Evo. Sugi made the 100-piece limited edition, and Sugimoto recalls some hard work to get it right.

"I visited Los Angeles in 2011 and traced all the details from Steve's guitar," Sugimoto says. "I took those back to Japan, and started my work." He asked ex-Fender custom shop man Jay Black about the art of relic'ing, and got pages of instructions in return. "We painted the special aged white colour first, then I had my tracing – all the dents and scratches in a kind of map – which I would stick on the body and then cut into the face. The relic job takes about two guitars a day, sometimes three a day. Sometimes I had blisters come up, you know?"[113] Vai himself praised the result and remained in awe of the original. "Although Evo is just made out of wire and wood, I'm afraid of how much emotional investment I have in her," he says. "I'm afraid at how much I love her, but I know that she is only on loan to me for a short time and will one day be dust. But for now, there's still quite a bit we have to say together."[114]

At the time of writing, Ibanez's electrics catalogue still proudly displays five JEM models, and the by-product RG guitars take pole position. The RG line still provides Ibanez's metal heart, from top-end Prestiges and Premiums, through guitars with and without vibrato, straightahead Iron Labels, multi-stringers and long-scale downtuners, the curvier RGAs, and down to the budget RG derivatives, the GRGs and GRXs. "This six-string is nothing new," wrote a reviewer who recently analysed a GRG250, "but that's only because Ibanez got it right many years ago."[115] The various S models form an equal tier of solid Ibanez achievement in the catalogue, while the X series brings together odd shapes, from Iceman to pointy metal axes. There are single-cutaway ARZs, ARTs, GARTs, and ARXs, retro-flavour FRs, and plenty of Artcore and Artstar hollows and semis.

Finally, in the current catalogue, an impressive team of artists lines up to present the various Ibanez signature models: Tosin Abasi, George Benson, Ben Bruce, Paul Gilbert, Herman Li, Cameron Lidell, Meshuggah, Pat Metheny, Munky, Noodles, Joe Satriani, John Scofield, Mick Thomson, Andy Timmons, Sam Totman, and Steve Vai. In 2012, there were even a couple of 25th anniversary editions of the RG and S models. "So here we are celebrating 25 years," ran the catalogue's blurb. "With more and more young players discovering the RG and the S series every day, don't worry if you can't celebrate our 25th anniversary with us. Our 50th will be here before you know it."

Bill Reim is the president of Hoshino USA, and in his 30-plus years with the company he's seen it all, from the hard times when it seemed no one would ever want an Ibanez guitar again, to the boom years and beyond. "But today, I think we still appeal to guys who are looking for a harder-edged hard rock guitar," he says. "And with the Artcores, we attract people looking to add a nice box guitar to their collection. Then there are guitars like the S model, which continues to appeal to people who don't really fit into any category. Originally, that was pegged as kind of a fusion guitar, but then we found we had death metal guys playing it and teachers at Berklee playing it. There's a practicality to it that people who can get beyond trends recognise."

Reim reckons that the strength of the Ibanez operation has always come back to an emphasis on teamwork, on guitar-makers and musicians and retailers and distributors all working together. "Anybody who tried to stand up and make themselves the hero was immediately shot down," Reim says, "because that's really not the way we work. We function as a team. And Japan has a very strong sense of morality. We try to do the right thing – and that's something it's not always easy to do in this world."[116]

2012 JEMEVO

■ Artist endorsement and signature models remain important to Ibanez, drawing attention to the regular lines that provide the brand's day-to-day sales. **Steve Vai**, who did much to kickstart Ibanez's revival in the late 80s, saw every ding and scratch of his favourite working guitar, Evo, echoed for the 2012 limited-edition **JEMEVO** (above; and rear, left). Slipknot's **Mick Thomson** moved from his first MTM signature model (2007 ad, opposite) to the **MTM100** (top), "like a Warlock got raped by a Randy Rhoads V," he says. Up at the top end, Ibanez has **J.Custom** and **Prestige** (**2012 ad**, opposite) and **Premium** (**2011 RG ad**, centre), while the latest retro new-oldie is the **Roadcore** (**RC320**, opposite). Whatever will they think of next?

2012 MTM100 Mick Thomson

2012 Roadcore RC320

Endnotes

1   Bank Of Japan governor Ichimada Naoto quoted in William Stueck *The Korean War In World History* (University Press of Kentucky 2004)

2   Author's interview July 11 2012

3   Author's interview May 18 2012

4   Author's interview July 11 2012

5   Author's correspondence July 18–November 29 2012

6   Author's interview June 27 2012

7   Author's interview May 23 2012

8   Author's interview October 4 2012

9   Author's interview October 4 2012

10 Author's interview May 23 2012

11 *Beat Instrumental* September 1973

12 Author's interview June 27 2012

13 Author's interview October 4 2012

14 Author's interview June 27 2012

15 *The Music Trades* July 1973

16 *Guitar Player* December 1973

17 Author's interview July 11 2012

18 Author's interview May 23 2012

19 George Gruhn *Guitar Player* February 1975

20 *The Guitars Friend* (Quick Fox 1977)

21 Author's interview October 4 2012

22 Author's interview October 4 2012

23 Author's correspondence July 18–November 29 2012

24 Author's interview October 4 2012

25 Tom Wheeler & Steve Rosen *Guitar Player* February 1979

26 Author's interview October 3 2012

27 Author's interview October 4 2012

28 Author's interview October 3 2012

29 Author's interview October 4 2012

30 Leonard Ferris *Guitar Player* May 1974

31 Author's interview October 4 2012

32 Author's correspondence December 3 2012

33 Author's interview October 4 2012

34 Brian McLaughlin *Guitar Player* January 1978

35 Author's interview January 11 2013

36 Author's interview December 5 2012

37 Author's interview October 4 2012

38 Author's interview October 4 2012

39 *Japan Music Trades* English Readers Edition October 1976

40 Author's interview October 8 & November 1 2012

41 Author's interview October 4 2012

42 Author's interview July 16 2012

43 Author's interview May 11 2011

44 Author's interview July 16 2012

45 Author's interview October 17 2012

46 Author's correspondence July 18–November 29 2012

47 Author's interview October 17 2012

48 Author's interview July 16 2012

49 Author's interview October 17 2012

50 Author's interview July 16 2012

51 Author's interview October 17 2012

52 Author's interview December 11 2012

53 Author's interview July 16 2012

54 Author's interview October 17 2012

55 Author's interview October 17 2012

56 Author's interview October 2 2012

57 Author's interview July 16 2012

58 John Swenson *Guitar World* March 1982

59 Author's interview June 21 2012

60 Author's interview January 11 2013

61 Author's interview June 21 2012

62 Author's interview January 11 2013

63 Jas Obrecht *Guitar Player* October 1986

64 Author's interview October 17 2012

65 vai.com accessed June 11 2004

66 Author's interview June 21 2012

67 Author's interview October 17 2012

68 Author's interview January 11 2013

69 Author's interview October 17 2012

70 Author's interview June 21 2012

71 Author's interview October 17 2012

72 Author's interview July 16 2012

73 Author's interview October 8 & November 1 2012

74 Author's interview October 17 2012

75 Author's interview October 8 & November 1 2012

76 Author's interview October 17 2012

77 Author's interview June 21 2012

78 Author's interview October 17 2012

79 Andy Brauer *Guitar Player* September 1988

80 Author's interview October 17 2012

81 Author's correspondence January 4 2013

82 Author's interview October 17 2012

83 Author's interview June 21 2012

84 Author's correspondence January 4 2013

85 Author's interview October 8 & November 1 2012

86 Author's interview June 21 2012

87 *Ibanez 2012 Electric Guitars Catalog*

88 Author's interview October 2 2012

89 Author's interview January 4 2013

90 Author's interview October 2 2012

91 Author's interview January 13 2013

92 Author's correspondence January 17 2013

93 Author's correspondence January 15 2013

94 Author's correspondence January 15 2013

95 Alan DiPerna *Ibanez Internazionale* catalogue 1992–93

96 Author's interview June 21 2012

97 Author's interview May 30 & October 26 2012

98 *Ibanez Guitars Basses* catalogue 1990

99 Author's interview May 30 & October 26 2012

100 Author's interview October 8 & November 1 2012

101 Author's interview May 30 & October 26 2012

102 Author's interview January 11 2013

103 Author's interview July 16 2012

104 Author's interview October 2 2012

105 Author's interview October 16 2012

106 Author's interview July 16 2012

107 Author's correspondence January 17 2013

108 Author's interview July 16 2012

109 Author's interview July 16 2012

110 Author's interview October 2 2012

111 Author's interview October 16 2012

112 Author's interview December 14 2012

113 Author's interview October 8 & November 1 2012

114 guitarvaults.com accessed January 20 2013

115 Matt Blackett reviewing GRG250DXB *Guitar Player* December 2012

116 Author's interview July 16 2012

THE
REFERENCE
LISTING

REFERENCE LISTING

This guide to Ibanez electric guitar models consists of an alphabetical list of series entries, some of which have detailed model listings, followed by an analysis of Ibanez's serial-number systems.

WHY IT'S HERE

We've designed this Reference Listing to help you identify Ibanez electric guitars made between the late 50s and 2012. The notes here should help you get the most from this unique inventory.

WHAT'S HERE

The Listing covers production models, with the following series covered in detail: Artist, George Benson, Copies, Paul Gilbert, Iceman, Jem, P, Pro, R, RG, Roadstar II, Roadster, S, Joe Satriani, Paul Stanley, T, and Universe. Other series have brief summaries.

Ibanez regularly offers different models in its various international markets, and we have tried to include as many of these as possible. We've checked all the catalogues and pricelists we could find from as many sources as possible, but we certainly don't claim that the listing here is complete. Don't be surprised if you come across a model without an entry here or if you find a model here that you didn't know existed. The Listing is meant to be a helpful guide, not an all-embracing catalogue.

UNDERSTANDING THE DATA

In the series entries that have detailed treatments, each model is listed by the alphabetical and/or numerical order of the model name, usually following published Ibanez catalogues and pricelists for style.

At the head of each model entry is that model name, in bold type. Next is a year or range of years indicating the production period of the particular model. Please be aware that these dates are necessarily approximate, because it's not easy to pinpoint manufacturing spans with accuracy. The dates shown are based on our extensive research as well as official data supplied by Ibanez, so they represent the best information available. But don't be surprised if, occasionally, you do find a guitar made a little earlier or a little later than the dates given.

Most entries then include a list of bullet points below the heading that relate to the particular model's specifications and other relevant features, followed by any notes, and a list of related models, where relevant. In order, these points refer to the following components and details, where present:

- Neck, fingerboard (meaning the playing surface, and not necessarily a separate board); scale, frets; string-guide; locking nut; headstock.
- Body; finish colour(s).
- Pickup(s).
- Controls; output jack.
- Pickguard.
- Bridge.
- Metalwork finish if gold-plated.

- *Any other information, including cross-references, alternative model names, and so on.*

* Model or models related to the main one above are listed here, with the model name in bold, production year or years, and a short description.

All this information is designed to tell you more about Ibanez electric guitars.

By using the general information and illustrations earlier in the book, combined with the data in this Reference Listing, you should be able to build up a fuller picture of any instrument and its pedigree.

AMERICAN MASTER

See **USA CUSTOM**.

APEX

See **MUNKY**.

ARTCORE

2002–current
Broad series name for extensive lines of mostly hollow and semi-solid models, including AF, AFS, AG, AGR, AM, AS lines.

ARTFIELD

1988
AFD models, sculpted PRS-like Artist style AFD25, and extended-top-horn natural-wood AFD40 and 45.

ARTSTAR

See **ARTIST & PRO**.

ARTIST & PRO

SOLIDBODY

Single-Cutaway
Artist or Pro or Professional

ARC100 2006–07
- Bound rosewood fingerboard, block markers; 22 frets; swirl inlay on headstock.
- Bound carved-top body; various colours.
- Two metal-cover humbuckers.
- Three controls (two volume, tone) plus three-way selector; side-mounted output jack.
- Six-saddle bridge plus separate fine-tuning tailpiece.

* **ARC300** 2006–07 *As ARC100 but pearl block markers, flame maple top. 06 07*
* **ARC500** 2007 *As ARC100 but ebony fingerboard, star markers, natural finish quilted maple top, gold-plated metalwork. 07*

ART90 2012–current
- Rosewood fingerboard, dot markers; 22 frets.
- Carved-top body; various colours.
- Two coverless humbuckers.
- Two controls (volume, tone) plus three-way selector; side-mounted output jack.
- Six-saddle bridge plus separate bar tailpiece.

ART100 2007–current
- Rosewood fingerboard, fancy marker at 12th fret; 22 frets.
- Carved-top body; various colours.
- Two coverless humbuckers.
- Three controls (two volume, tone) plus three-way selector; side-mounted output jack.
- Six-saddle bridge plus separate bar tailpiece.
* **ART200** 2012–current *As ART100 but flame maple top, block markers.*
* **ART300** 2008–10 *As ART100 but diamond markers plus fancy marker at 12th fret, textured top, two black-cover humbuckers.*
* **ART320** 2010–11 *As ART100 but diamond markers plus fancy marker at 12th fret, blue flame-maple top, two black-cover humbuckers.*
* **ART420** 2009–10 *As ART100 but diamond markers plus fancy marker at 12th fret, spalted maple top, two black-cover humbuckers.*
* **ART500** 2008 *As ART100 but all fancy markers, quilted maple top, two black-cover humbuckers.*
* **ART600** 2010 *As ART100 but pearl block markers, quilted maple top, two black-cover humbuckers.*

ARZ307 2011–current
- Rosewood fingerboard, no markers; 24 frets; fancy headstock inlay.
- Carved-top body; various colours.
- Two coverless humbuckers.
- Two controls (volume, tone) plus three-way selector; side-mounted output jack.
- Six-saddle bridge plus separate bar tailpiece.
* **ARZ400** 2011–current *As ARZ307 but two black-cover humbuckers.*
* **ARZ800** 2011–current *As ARZ307 but quilted maple top, two black-cover humbuckers.*

Custom Agent *See 2405.*

GART30 2009–10
- Rosewood fingerboard, dot markers; 22 frets.

- Solid body; grey or red.
- Two coverless humbuckers.
- Two controls (volume, tone) plus three-way selector; side-mounted output jack.
- Six-saddle bridge/tailpiece.

GART60 2010–current
- Rosewood fingerboard, dot markers; 22 frets.
- Solid body; various colours.
- Two coverless humbuckers.
- Three controls (two volume, tone) plus three-way selector; side-mounted output jack.
- Six-saddle bridge plus separate bar tailpiece.
* **GART50** 2010–11 *As GART60 but quilted maple top, six-saddle bridge/tailpiece.*
* **GART80** 2011 *As GART60 but flame maple top, two black-cover humbuckers.*
* **GARTS70** 2010–11 *As GART60 but two metal-cover humbuckers.*

Randy Scruggs *See 2671.*

Single Cutaway *See 2671.*

2405 1976
- Bound rosewood fingerboard, fancy-shapes markers; 22 frets; fancy inlay on mandolin-style scrolled headstock.
- Solid body with fancy pearl inlay below tailpiece; sunburst.
- Two metal-cover humbuckers.
- Four controls (two volume, two tone), three-way selector; side-mounted output jack.
- Six-saddle bridge plus separate bar tailpiece.
- Black scrolled pickguard.
- Gold-plated metalwork.
- *Known as Custom Agent model.*

2671 1976–78
- Bound ebony fingerboard, vine inlay; 22 frets; fancy inlay on headstock; fancy headstock shape.
- Bound carved-top ash body; natural.
- Two metal-cover humbuckers.
- Four controls (two volume, two tone), three-way selector, and mini-switch; side-mounted output jack.
- Six-saddle bridge plus separate fancy 'harmonica' tailpiece.
- Gold-plated metalwork.
- *Known at first as Randy Scruggs model, then Single Cutaway.*
* **2671S** 1976–77 *As 2671 but dot markers.*

2674 1976–78
- Bound ebony fingerboard, vine inlay; 22 frets; fancy inlay on headstock.

- Solid body with fancy pearl inlay; black.
- Two black coverless humbuckers.
- Four controls (two volume, two tone), three-way selector, and mini-switch; side-mounted output jack.
- Six-saddle bridge plus separate fancy 'harmonica' tailpiece.
- Black pickguard.
- Gold-plated metalwork.
* **2675** 1976–78 *As 2674 but fancy-shapes fingerboard markers, mandolin-style scrolled headstock, sunburst finish, one metal-cover and one coverless humbucker, bar tailpiece, scrolled pickguard.*
* **2676** 1976 *As 2674 but pearl block markers, red finish, two metal-cover humbuckers, bar tailpiece.*

Double-Cutaway
Artist

AR50 1979–82
- Bound rosewood fingerboard, dot markers; 22 frets; most with fancy inlay on headstock.
- Carved-top body; black.
- Two coverless humbuckers.
- Four controls (two volume, two tone) plus three-way selector; side-mounted output jack.
- Six-saddle bridge plus separate bar tailpiece.

AR100 1979–83
- Bound rosewood fingerboard, dot markers; 22 frets; fancy inlay on headstock.
- Bound carved-top body; sunburst, natural, or black.
- Two coverless humbuckers.
- Four controls (two volume, two tone) plus three-way selector; side-mounted output jack.
- Six-saddle bridge plus separate triangular tailpiece.
- Gold-plated metalwork.
- *See next entry for 90s AR100.*
* **AR105** 1981–83 *As AR100 but sunburst burl-mahogany body, two metal-cover humbuckers.*
* **AR112** 1980–83 *As AR100 but 12-string, 24 frets, two metal-cover humbuckers.*
* **AR120** 1985–86 *As AR100 but no headstock inlay, two black-cover humbuckers, combined bridge/tailpiece.*
* **AR200** 1979 *As AR100 but two metal-cover humbuckers, mini-switch. Also known as AR250. (See next entry for 90s AR200.)*
* **AR300** 1979–86 *As AR100 but ebony fingerboard, pearl block markers, two metal-cover humbuckers, two mini-switches. (See next entry for 90s AR300, and entry following that for 00s AR300.)*

* **AR305** 1981–83 *As AR100 but ebony fingerboard, pearl block markers, sunburst burl-mahogany body, two metal-cover humbuckers, two mini-switches.*
* **AR350** 1985–86 *As AR100 but ebony fingerboard, pearl block markers, locking nut, two metal-cover humbuckers, two mini-switches, two-pivot fine-tuning and/or locking bridge/vibrato unit.*
* **AR400** 1979 *As AR100 but ebony fingerboard, pearl block markers, two metal-cover humbuckers, four controls (one volume, three tone), two mini-switches.*
* **AR500** *See 2622 for 70s–80s AR500; see next entry for 90s AR500.*

AR100 1990–91
- Bound rosewood fingerboard, dot markers; 22 frets; fancy inlay on headstock.
- Bound carved-top body; sunburst or black.
- Two coverless humbuckers.
- Four controls (two volume, two tone) plus three-way selector; side-mounted output jack.
- Six-saddle bridge plus separate bar tailpiece.
- Gold-plated metalwork.
- *See previous entry for 70s/80s AR100.*
  * **AR200** 1990–92 *As AR100 but block markers, also red or blue finish. (See previous entry for 70s AR200.)*
  * **AR300** 1990–92 *As AR100 but ebony fingerboard, block markers. (See previous entry for 70s/80s AR300, and next entry for 00s AR300.)*
  * **AR500** 1990–92 *As AR100 but ebony fingerboard, pearl block markers, flame maple top. (See 2622 for 70s–80s AR500.)*

AR250 1999–2003
- Bound rosewood fingerboard, dot markers; 22 frets; fancy inlay on headstock.
- Bound carved-top flame-maple body; sunburst.
- Two coverless humbuckers.
- Four controls (two volume, two tone) plus three-way selector; side-mounted output jack.
- Six-saddle bridge plus separate bar tailpiece.
- *See 1979 AR200, under AR100, for related model.*
  * **AR300** 2004–07 *As AR250 but pearl block markers, two metal-cover humbuckers. (See earlier entry for 70s/80s AR300, and previous entry for 90s AR300.)*
  * **AR325** 2012–current *As AR250 but pearl block markers, figured bubinga top, two metal-cover humbuckers, two mini-switches, triangular tailpiece.*
  * **AR300RE** 2008–10 *As AR250 but pearl block markers, two metal-cover humbuckers, two*

mini-switches, six-saddle bridge plus separate triangular tailpiece.
  * **AR420** 2102-current *As AR250 but pearl block markers, two metal-cover humbuckers, two mini-switches, triangular tailpiece.*

AR1200 *See 2640.*

AR1500 1983
- Bound ebony fingerboard, pearl block markers; 22 frets; fancy inlay on headstock.
- Bound carved-top maple/mahogany body; sunburst.
- Two metal-cover humbuckers.
- Four controls (two volume, two tone) and three-way selector; side-mounted output jack.
- Six-saddle bridge plus separate triangular tailpiece.
- Gold-plated metalwork.
  * **AR1505** 1983 *As AR1500 but rosewood fingerboard, spruce/mahogany body.*

AR2000 1998–2003
- Bound rosewood fingerboard, dot markers; 22 frets; fancy inlay on headstock.
- Bound carved-top flame-maple body; sunburst.
- Two metal-cover humbuckers.
- Four controls (two volume, two tone) plus three-way selector; side-mounted output jack.
- Six-saddle bridge plus separate bar tailpiece.
- Gold-plated metalwork.
  * **AR3000** 2004 *As AR2000 but pearl block markers, triangular tailpiece. (See next entry for 80s AR3000.)*

AR3000 1980
- Bound ebony fingerboard, pearl block markers; 22 frets; fancy inlay on headstock.
- Bound carved-top body; sunburst.
- Two metal-cover humbuckers.
- Six controls (volume, boost, four tone) and three mini-switches, plus three-way selector; side-mounted output jack.
- Six-saddle bridge plus separate triangular tailpiece.
- Gold-plated metalwork.
- *See previous entry for 90s/00s AR3000.*
  * **AR5000** 1980–82 *As AR3000 but vine fingerboard and headstock inlay.*

Artist EQ *See 2622.*

Artist 22 *See 2619.*

Artist 24 *See 2618.*

Artwood Artist *See 2617.*

Artwood Twin *See 2670.*

ARX100 2006
- Bound rosewood fingerboard, dot markers; 22 frets.
- Carved-top body; various colours.
- Two coverless humbuckers.
- Three controls (two volume, tone) plus three-way selector; side-mounted output jack.
- Six-saddle bridge plus separate triangular tailpiece.
  * **ARX120** 2007 *As ARX100 but cross markers, black finish, six-saddle bridge plus separate bar tailpiece.*
  * **ARX140** 2008–09 *As ARX 100 but black or white finish, six-saddle bridge plus separate bar tailpiece.*
  * **ARX320** 2007–current *As ARX100 but cross markers, quilted maple top, six-saddle bridge plus separate bar tailpiece.*
  * **ARX500** 2007–08 *As ARX100 but cross markers, sunburst finish, two metal-cover humbuckers, gold-plated metalwork.*

AX120 2000–04
- Bound rosewood fingerboard, dot markers; 22 frets.
- Carved-top body; various colours.
- Two coverless humbuckers.
- Four controls (two volume, two tone) plus three-way selector; side-mounted output jack.
- Six-saddle bridge/tailpiece.
  * **AX125** 2001–03 *As AX120 but bridge with D-tuner.*
  * **AX220** 2001–06 *As DX100 but quilted maple top.*
  * **AX320H** 1999 *As AX120 but six-saddle bridge plus separate bar tailpiece.*
  * **AX320V** 1999 *As AX120 but single-bar string guide, locking nut, two-pivot locking bridge/vibrato unit.*
  * **AX1220** 2003 *As AX120 but fancy marker at 12th fret, black finish, limited edition.*
  * **AX7221** 2002–03, 2006 *As AX120 but seven-string.*

AXS32 2003–05
- Bound rosewood fingerboard, double-dot marker at 12th fret; 22 frets.
- Carved-top body; red or black.
- Two coverless humbuckers.
- Four controls (two volume, two tone) plus three-way selector on large pickguard; side-mounted output jack.
- Six-saddle bridge and through-body stringing.
  * **AXS42** 2006 *As AXS32 but pearl block markers, two metal-cover humbuckers, six-saddle bridge plus separate bar tailpiece.*

EQ model *See 2622.*

GAX30 2004–11
■ Rosewood fingerboard, dot markers; 22 frets.
■ Solid body; various colours.
■ Two coverless humbuckers.
■ Two controls (volume, tone) plus three-way selector; side-mounted output jack.
■ Black pickguard.
■ Six-saddle bridge/tailpiece.

GAX70 1999–2007
■ Rosewood fingerboard, dot markers; 22 frets.
■ Solid body; various colours.
■ Two coverless humbuckers.
■ Four controls (two volume, two tone) plus three-way selector; side-mounted output jack.
■ Six-saddle bridge plus separate bar tailpiece.
* **GAX75** 2001–06 *As GAX70 but bridge/tailpiece with D-tuner.*

Bob Weir *See 2680.*

2611 1973–76
■ Bound rosewood fingerboard, star-in-block markers; fancy inlay on headstock.
■ Bound carved-top body; black.
■ Two metal-cover humbuckers.
■ Four controls (two volume, two tone) plus three-way selector; side-mounted output jack (some with controls and output jack on body-face plate).
■ Black pickguard.
■ Six-saddle bridge plus separate vibrato tailpiece.
■ Gold-plated metalwork.
* **2612** 1973–76 *As 2611 but separate bar tailpiece.*
* **2613** 1973–76 *As 2611 but bound maple fingerboard, natural finish, separate bar tailpiece, chrome-plated metalwork.*
* **2614** 1973–76 *As 2611 but brown finish, chrome-plated metalwork, separate bar tailpiece.*

2617 1975–79
■ Bound ebony fingerboard, pearl block markers; 22 frets; fancy inlay on headstock.
■ Bound carved-top ash body; natural or sunburst.
■ Two metal-cover humbuckers.
■ Four controls (two volume, two tone) plus three-way selector; side-mounted output jack.
■ Six-saddle bridge plus separate bar tailpiece (later triangular tailpiece).
■ Gold-plated metalwork.
- *Also known as Artwood Artist.*
* **2618** 1976–79 *As 2617 but dot markers, 24*

frets, various finishes mahogany/maple body. Also known as Artist 24.*
* **2618/12** 1977–80 *As 2617 but 12-string, dot markers, 24 frets, various finishes.*
* **2619** 1976–79 *As 2617 but various finishes mahogany/maple body, one mini-switch (later two). Also known as Artist 22.*

2622 1977–79
■ Bound ebony fingerboard, pearl block markers; 22 frets; fancy inlay on headstock.
■ Bound carved-top mahogany/maple body; sunburst, red, or black.
■ Two metal-cover humbuckers.
■ Five controls (volume, pre-amp, three tone), mini-switch, and three-way selector; side-mounted output jack; battery or external power.
■ Six-saddle bridge plus separate triangular tailpiece.
■ Gold-plated metalwork.
- *Known as Artist EQ model.*
* Renamed **AR500** 1979–82 *As 2622 but six controls (volume, boost, four tone) and three mini-switches.*

2640 1977–79
■ Two necks, each with bound ebony fingerboard, dot markers, 22 frets, fancy inlay on headstocks.
■ Bound carved-top mahogany/maple body; sunburst or red.
■ Four metal-cover humbuckers.
■ Five controls (three volume, two tone) plus neck selector; three-way selector and two mini-switches for each neck; side-mounted output jack.
■ Two six-saddle bridges each with separate triangular tailpiece.
■ Gold-plated metalwork.
* Renamed **AR1200** 1980–83 *As 2640 but ash body.*

2662 1975
■ Bound rosewood fingerboard, block markers; 22 frets.
■ Body with very shallow cutaways; sunburst.
■ Two metal-cover humbuckers.
■ Four controls (two volume, two tone), three-way selector, and output jack, all on body.
■ White pickguard.
■ Six-saddle bridge and separate long tailpiece.
■ Gold-plated metalwork.

2670 1975–78
■ Two necks, each with bound ebony fingerboard, vine inlay, 22 frets, fancy inlay on headstock, fancy headstock shape.

■ Bound carved-top ash body; natural.
■ Four metal-cover humbuckers.
■ Five controls (three volume, two tone) plus neck selector; three-way selector and two mini-switches for each neck; output jack on body face.
■ Two six-saddle bridges each with separate triangular tailpiece.
■ Gold-plated metalwork.
- *Known as Artwood Twin model.*

2680 1976–78
■ Bound ebony fingerboard, dot markers; 22 frets; fancy headstock shape.
■ Bound carved-top ash body, shallow cutaways; natural or sunburst.
■ Two metal-cover humbuckers.
■ Four controls (two volume, two tone) plus three-way selector; side-mounted output jack.
■ Six-saddle bridge plus triangular tailpiece.
■ Gold-plated metalwork.
- *Known as Bob Weir Standard.*
* **2681** 1976–78 *As 2680 but vine inlay on fingerboard and headstock. Known as Bob Weir Pro.*

2683 1976
■ Bound ebony fingerboard, dot markers; 24 frets.
■ Bound carved-top maple body, shallow cutaways; sunburst.
■ Two metal-cover humbuckers.
■ Four controls (two volume, two tone) plus three-way selector; side-mounted output jack.
■ Six-saddle bridge plus bar tailpiece.

2700 1977
■ Through-neck; ebony fingerboard, dot markers; 24 frets.
■ Carved-top laminated "exotic wood" body; natural with through-neck stripes.
■ Two black-cover pickups.
■ Five controls (volume, pre-amp, three tone), three mini-switches, and three-way selector; output jack on body face.
■ Six-saddle bridge plus triangular tailpiece.
■ Gold-plated metalwork.
* **2710** 1977 *As 2700 but four controls and two mini-switches.*

SEMI-SOLID & HOLLOWBODY

Single-Cutaway
Artist or Artstar

AC50 1990–92
■ Bound rosewood fingerboard, dot markers.

- Hollow body with f-holes; black or sunburst.
- Two metal-cover humbuckers.
- Two controls (volume, tone) and three-way selector, output jack, all on body.
- Black pickguard.
- One-saddle bridge, bar tailpiece.

AF80 1994–96
- Bound rosewood fingerboard, dot markers; fancy inlay on headstock.
- Hollow bound body with f-holes; sunburst.
- Two metal-cover humbuckers.
- Four controls (two volume, two tone) and three-way selector, all on body; side-mounted output jack.
- Black pickguard.
- One-saddle bridge, fancy tailpiece.
- * **AF120** 1995–2000 *As AF80 but pearl block markers, also black finish.*

AF200 1988–2000
- Bound ebony fingerboard, pearl block markers; fancy inlay on headstock.
- Hollow bound body with f-holes; sunburst.
- Two metal-cover humbuckers.
- Four controls (two volume, two tone) and three-way selector, all on body; side-mounted output jack.
- Black or matching pickguard.
- One-saddle bridge, fancy tailpiece.
- Gold-plated metalwork.
- * **AF207** 1998–2003 *As AF200 but one metal-cover humbucker (at neck), two controls.*
- * **AF220** 1998 *As AF200 but natural finish, no pickguard, six-saddle bridge.*

Artist Semi Acoustic *See 2629.*

2616 1976
- Bound rosewood fingerboard, star-in-block markers; fancy inlay on headstock.
- Hollow bound body with f-holes; natural or sunburst.
- Two metal-cover humbuckers.
- Four controls (two volume, two tone) and three-way selector, all on body; side-mounted output jack.
- Black pickguard.
- One-saddle bridge, fancy tailpiece.
- Gold-plated metalwork.

Double-Cutaway
Artist or Stagemaster

AM50 1982–83, 1990–92
- Bound rosewood fingerboard, dot markers.
- Small semi-solid bound body with f-holes;

sunburst or black.
- Two metal-cover humbuckers.
- Four controls (two volume, two tone), three-way selector, and output jack, all on body.
- Six-saddle bridge plus separate bar tailpiece.
- * **AM70** 1985–86 *As AM50 but black finish, two black-cover humbuckers, combined bridge/tailpiece.*
- * **AM75** 1985–86 *As AM50 but locking nut, two black-cover humbuckers, two-pivot fine-tuning and/or locking bridge/vibrato unit.*
- * **AM80** 1990–92 *As AM50 but two controls.*
- * **AM100** 1983 *As AM50 but metallic black finish, white pickguard.*
- * **AM200** 1988–2000 *As AM50 but ebony fingerboard, pearl block markers, burl-mahogany body, pickguard, gold-plated metalwork.*
- * **AM205** 1982–86 *As AM50 but ebony fingerboard, pearl block markers, black pickguard, gold-plated metalwork.*
- * **AM255** 1983–84 *As AM50 but pearl block markers, vibrato.*
- * **AM400** 1988–90 *As AM50 but ebony fingerboard, pearl block markers, two controls (volume, tone), gold-plated metalwork.*

AS50 1980–82
- Bound rosewood fingerboard, dot markers.
- Semi-solid bound body with f-holes; sunburst.
- Two coverless humbuckers.
- Four controls (two volume, two tone), three-way selector, and output jack, all on body.
- Black pickguard.
- Six-saddle bridge plus separate bar tailpiece.
- * **AS80** 1983–86, 1994–2002 *As AS50 but two metal-cover humbuckers, also red finish.*
- * **AS100** *See 2629.*
- * **AS120** 1995–2003 *As AS50 but pearl block markers, also in white or red finish, two metal-cover humbuckers, gold-plated metalwork.*
- * **AS180** 1997–99 *As AS50 but two metal-cover humbuckers.*
- * **AS200** *See 2630.*

2629 1977–78
- Bound ebony fingerboard, dot markers; fancy inlay on headstock.
- Semi-solid bound body with f-holes; sunburst.
- Two metal-cover humbuckers.
- Four controls (two volume, two tone) and three-way selector, all on body; side-mounted output jack.
- Black pickguard.
- Six-saddle bridge plus separate triangular tailpiece.
- *Known as Artist Semi Acoustic.*
- * Renamed **AS100** 1979–82 *As 2629 but*

output jack on body face, bar tailpiece, also red finish.
- * **2630** 1977–79 *As 2629 but pearl block markers, mini-switch, gold-plated metalwork.*
- * Renamed **AS200** 1979–2003 *As 2630 but output jack on body face, bar tailpiece, later mini-switch.*

AXSTAR
1985
AX smooth-pointy models and some headless models.

MATT BACHAND
2007–10
MBM signature models, based on RG style with elaborate skull graphic on body.

REB BEACH
1991–95
Voyager RBM signature models with wedge-shape "end cutaways" in body and EMG r IBZ pickups.

GEORGE BENSON

GB2K Masquerade 2000
- Bound ebony fingerboard, pearl block markers; fancy inlay on headstock; 22 frets.
- Hollow single-cutaway pearl-bound body with f-holes; natural.
- Two floating wood-cover humbuckers.
- Four controls (two volume, two tone) and three-way selector, all on body; side-mounted output jack.
- Ebony pickguard with fancy inlay.
- One-saddle bridge and separate fancy two-prong tailpiece.

GB5 1994–96
- Bound ebony fingerboard, diagonal-split block markers; fancy inlay on headstock; 20 frets.
- Hollow single-cutaway bound body with f-holes; sunburst.
- Two metal-cover humbuckers.
- Four controls (two volume, two tone) and three-way selector, all on body; side-mounted output jack.
- Brown pickguard.
- One-saddle bridge and separate wooden two-prong tailpiece.
- Gold-plated metalwork.

GB10 1977–current
- Bound ebony fingerboard, pearl block

markers; fancy inlay on headstock; 22 frets (early examples with 21), "George Benson" inlay at penultimate fret (until about 1992).
- Hollow single-cutaway bound body with f-holes; sunburst or natural.
- Two floating metal-cover humbuckers.
- Four controls (two volume, two tone) and three-way selector, all on body; side-mounted output jack.
- Tortoiseshell or black pickguard.
- One-saddle bridge and separate fancy two-prong tailpiece.
- Gold-plated metalwork.

* **GB10JS** 1997–98 *As GB10 but rosewood fingerboard, black pickguard.*

* **GB12** 1990–92 *As GB10 but 12th anniversary model, "12" inlay on headstock, fancy fingerboard markers, flame maple top, maple-finish pickguard.*

* **GB15** 2006–10 *As GB10 but red finish, one floating humbucker, two controls (volume, tone).*

* **GB100** 1993–96 *As GB10 but fancy fingerboard markers, slightly deeper body, flame maple top, maple-finish pickguard.*

GB20 1977–82
- Bound ebony fingerboard, pearl block markers; fancy inlay on headstock; 21 frets, "George Benson" inlay at 20th.
- Hollow single-cutaway bound body with f-holes; sunburst or natural.
- One floating metal-cover humbucker.
- One control (volume) and output jack on pickguard.
- Tortoiseshell pickguard.
- One-saddle bridge and separate fancy two-prong tailpiece.
- Gold-plated metalwork.

GB30 1986–92
- Bound ebony fingerboard, offset dot markers; fancy inlay on headstock; 22 frets, "George Benson" inlay at 21st.
- Semi-hollow single-cutaway bound body with f-holes; black or red.
- Two metal-cover humbuckers.
- Four controls (two volume, two tone), three-way selector, and output jack, all on body.
- Black pickguard.
- Six-saddle bridge and separate bar tailpiece.
- Black-plated metalwork.

GB200 1999–2011
- Bound ebony fingerboard, diagonal-split block markers; fancy inlay on headstock; 20 frets.
- Hollow single-cutaway bound body with f-holes; sunburst.

- Two metal-cover humbuckers.
- Four controls (two volume, two tone) and three-way selector, all on body; side-mounted output jack.
- Brown pickguard.
- One-saddle bridge and separate wooden two-prong tailpiece.
- Gold-plated metalwork.

LGB300 2012–current
- Bound ebony fingerboard, pearl block markers; fancy inlay on headstock; 20 frets.
- Hollow single-cutaway bound body with f-holes; sunburst.
- Two metal-cover humbuckers.
- Four controls (two volume, two tone) and three-way selector, all on body; side-mounted output jack.
- Matching pickguard.
- One-saddle bridge and separate wooden two-prong tailpiece.
- Gold-plated metalwork.

BLAZER
1980–82, 1997–98
BL Strat-like budget models, revived in 90s.

CHALLENGER
1977–78
Lawyer-friendly Strat-style models.

CONCERT
1978–79
CN models with Les Paul-type carved maple tops on bound mahogany Strat-like bodies.

COPIES
These are arranged here by the brands and models that were copied. A name in "double quotes" is the name given to the model in Elger USA's pricelists, and it's followed by a description where necessary or possible. Other information comes from dated catalogues. More models exist that were not listed in catalogues or pricelists.

DAN ARMSTRONG
2364 Dan Armstrong See-Through 1972

EPIPHONE
2358R *Al Caiola-style, rosewood* 1974
* **2358M** *Same, maple* 1974

FENDER
Jazzmaster
2365 *Jazzmaster-like, no switches* 1972

Stratocaster
2334 "Old Style Strat" 1976–78
2375 "Strato" *Sunburst* 1972–78
* **2375ASH** *Same, natural ash* 1972–78
* **2375BK** *Same, black* 1976–78
* **2375N** *Same, natural* 1973–77
* **2375W** or **2375WH** *Same, white* 1973–78
* **2375** "W Neck" *6/12 double-neck, white* 1975
2407 "Strato Jazz" *6/4 double-neck, sunburst* 1974–78
2408-2 "Artwood Nouveau" *Carved flowery body and head* 1975
2408-1 "Artwood Orient" *Carved dragon body and head* 1975
2408-3 "Artwood Eagle" *Carved eagle body and head* 1975
2655ZB "Burned ash body" 1976

Telecaster
2352 "Telly" *Blond* 1972–78
* **2352 Custom** or **2352CT** "Telly Custom" 1974–78
* **2352DX** "Telly Deluxe" 1973–78
2368 "Telly Thinline" 1972–77
2384 "Tele Thinline" *Two humbuckers* 1973–76

GIBSON
ES series
2355 "Jazz Model" or "ES-175" *Sunburst* 1972–77
* **2355M** *Same, natural* 1972–77
2370 "Thin hollow body" or "ES-345" *Cherry* 1972–76
2374 "Crest model" *Walnut* 1972–76
2390 "Thin hollow body" *ES-345, walnut* 1974–76
2395 "Thin hollow body" *ES-300-series, natural* 1973–76
2454 "ES335" *ES-300-series composite* 1974–77
2457 "Thinline stereo" *ES-355, cherry* 1975–77
2467 "El. jazz guitar stereo model" *ES-345, cherry* 1976–77
* **2467WN** *Same, walnut* 1976–77

Hollowbody various
2356 *Barney Kessel-style* 1972
2453 "Howie Roberts" *Howard Roberts-style, natural* 1974–76
* **2453CW** *Same, cherry* 1976–77
2455 "Jazz model" *L-5CES* 1974–77
2460 "L5 natural" *L-5CES, natural* 1975–77
2461 "J. Smith model" *Johnny Smith Artist,*

natural 1975–77
* **2461BS** *Same, sunburst* 1976
2464 "Byrdland-style" *Natural* 1975–77
2470 "Natural venetian cutaway" *L-5CES* 1976–77

Les Paul Custom
2335 "Black Beauty" *Two P90s, black* 1976
2341 "Les Custom" *Three humbuckers, black* 1974–77
2350 "Les Custom" *Two humbuckers, black* 1973–77
* **2350CS** or **2350 Custom** *Same, sunburst* 1974–77
* **2350W** or **2350WH** *Same, white* 1974–77
2650 "Les model" *Black, sunburst, or cherry* 1976

Les Paul Goldtop
2351 "Les Std" *Two humbuckers* 1972–77
2351DX *Deluxe-style, mini-humbuckers* 1974–75

Les Paul Junior and Special
2336 "Les Jr. model" *Single-cut, natural* 1974–76
2337 "Les Special" *Single-cut, sunburst* 1976
* **2337DX** *Same, but set-neck* 1974–76
2342 "Moonlight Special" *Single-cut, humbuckers, black* 1974–77
* **2342IV** or **2342IVORY** "Sunlight Special" *As 2342 but white* 1974–77
2343 "FM Jr." *Double-cut, cherry* 1974–76
* **2343CUST** "FM Custom" *As 2343 but humbucker* 1976

Les Paul Standard
2340 "Deluxe 59'er" *Coverless humbuckers* 1974–77
2351BS "Les Std." *Tobacco sunburst* 1976–77
* **2351AV** "Les model" *Same, antique violin finish* 1976–77
* **2351CW** "Les model" *Same, dark cherry* 1976–77
* **2351M** "Les model" *Same, sunburst* 1972–76
* **2351WN** *Same, walnut* 1976–77
2386 "Les Std." *Sunburst, zebra pickups* 1973–77
2651 *Two humbuckers, black* 1976
* **2651BS** *Same, tobacco brown sunburst* 1976
* **2651CW** *Same, dark cherry* 1976

Les Paul various
2372 "Les Pro" *Professional* 1972–74
* **2372DX** *Same, gold-plated metalwork* 1973
2380 "Les Recording" 1972–76
2391 "Les model" *Natural, see-through pickups* 1974–76

2392 "Les model" *Cloud markers* 1974–76
2393 "Les model" *Mahogany finish, maple fingerboard* 1974–77
2397 "Signature" *Thin hollow goldtop* 1973–74
* **2401** *As 2397 but bolt-on neck* 1974
2398 "Les model" *Maple finish, maple fingerboard* 1973–76
2405 "Custom Agent" *Scroll head* 1974–77
2420 "Les custom" *Natural, gold-plated metalwork* 1976–77
* **2420CW** *Same, cherry* 1976–77
2458 *Natural, maple fingerboard, white markers* 1974–75
2660 "Les model" *Vine fingerboard inlay, black* 1975–77
* **2662** *Same, sunburst* 1975–77

SG Custom
2345 "SG Custom old style" *Cherry, walnut* 1974–76
* **2345W** *Same, white* 1974–76
2383 "SG Custom late 60s model" *Mahogany, walnut* 1972–76
* **2383W** or **2383WH** *Same, white* 1976

SG Junior
2347 "SG TV old style" *cherry* 1974–76
* **2347W** *Same, white* 1974–76

SG Standard
2346 "Double cutaway" *Cherry* 1974–75
2354 "SG Mid 60s model" *Walnut* 1972–77
* **2354S** *Same, no vibrato* 1972–77

SG double-neck
2402 "Double Axe" *12/6 double-neck, cherry, walnut* 1974–77
* **2402DX** or **2402WH** *Same, white, gold-plated metalwork* 1974–76
* **2402S** or **2402SWH** *Same, set neck* 1976–77
2404 "Double Axe" *6/4, walnut* 1974–77
* **2404WH** *Same, white, gold-plated metalwork* 1976–77
2406 "Double Axe" *6/6, cherry* 1974–76
* **2406WH** *Same, white* 1974–76

SG various
2377 *SG Pro-like* 1972–73
2382 "SG Std." *SG Deluxe-like* 1972–76
2394 "SG Std." *Natural, maple fingerboard* 1975–76
2440 *Walnut, small-block markers* 1976
2441 *White, gold-plated metalwork* 1976
2654 *Walnut, large block markers* 1976

Solidbody various
2344 "Melody Maker" 1974–76

2348 "Firebrand reverse body" *Sunburst* 1974–77
* **2348W** *Same, white* 1975–77
2387 "Rocket Style" or "Rocket Roll" *Flying V 67-style* 1972–76
* **2387CT** or **2387 Custom** "Rocket Roll Sr." *Flying V 58-style* 1975–77
* **2387DX** *As 2387 but set-neck* 1972–76
2399 or **2399DX** "L5S model" 1974–76
2451 "L6S" 1974–77
2456 *L5S-like, fancy tailpiece* 1974–75
2459 "The Destroyer" *Explorer* 1975–77
2469 "The Futura" *Moderne* 1976–77
2803 "Flamingbird" *Walnut, unknown model, possibly Firebird* 1974

GRETSCH
2362 *Gretsch-composite hollowbody* 1972

RICKENBACKER
2388 "Rick 480 model" 1974–76

DN
2009–current
Darkstone double-cutaway models with Iceman-like body-tail point.

EARLY MODELS
1957–1968
Preceding the copy guitars, these were loose interpretations of designs by Fender (mostly Jazzmaster, Jaguar, and Stratocaster), Burns, Gibson (hollowbody), and others. Some were quirky, known as Bizarre models; many were rudimentary.

EX
1988–93
Budget RG-derived models.

EXOTIC WOOD
See **USA CUSTOM**.

FA / FG
1978–87
Large hollowbody single-cutaway models, most with floating pickups.

FR
2008–current
Tele-like retro models with two humbuckers.

MARTY FRIEDMAN
2006–08
MFM signature models, based on SZ style with star body logo and fingerboard markers.

FRANK GAMBALE
1991–98
FGM signature models, based on 540S with different pickups, smaller frets, All Access neck joint.

GHOSTRIDER
1994–96
GR retro models based on Artist double-cutaway design, with smaller alder bodies and pointier horns.

PAUL GILBERT

FRM1 2009
- Rosewood fingerboard; 22 frets; dot markers; three-tuners-each-side headstock.
- "Flipped Iceman" body; natural finish.
- Three white angled six-polepiece pickups.
- Two controls (volume, tone) and five-way selector, all on pickguard; side-mounted output jack.
- Tortoiseshell pickguard.
- Six-saddle bridge and separate bar tailpiece.
- Limited edition. Also known as Fireman model.
* **FRM2** 2009 As FRM1 but two metal-cover humbuckers, no pickguard.
* **FRM100** 2011–current As FRM1 but regular production model, red finish.

PGM30 1995–2003
- Rosewood fingerboard; 24 frets; dot markers; single-bar string-guide; locking nut; reversed headstock.
- Blue finish with pink painted f-holes.
- Two black coverless humbuckers and one black six-polepiece pickup (in centre).
- One control (volume) and five-way selector; side-mounted output jack.
- Two-pivot locking bridge/vibrato unit.

PGM10TH 2002
- Bound rosewood fingerboard; 25 frets; pearl block markers; reversed headstock.
- Natural finish with black painted f-holes.
- Two coverless humbuckers and one six-polepiece pickup (in centre).
- One control (volume) and five-way selector; side-mounted output jack.
- Six-saddle fixed bridge.

- Gold-plated metalwork.
- 10th anniversary model.

PGM100 1990–93
- Bound rosewood fingerboard; 24 frets; sharktooth markers; single-bar string-guide; locking nut.
- Blue finish with pink painted f-holes.
- Two pink coverless humbuckers and one pink six-polepiece pickup (in centre).
- One control (volume) and five-way selector; side-mounted output jack.
- Two-pivot locking bridge/vibrato unit.
- Sold in Japan only.
* **PGM200** 1990 As PGM100 but no string guide or locking nut, light blue finish with pink painted f-holes, three pink coverless humbuckers, six-saddle fixed bridge.
* **PGM300** 1992 As PGM100 but maple fingerboard with dot markers, reversed headstock, white finish with black painted f-holes, white pickups.
* **PGM301** 2004–08 As PGM100 but maple fingerboard with dot markers, reversed headstock, no string-guide or locking nut, white finish with black painted f-holes, white pickups, six-saddle fixed bridge.
* **PGM401** 2009–11 As PGM100 but dot markers, no string-guide or locking nut, sunburst finish with black painted f-holes, two metal-cover humbuckers, six-saddle fixed bridge.
* **PGM500** 1994–96 As PGM100 but dot markers, no string-guide or locking nut, red finish with white painted f-holes, white pickups, six-saddle fixed bridge, gold-plated metalwork.
* **PGM90HAM** 1998 As PGM100 but Hoshino 90th anniversary model (edition estimated at 337), ebony fingerboard, fancy inlay at 12th fret, no string guide or locking nut, reversed headstock, blue textured headstock, blue finish with white painted f-holes, white pickups, six-saddle fixed bridge.

PGM900 1998
- Rosewood fingerboard; 22 frets; dot markers; three-tuners-each-side headstock.
- Red finish with black painted f-holes.
- Two metal-cover humbuckers.
- One control (volume) and five-way selector; side-mounted output jack.
- Six-saddle fixed brdge.
- Gold-plated metalwork.
Based on Talman TC design.

GRX
1998–current
Budget RG-derived models.

ALLAN HOLDSWORTH
1985–87
AH signature models, based on Roadstar II, with "sound cavity" below pickguard, modified vibrato, spider logo.

ICEMAN & PAUL STANLEY
All have angular body with curved, pointed base and hooked lower horn, and a long, pointy headstock.

Flash See 2663.

IC50 1979–81
- Three-tuners-each-side headstock; rosewood fingerboard, dot markers; 22 frets.
- Black finish.
- Two coverless humbuckers.
- Three controls (two volume, tone), three-way selector, and output jack, all on body.
- Six-saddle bridge plus separate bar tailpiece.
- For 1982 model see Iceman II IC50.

IC100 1978–79
- Three-tuners-each-side headstock; bound rosewood fingerboard, dot or angled block markers; 22 frets.
- Bound body; black or white.
- Two metal-cover or coverless humbuckers.
- Four controls (two volume, two tone), three-way selector, and output jack, all on body.
- Six-saddle bridge plus separate bar tailpiece.
* **IC200** See 2663.
* **IC210** See 2663TC.
* **IC250** 1978–79 As IC100 but flame maple top, gold-plated metalwork.
* **IC300** 1978–79 As IC100 but unbound fingerboard, natural finish. See next entry for 90s IC300.
* **IC400** 1978–79 As IC100 but angled block markers, gold-plated metalwork. (For 1982 model see Iceman II IC400. For 00s model see under IC300.)

IC300 1995–2003
- Three-tuners-each-side headstock; bound rosewood fingerboard, dot markers; 22 frets.
- Bound body; black or white.
- Two coverless humbuckers.
- Two controls (volume, tone), three-way selector; side-mounted output jack.
- Early models with white pickguard, then no pickguard.
- Six-saddle bridge plus separate bar tailpiece.
- See previous entry for 70s IC300.

* **IC350** 1995 *As IC300 but string guide, locking nut, no pickguard, two-pivot locking bridge/vibrato unit.*
* **IC400** 2004–07 *As IC300 but angled block markers, four controls (two volume, two tone), no pickguard. (For 70s model see under IC100. For 1982 model see Iceman II IC400.)*

Iceman SL / Std./ 3 *See 2663.*

Iceman II IC50 1982
▨ Six-tuners-one-side headstock; rosewood fingerboard, dot markers; 22 frets.
▨ Blue finish.
▨ One coverless humbucker (at bridge) and one metal-cover humbucker (at neck).
▨ Three controls (two volume, tone), three-way selector, and output jack, all on body.
▨ Six-saddle bridge plus separate bar tailpiece.
- For earlier model see IC50.

Iceman II IC400 1982
▨ Six-tuners-one-side headstock; bound rosewood fingerboard, pearl block markers; 22 frets.
▨ Bound flame-maple body; sunburst.
▨ One coverless humbucker (at bridge) and one metal-cover humbucker (at neck).
▨ Three controls (two volume, tone) and three-way selector; side-mounted output jack.
▨ Six-saddle bridge plus separate bar tailpiece.
- For 70s model see under IC100. For 00s model see under IC300.

ICJ100WZ 1996–99
▨ Three-tuners-each-side headstock with star inlay; bound ebony fingerboard, pearl block markers; 22 frets; single-bar string-guide, locking nut.
▨ Bound body; green finish with white stars graphic.
▨ Two coverless humbuckers.
▨ Three controls (two volume, tone), three-way selector; side-mounted output jack.
▨ Two-pivot locking bridge/vibrato unit.
- J (White Zombie) model.

ICT700 2008–current
▨ Six-tuners-one-side reversed headstock; bound rosewood fingerboard, sharktooth markers; 24 frets.
▨ Bound body; black or white.
▨ Two coverless humbuckers.
▨ Two controls (volume, tone), three-way selector; side-mounted output jack.
▨ Six-saddle bridge plus through-body stringing.

ICX120 2001–03
▨ Six-tuners-one-side headstock; bound rosewood fingerboard, dot markers; 22 frets.
▨ Bound smaller modified-shape body; black.
▨ Two coverless humbuckers.
▨ Two controls (volume, tone), three-way selector; side-mounted output jack.
▨ Six-saddle bridge plus separate bar tailpiece.
* **ICX220** 2006 As ICX120 but sharktooth markers, 24 frets, unbound body.

J (White Zombie) *See ICJ100WZ.*

PS10 1978–81
▨ Three-tuners-each-side headstock; bound rosewood fingerboard, pearl block markers; 22 frets, "Paul Stanley" inlay at 21st.
▨ Pearl-bound body; black.
▨ Two coverless humbuckers.
▨ Three controls (two volume, tone) and three-way selector on body; side-mounted output jack.
▨ Chrome-plated pickguard.
▨ Six-saddle bridge plus separate fancy-shape tailpiece.
- Paul Stanley model.
* **PS10II** 1995–96 *As PS10 but reissue.*
* **PS10CL** 1996 *As PS10 but clear plastic pickguard.*
* **PS10LTD** 1995–96 *As PS10 but ebony fingerboard, gold-plated metalwork.*

Paul Stanley *See PS10.*

STM1 2008–10
▨ Six-tuners-one-side headstock; bound rosewood fingerboard, angled block markers; 24 frets; single-bar string-guide, locking nut.
▨ Bound body; white finish.
▨ One black/white coverless humbucker (at bridge) and one black coverless humbucker (at neck).
▨ One control (volume), three-way selector; side-mounted output jack.
▨ Two-pivot locking bridge/vibrato unit.
- Sam Totman model.
* **STM2** 2011–current *As STM1 but blue finish on flame maple top.*

Sam Totman *See STM1.*

2663 1975–78
▨ Three-tuners-each-side headstock; bound rosewood fingerboard, angled block markers; 22 frets.
▨ Bound body; sunburst.
▨ Two metal-cover exposed humbuckers.
▨ Four controls (two volume, two tone), three-way selector, and output jack, all on body.

▨ Six-saddle bridge plus separate long tailpiece.
- Known at first as The Flash I or Iceman Std.
* Renamed **IC-200** 1978–79 *As 2663 but metal-cover or coverless humbuckers and bar tailpiece.*
* **2663SL** 1975–78 *As 2663 but one sliding metal-cover exposed three-coil pickup, three controls (volume, two tone), no selector. Known at first as The Flash III or Iceman SL.*
* **2663TC / 2663-3P** 1975–78 *As 2663 but one metal-cover exposed three-coil pickup, three controls (volume, tone, 4-way tone), no selector. Known at first as The Flash II or Iceman 3.*
* Renamed **IC-210** 1978–79 *As 2663TC but bar tailpiece.*

J CUSTOM
1996–current
Series name for generally upscale models (with no obvious common theme).

JEM
To avoid repetition, we've considered a few features as common to all JEM models, and so these are not shown in every entry. Unless stated otherwise, you can always assume the following:

* Twenty-four frets.
* Single-bar string-guide and locking nut.
* Solid offset-double-cutaway body with "Monkey Grip" handle hole.

JEMEVO 2012
▨ Rosewood fingerboard; vine inlay; 21st to 24th frets scalloped; white headstock.
▨ Aged white.
▨ Two white coverless humbuckers and one white six-polepiece pickup (in centre).
▨ One white and one black control (volume, tone) and white five-way selector, all on pickguard; side-mounted output jack.
▨ Pearl pickguard.
▨ Two-pivot locking bridge/vibrato unit with 'lion's claw' cavity.

JEM-JR 2003–11
▨ Rosewood fingerboard; dot inlay.
▨ Black, white, or 'wine'.
▨ Two black or white coverless humbuckers and one black or white six-polepiece pickup (in centre).
▨ Two controls (volume, tone) and five-way selector, all on pickguard; side-mounted output jack.

- Black or white pickguard.
- Two-pivot locking bridge/vibrato unit with 'lion's claw' cavity.
- *Also known as JEM333*

JEM2KDNA 2000
- Rosewood fingerboard; 'DNA' vine inlay; 21st to 24th frets scalloped.
- Multicolour swirl finish, incorporates Steve Vai's blood.
- Two green and black coverless humbuckers and one red six-polepiece pickup (in centre).
- Two green controls (volume, tone) and green five-way selector, all on see-through pickguard; side-mounted output jack.
- See-through luminous pickguard.
- Two-pivot locking bridge/vibrato unit with 'lion's claw' cavity.
- *Limited edition of 300.*

JEM7 1988–89
- Rosewood fingerboard; dot inlay; 21st to 24th frets scalloped.
- Brown.
- Two pink coverless humbuckers and one pink six-polepiece pickup (in centre).
- Two controls (volume, tone) and five-way selector, all on pickguard; side-mounted output jack.
- Black pickguard.
- Two-pivot locking bridge/vibrato unit with 'lion's claw' cavity.
- ★ **JEM7BSB** 1996–2001 *As JEM7 but circle-dot inlay, 'monkey grip' handle, 'burnt blue' finish.*
- ★ **JEM7DBK** 1999–2004 *As JEM7 but circle-dot inlay, 'monkey grip' handle, 'textured black' finish, metal pickguard.*
- ★ **JEM7EAFXBK** 2009 *As JEM7 but white vine inlay, regular nut, 'monkey grip' handle in black body, black pickups and controls, metal pickguard, hardtail (non-vibrato) bridge.*
- ★ **JEM7PBK** 1988–91 *As JEM7 but white pyramid inlay, black body.*
- ★ **JEM7VSBL** 2002–04 *As JEM7 but blue vine inlay, 'monkey grip' handle, sparkle blue finish, white pickups, chrome-plated controls, white pickguard.*
- ★ **JEM7VWH** 1993–current *As JEM7 but white vine inlay, rounded body/neck join, 'monkey grip' handle, white body, white pickups and controls, pearl pickguard, gold-plated metalwork.*

JEM10th 1996
- Bound ebony fingerboard; vine inlay; bound metal headstock with pyramid/eye engraving.
- Black.
- Two white coverless humbuckers and one white six-polepiece pickup (in centre).

- Two chrome-plated controls (volume, tone) and black five-way selector, all on pickguard; side-mounted output jack.
- Metal pickguard with engraved design and inscription: '10th Anniversary IBANEZ JEM 1986–1996 Serial No. XXX'.
- Two-pivot locking bridge/vibrato unit with 'lion's claw' cavity.
- *Production run estimated at 852.*

JEM20TH 2007
- Rosewood fingerboard; pearl vine inlay.
- Acrylic see-through body with eight internal LEDs.
- Two pink-and-green coverless humbuckers and one green six-polepiece pickup (in centre).
- One yellow, one green control (volume, tone) and pink five-way selector, all on clear pickguard; side-mounted output jack.
- See-through pickguard.
- Two-pivot locking bridge/vibrato unit with 'lion's claw' cavity.
- *Limited edition of 500.*

JEM70VSFG 2012–current
- Rosewood fingerboard; vine inlay; green headstock.
- Green.
- Two white coverless humbuckers and one white six-polepiece pickup (in centre).
- Two white controls (volume, tone) and white five-way selector, all on pickguard; side-mounted output jack.
- Pearl pickguard.
- Two-pivot locking bridge/vibrato unit with 'lion's claw' cavity.

JEM77FP 1988–2004
- Rosewood fingerboard; vine inlay; 21st to 24th frets scalloped; coloured headstock.
- Black with green and pink flowers.
- Two pink coverless humbuckers and one pink six-polepiece pickup (in centre).
- Two pink controls (volume, tone) and pink five-way selector, all on pickguard; side-mounted output jack.
- See-through pickguard.
- Two-pivot locking bridge/vibrato unit with 'lion's claw' cavity.
- ★ **JEM77BFP** 1991–95 *As JEM77FP but maple fingerboard, blue vine inlay, black body with blue flowers, blue pickups and controls.*
- ★ **JEM77BRMR** 2005–06 *As JEM77FP but dot inlay, mirror finish, black pickups and controls.*
- ★ **JEM77FP2** 2011–current *As JEM77FP but red and white vine inlay, black pickups and controls.*
- ★ **JEM77GMC** 1992–93 *As JEM77FP but black*

headstock, green swirl finish, green pickups and controls.
- ★ **JEM77PMC** 1992 *As JEM77FP but black headstock, maple fingerboard, coloured pyramid inlay, multicolour swirl finish, purple pickups, green controls.*
- ★ **JEM77VBK** 2007–11 *As JEM77FP but white vine inlay, bound black body, black pickups and controls, metal pickguard.*

JEM90HAM 1998
- Ebony fingerboard; fancy inlay at 12th fret; blue textured headstock.
- Blue textured finish.
- Two black coverless humbuckers and one black six-polepiece pickup (in centre).
- Two controls (volume, tone) and five-way selector, all on mirror pickguard; side-mounted output jack.
- Mirror-finish metal pickguard.
- Two-pivot locking bridge/vibrato unit with 'lion's claw' cavity.
- *Limited edition of 759 to celebrate 90th anniversary of Hoshino.*

JEM333 See JEM-JR.

JEM505 2010–11
- Maple fingerboard; vine inlay; black or white headstock.
- Black or white.
- Two black or white coverless humbuckers and one black or white six-polepiece pickup (in centre).
- Two black or white controls (volume, tone) and black or white five-way selector, all on pickguard; side-mounted output jack.
- Dark pearl or pearl pickguard.
- Two-pivot locking bridge/vibrato unit.

JEM555 1994–2008
- Rosewood fingerboard; vine and dots inlay; 'Steve Vai' inlay at 24th fret; black or white headstock.
- Black or white.
- Two coverless humbuckers and one six-polepiece pickup (in centre).
- Two controls (volume, tone) and five-way selector, all on pickguard; side-mounted output jack.
- Pearl pickguard.
- Two-pivot locking bridge/vibrato unit with 'lion's claw' cavity.

JEM777LG 1987
- Maple fingerboard; coloured pyramid inlay; 21st to 24th frets scalloped; green headstock.
- Green.

- Two pink coverless humbuckers and one pink six-polepiece pickup (in centre).
- Two yellow controls (volume, tone) and pink five-way selector, all on pickguard; side-mounted output jack.
- Black pickguard.
- Two-pivot locking bridge/vibrato unit with 'lion's claw' cavity.
- Limited edition of 777
* **JEM777DY** 1987–96 *As 777 but yellow body and head, green controls.*
* **JEM777SK** 1988–89 *As 777 but pink body and head, yellow controls, green five-way.*
* **JEM777VBK** 1988–93 *As 777 but black body and head, green pickups, controls, and five-way, rosewood fingerboard, green vine inlay.*
* **JEM777VDY** 1988–91 *As 777 but yellow body and head, rosewood fingerboard, yellow vine inlay.*

JET KING
2005–10
JTK Talman-like retro models in two body shapes.

KORN
2001–06
K7 seven-string signature model, superseded by Munky model.

HERMAN LI
2008–current
EGEN signature models, based on S style, with hand-shaped scoop cutaway.

MAXXAS
1987–89
MX models with extended upper horn, some with semi-solid body, also have thin body shape, All Access neck joint.

MESHUGGAH
2012–current
M8M eight-string signature model.

PAT METHENY
1996–current
PM hollowbody signature models with offset-cutaways.

MIDI GUITAR SYSTEM
1985–86
IMG2010 MIDI Electronic Guitar, MC1 MIDI Controller, IFC60 Intelligent Foot Controller, MIU8 MIDI Interface; some with "X-ING" logo.

VINNIE MOORE
1989
VM1 Star-4 signature model based on old-style RG, with locking tuners.

MUNKY
2007–current
Apex seven-string signature models.

MIKE MUSHOK
2003–07
MMM1 long-scale baritone signature model.

MUSICIAN
1978–82
MC models with 24-fret laminated through-necks, brass hardware, some active with complex electronics.

NOODLES
2003–current
NDM signature models, based on Talman TV model.

P
Unless stated, all have offset-double-cutaway P body profile, with deep, chunky, angled cross-section.

Pro540 Power 1987–88
- Rosewood fingerboard, dot markers; 22 frets; single-bar string-guide; locking nut.
- Various colours.
- One black coverless humbucker (at bridge) and two black six-polepiece pickups.
- One control (volume) and three mini-switches on body; side-mounted output jack.
- Two-pivot locking bridge/vibrato unit
- *Also known as 540P. Some with two controls (volume, tone).*
- *Custom 1988, Hoshino 80th anniversary guitars.*
* **540PTC** 1988 *As Pro540 Power but one three-coil pickup (at bridge), two mini-switches.*

540P *See Pro540 Power.*

540PHH 1988–90
- Rosewood fingerboard, sharktooth markers; 24 frets; single-bar string-guide; locking nut; reversed headstock.
- Pointy body with extended lower horn; various colours.
- Two black coverless humbuckers.
- One control (volume) and three-way selector on body; side-mounted output jack.
- With or without pickguard.
- Two-pivot locking bridge/vibrato unit.
- *Also known as 540PII.*
* **540PSH** 1988–90 *As 540PII but h-s pickup layout. Also known as 540PIISH.*

540PII *See 540PHH.*
540PIISH *See 540PSH under 540PHH.*

JOE PASS
1981–90
JP20 hollowbody signature model.

PERFORMER
1978–81
PF lawyer-friendly Les Paul-style models.

JOHN PETRUCCI
1996–99
JPM signature model, based on RG style with thicker Ultra neck, coil-tap switching, brash graphics.

PRO
See **ARTIST & PRO**.

PRO LINE
1985–87
PL Jackson Randy Rhoads-style V model and two superstrat-like models with odd five-button pickup-preset system.

PROFESSIONAL
See **ARTIST & PRO**.

R
All have offset-double-cutaway R body profile, with wedge-shape cross-section.

442R 1992
- Maple fingerboard, dot markers; 22 frets.
- Various colours.

- One black coverless humbucker (at bridge) and two black six-polepiece pickups.
- Two controls (volume, tone) and five-way selector on body; side-mounted output jack.
- Two-pivot bridge/vibrato unit.
* **542R** 1992 *As 442R but rosewood fingerboard, oval markers, s-s-s pickup layout.*

Pro540 Radius 1987
- Rosewood fingerboard, dot markers; 22 frets; single-bar string-guide; locking nut.
- Various colours.
- One black coverless humbucker (at bridge) and two black six-polepiece pickups.
- Two controls (volume, tone) and three mini-switches on body; side-mounted output jack.
- Two-pivot locking bridge/vibrato unit

R540 *See 540R.*

540R 1988–92
- Rosewood fingerboard, dot markers; 22 frets; single-bar string-guide; locking nut.
- Various colours.
- One black coverless humbucker (at bridge) and two black six-polepiece pickups.
- Two controls (volume, tone) and five-way selector on body; side-mounted output jack.
- Two-pivot locking bridge/vibrato unit
* **540RHH** 1989–92 *As 540R but h-h pickup layout, three-way selector.*
* **540RLTD** 1991–93 *As 540R but sharktooth markers, h-s-h pickup layout.*
- *Some 540R-series models circa 1990–92 have "Custom Made" inlay at 21st fret.*
- *Custom 1988, Hoshino 80th anniversary guitars.*

R355GF 1992
- Rosewood fingerboard, dot markers; 22 frets.
- Gravure Flame printed finish.
- Two black coverless humbuckers and one black six-polepiece pickup (in centre).
- Two controls (volume, tone) and five-way selector on body; side-mounted output jack.
- Pickguard.
- Two-pivot bridge/vibrato unit.
- Gold-plated metalwork.

R470 1992
- Rosewood fingerboard, dot markers; 22 frets; single-bar string-guide; locking nut.
- Various colours.
- Two black coverless humbuckers and one black six-polepiece pickup (in centre).
- Two controls (volume, tone) and five-way selector on body; side-mounted output jack.
- Two-pivot locking bridge/vibrato unit

RV470 1993
- Rosewood fingerboard, dot markers; 22 frets.
- Gravure Flame printed finish.
- Two black coverless humbuckers and one black six-polepiece pickup (in centre).
- Two controls (volume, tone) and five-way selector on body; side-mounted output jack.
- Transparent pickguard.
- Two-pivot bridge/vibrato unit.
- Gold-plated metalwork.

RG NEW STYLE

This listing covers the new pointy-horn body style of RG first seen in 1987 with the RG550. For the previous stumpier-horn RGs, see ROADSTAR II – RG.

Because of the widespread appeal of the RG and its importance in the Ibanez line, we have included as many models as possible in the listing, including some that were only available in certain territories. Nonetheless, this inventory cannot claim completeness.

We've included a number of sub-RG models here, too. RG is, of course, the original and now primary RG-style series. GRG is the budget-price series. RGA models have an archtop body and usually a fixed bridge. RGD models have a longer scale, for down-tuning, and an extra-sharp body cut. RGT models have a through-neck. You'll also see RGR-prefix models, which have reversed headstocks, included in the main RG entries.

For ease of reference we've divided the models into sections based on pickup configurations. They are arranged in the following order:

H   One humbucker (at bridge).
HH   Two humbuckers.
HS   One humbucker (at bridge) and one single-coil (at neck).
HSH   Two humbuckers and one single-coil (in centre).
HSS   One humbucker (at bridge) and two single-coils.

And at the end, we've grouped together the seven-string and eight-string versions.

To avoid needless repetition, we've considered certain features as common to all RG and sub-RG models, and so these are not shown in every entry. Unless stated otherwise, you can always assume the following:

*   Fingerboard with dot position markers.
*   Twenty-five-and-a-half-inch (648mm) scale.
*   Twenty-four frets.
*   Solid offset-double-cutaway body.

H   ONE HUMBUCKER (AT BRIDGE)

RG2610 2007–08
- Bound rosewood fingerboard; sharktooth markers; single-bar string-guide; locking nut.
- Solid offset-double-cutaway bound body; black.
- One black coverless humbucker (at bridge).
- One control; side-mounted output jack.
- Two-pivot locking bridge/vibrato unit.

HH   TWO HUMBUCKERS

GRG121 2007
- Bound rosewood fingerboard.
- Various colours.
- Two black coverless humbuckers.
- Two controls (volume, tone) and five-way selector on body; side-mounted output jack.
- Six-saddle fixed bridge.
* **GRG121DX** 2012–current *As GRG121 but sharktooth markers.*
* **GRG121EX** 2010 *As GRG121 but reversed headstock, unbound fingerboard, two black-cover humbuckers.*
* **GRGR121EX** 2011 *As GRG121 but reversed headstock, unbound fingerboard.*

GRG150DX 2011–current
- Rosewood fingerboard; coloured sharktooth markers.
- Black.
- Two black coverless humbuckers and one black six-polepiece pickup (in centre).
- Two controls (volume, tone) and five-way selector on body; side-mounted output jack.
- Coloured pickguard.
- Two-pivot bridge/vibrato unit. 11 12

GRG170DX 2004–11
- vBound rosewood fingerboard; sharktooth markers.
- Various colours.
- Two black coverless humbuckers and one black six-polepiece pickup (in centre).
- Two controls (volume, tone) and five-way selector on body; side-mounted output jack.
- Two-pivot bridge/vibrato unit.

GRG220DEX 2007
- Bound rosewood fingerboard; sharktooth markers; single-bar string-guide; locking nut.
- Various colours.
- Two black-cover humbuckers.
- Two controls (volume, tone) and five-way selector on body; side-mounted output jack.
- Two-pivot locking bridge/vibrato unit.

GRGA42 2011
- Rosewood fingerboard; locking nut.
- Black.
- Two black-cover humbuckers.
- Two controls (volume, tone) and five-way selector on body; side-mounted output jack.
- Two-pivot locking bridge/vibrato unit.
- * **GRGA42QA** 2012–current *As GRGA42 but no locking nut, flame maple top, six-saddle fixed bridge.*
- * **GRGA42TQA** 2012–current *As GRGA42 but flame maple top.*

GRGR121EX *See GRG121.*

RG120 2001–2009 *Guitar Center-only model.*

RG220 1999
- Rosewood fingerboard; single-bar string-guide; locking nut.
- Various colours.
- Two black coverless humbuckers.
- Two controls (volume, tone) and five-way selector; side-mounted output jack.
- Two-pivot locking bridge/vibrato unit.
- * **RGR220DX** 2002 *As RG220 but reversed headstock, sharktooth markers.*
- * **RGT220** 2005–06 *As RG220 but through-neck, with stripes on natural body.*

RG320 1998–2007
- Rosewood fingerboard; single-bar string-guide; locking nut.
- Various colours.
- Two black coverless humbuckers.
- Two controls (volume, tone) and five-way selector; side-mounted output jack.
- Two-pivot locking bridge/vibrato unit.
- * **RG320PG** 2008–09 *As RG320 but sharktooth markers, custom graphic finishes.*
- * **RGR320** 2001 *As RG320 but reversed headstock.*
- * **RGR320DX** 2003 *As RG320 but reversed headstock, sharktooth markers.*
- * **RGR320DXQM** 2003 *As RG320 but reversed headstock, sharktooth markers, quilted maple top.*
- * **RGR320EX** 2007 *As RG320 but reversed headstock, sharktooth markers.*
- * **RG321** 2003–current *As RG320 but six-saddle fixed bridge.*
- * **RGR321** 2007 *As RG320 but reversed headstock.*
- * **RGR321EX** 2011 *As RG320 but reversed headstock, black-cover humbuckers.*
- * **RGT320** 2005–09 *As RG320 but quilted maple top, through neck, some with stripes on body.*

RG420 1998–99
- Rosewood fingerboard; single-bar string-guide; locking nut.
- Various colours.
- Two black coverless humbuckers.
- Two controls (volume, tone) and five-way selector; side-mounted output jack.
- Two-pivot locking bridge/vibrato unit.
- * **RG420CM** 2009 *As RG420 but sharktooth markers, figured mahogany body.*
- * **RG420EG** 2008–10 *As RG420 but two black-cover humbuckers, sharktooth markers.*
- * **RG420FB** 2010–11 *As RG420 but sharktooth markers, figured bubinga top.*
- * **RG420GK** 2001–02 *As RG420 but additional slim black Roland GK synthesiser pickup (at bridge), three controls plus two-mini-switches and five-way.*
- * **RG421** 2001–02 *As RG420 but six-saddle fixed bridge.*
- * **RGR420EX** 2008 *As RG420 but reversed headstock, sharktooth markers, two black-cover humbuckers.*
- * **RGR421EX** 2008–09 *As RG420 but reversed headstock, six-saddle fixed bridge, black-cover humbuckers.*
- * **RGT42** 2002–04 *As RG420 but through-neck, bound fingerboard.*
- * **RGT42DX** 2005–10 *As RG420 but through neck, bound fingerboard, sharktooth markers.*
- * **RGT42MDX** 2009 *As RG420 but through neck, maple fingerboard, sharktooth markers.*
- * **RGT42(DX)FX** 2005–06 *As RG420 but through neck, offset sharktooth markers, no vibrato.*
- * **RG7-420** *See RG7420.*
- * **RG7-421** *See RG7421.*

RG520 1998–2001
- Rosewood fingerboard; single-bar string-guide; locking nut.
- Various colours on quilted sapele.
- Two black coverless humbuckers.
- Two controls (volume, tone) and five-way selector; side-mounted output jack.
- Two-pivot locking bridge/vibrato unit.

RG620 1997–98
- Rosewood fingerboard; single-bar string-guide; locking nut.
- Various colours.
- Two black coverless humbuckers.
- Two controls (volume, tone) and five-way selector, all on pickguard; side-mounted output jack.
- Two-pivot locking bridge/vibrato unit.
- Some with gold-plated metalwork.
- * **RG620QM** 2002 *As RG620 but quilted maple top.*

- * **RG620X** 2002 *As RG620 but piezo pickups in bridge, three controls plus mini-switch and five-way.*
- * **RG7-620** *See RG6720.*
- * **RG7-621** *See RG6721.*

RG920Q 2012–current
- Bound rosewood fingerboard; offset dot markers; locking nut.
- Solid offset-double-cutaway bound body; various transparent colours on quilted maple.
- Two black coverless humbuckers.
- Two controls (volume, tone) and five-way selector; side-mounted output jack.
- Two-pivot locking bridge/vibrato unit.
- * **RG920BK** 2012–current *As RG920Q but black finish.*
- * **RG921Q** 2012–current *As RG920Q but no vibrato.*

RG1520 2003–07
- Rosewood fingerboard; single-bar string-guide; locking nut.
- Solid offset-double-cutaway bound body; black.
- Two black coverless humbuckers.
- Three controls, two mini-switches, and five-way selector; two side-mounted output jacks.
- Two-pivot locking bridge/vibrato unit with piezo pickups to drive Roland GK system.

RG1527 2003–11
- Rosewood fingerboard; single-bar string-guide; locking nut.
- Solid offset-double-cutaway bound body; black.
- Two black coverless humbuckers.
- Two controls (volume, tone) and five-way selector; side-mounted output jack.
- Two-pivot locking bridge/vibrato unit.

RG1620X 2003–04
- Rosewood fingerboard; single-bar string-guide; locking nut.
- Solid offset-double-cutaway bound body; black.
- Two black coverless humbuckers.
- Three controls (regular volume, tone; piezo volume), 3-way switch (piezo), and five-way selector; two side-mounted output jacks.
- Two-pivot locking bridge/vibrato unit with piezo pickups.

RG1820X 2005–07
- Rosewood fingerboard; single-bar string-guide; locking nut.
- Solid offset-double-cutaway bound body; black.

- Two black coverless humbuckers.
- Three controls plus one stacked control, one mini-switch, one five-way selector; two side-mounted output jacks.
- Two-pivot locking bridge/vibrato unit with piezo pickups.

RG2020X 2000–01
- Rosewood fingerboard; offset dot markers at 12th fret only; single-bar string-guide; locking nut.
- Solid offset-double-cutaway bound body; various colours.
- Two black coverless humbuckers.
- Three controls (regular volume, tone; piezo volume), one mini-switch (piezo output), one output-select pushbutton, one five-way selector; two side-mounted output jacks.
- Two-pivot locking bridge/vibrato unit with piezo pickups.
- * **RG2120X** 2002–04 As RG2020X but four controls (one stacked), one mini-switch, five-way.

RG2620 2003–06
- Rosewood fingerboard; single-bar string-guide; locking nut.
- Solid offset-double-cutaway bound body; various colours, most on quilted maple.
- Two black coverless humbuckers.
- Two controls (volume, tone) and one mini-switch; side-mounted output jack.
- Two-pivot locking bridge/vibrato unit.
- * **RG2620E** 2007 As RG2620 but sharktooth markers.

RG3020 2003
- Rosewood fingerboard; offset dot markers; single-bar string-guide; locking nut.
- Solid offset-double-cutaway bound body; various transparent colours on figured maple.
- Two black coverless humbuckers.
- Two controls (volume, tone) and five-way selector; side-mounted output jack.
- Two-pivot locking bridge/vibrato unit.
- * **RGT3020** 2003–04 As RG3020 but through-neck, some early examples with regular dot markers.

RG3120 1997–2006
- Rosewood fingerboard; offset-dot or regular dot markers; some early examples with 'Prestige' inlay at 24th fret; single-bar string-guide; locking nut.
- Solid offset-double-cutaway bound body; natural or various transparent colours on flame-maple top.
- Two black coverless humbuckers.

- Two controls (volume, tone) and five-way selector; side-mounted output jack.
- Two-pivot locking bridge/vibrato unit.
- * **RGT3120** 2002–03 As RG3120 but through-neck.

RG3521 2012–current
- Rosewood fingerboard; sharktooth markers.
- Solid offset-double-cutaway bound body; black.
- Two black coverless humbuckers.
- Two controls (volume, tone) and five-way selector; side-mounted output jack.
- Six-saddle fixed bridge.

RGA32 2010–11
- Rosewood fingerboard.
- Solid carved offset-double-cutaway body; various colours.
- Two black-cover humbuckers.
- Two controls (volume, tone) and five-way selector; side-mounted output jack.
- Six-saddle fixed bridge.

RGA42 2009–current
- Rosewood fingerboard.
- Solid carved offset-double-cutaway body; black.
- Two black-cover humbuckers.
- Two controls (volume, tone) and five-way selector; side-mounted output jack.
- Six-saddle fixed bridge.
- * **RGA42FM** 2009 As RGA42 but flame maple top.
- * **RGA42T / RGA42TE** 2010–current As RGA42 but bound fingerboard, locking nut, two-pivot locking bridge/vibrato unit.
- * **RGA42TFMZ** 2011 As RGA42 but bound fingerboard, locking nut, flame maple top, two-pivot locking bridge/vibrato unit.
- * **RGA72TQM** 2010–current As RGA42 but bound fingerboard with fancy markers, locking nut, quilted maple top, two-pivot locking bridge/vibrato unit.

RGA121 2005–08
- Rosewood fingerboard.
- Solid carved offset-double-cutaway body; various finishes.
- Two black coverless humbuckers.
- Two controls (volume, tone) and five-way selector; side-mounted output jack.
- Six-saddle fixed bridge.

RGA220Z 2010–11
- Rosewood fingerboard; locking nut.
- Solid carved offset-double-cutaway body; various colours.

- Two black-cover humbuckers.
- Two controls (volume, tone) and five-way selector; side-mounted output jack.
- Two-pivot locking bridge/vibrato unit.

RGA321F 2005–08
- Rosewood fingerboard.
- Solid carved offset-double-cutaway body; flamed maple top.
- Two black coverless humbuckers.
- Two controls (volume, tone) and five-way selector; side-mounted output jack.
- Six-saddle fixed bridge.
- * **RGA321** 2009 As RGA321F but regular top.

RGA420Z 2010–current
- Rosewood fingerboard; locking nut.
- Solid carved offset-double-cutaway body; flamed maple top.
- Two black-cover humbuckers.
- Two controls (volume, tone) and five-way selector; side-mounted output jack.
- Two-pivot locking bridge/vibrato unit.

RGD320Z 2010–11
- Rosewood fingerboard; fancy markers; long scale 26 1/2-inch; locking nut.
- Solid offset-double-cutaway bevel-cut body; various finishes.
- Two twin-blade or coverless humbuckers.
- Two controls (volume, tone) and five-way selector; side-mounted output jack.
- Two-pivot locking bridge/vibrato unit.

RGD420 2012–current
- Rosewood fingerboard; long scale 26 1/2-inch; locking nut.
- Solid offset-double-cutaway bevel-cut body; black.
- Two coverless humbuckers.
- One control (volume) and three-way selector; side-mounted output jack.
- Two-pivot locking bridge/vibrato unit.
- * **RGD421** 2012–current As RGD420 but no locking nut, six-saddle fixed bridge.

RGD2120Z 2010–current
- Rosewood fingerboard; long scale 26 1/2-inch; locking nut.
- Solid offset-double-cutaway bevel-cut body; metallic finish.
- Two coverless humbuckers.
- One control (volume) and three-way selector; side-mounted output jack.
- Two-pivot locking bridge/vibrato unit.

RGR models See under RG model number.

RGT6EX 2008–current
- Bound rosewood fingerboard; offset dot markers; through neck.
- Black.
- Two black-cover humbuckers.
- Two controls (volume, tone) and five-way selector; side-mounted output jack.
- Six-saddle fixed bridge.

RGT42 See RG420.

RGT220 See RG220.

RGT320 See RG320.

RGT2020 2003–04
- Rosewood fingerboard; offset-dot markers; through neck; single-bar string-guide; locking nut.
- Solid offset-double-cutaway bound body; natural, through-neck wood stripes visible.
- Two black coverless humbuckers.
- Two controls (volume, tone) and five-way selector; side-mounted output jack.
- Two-pivot locking bridge/vibrato unit.

RGT3020 See RG3020.

RGT3120 See RG3120.

HS ONE HUMBUCKER (AT BRIDGE) AND ONE SINGLE-COIL (AT NECK)

RG565 1990–92
- Maple fingerboard; coloured dot markers; reversed headstock; single-bar string-guide; locking nut.
- Various colours.
- One black coverless humbucker (at bridge, with one blade magnet) and one black blade pickup (at neck).
- Two controls (volume, tone) and five-way selector; side-mounted output jack.
- Two-pivot locking bridge/vibrato unit.

HSH TWO HUMBUCKERS AND ONE SINGLE-COIL (IN CENTRE)

GRG250DX 2010–current
- Rosewood fingerboard; coloured sharktooth markers; single-bar string-guide; locking nut.
- Various colours.
- Two black coverless humbuckers and one black six-polepiece pickup (in centre).
- Two controls (volume, tone) and five-way

selector on body; side-mounted output jack.
- Coloured pickguard.
- Two-pivot locking bridge/vibrato unit.

GRG270 / GRG270B 2004–07, 2010–11
- Rosewood fingerboard; single-bar string-guide; locking nut.
- Various colours.
- Two black coverless humbuckers and one black six-polepiece pickup (in centre).
- Two controls (volume, tone) and five-way selector on body; side-mounted output jack.
- Two-pivot locking bridge/vibrato unit.
- *** GRG270DX** 2012–current As GRG270 but bound fingerboard with sharktooth markers.

RG1XXV 2012
- Rosewood fingerboard; coloured sharktooth markers; locking nut.
- Yellow or pink.
- Two yellow or pink coverless humbuckers and one yellow or pink six-polepiece pickup (in centre).
- Two yellow or pink controls (volume, tone) and yellow or pink five-way selector; side-mounted output jack.
- Two-pivot locking bridge/vibrato unit.
- 25th anniversary model.

RG4EX1 2007–07. Guitar Center-only model.

RG170 1997–2003
- Maple fingerboard.
- Various colours.
- Two black coverless humbuckers and one black six-polepiece pickup (in centre).
- Two controls (volume, tone) and five-way selector; side-mounted output jack.
- Six-pivot bridge/vibrato unit.
- *** RG170DX** 2003 As RG170 but sharktooth markers.

RG250 1995–96
- Rosewood fingerboard; single-bar string-guide; locking nut.
- Various colours.
- Two black coverless humbuckers and one black six-polepiece pickup (in centre).
- Two controls (volume, tone) and five-way selector, all on pickguard; side-mounted output jack.
- Black pickguard.
- Two-pivot locking bridge/vibrato unit.
- *** RG250DX** 2002 As RG250 but sharktooth markers, bound neck.
- *** RG250LTD** 2000–01 As RG250 but with mirror pickguard.
- *** RG270** 1994–2002 As RG250 but no

pickguard; some with maple fingerboard.
- *** RG270DX** 1996–2002 As RG250 but no pickguard, sharktooth markers, bound neck.
- *** RGR270DX** 1998–2001 As RG250 but no pickguard, sharktooth markers, bound neck; some with reversed headstock.

RG350 1988–90
- Rosewood or maple fingerboard; 22 frets; single-bar string-guide; locking nut.
- Various colours.
- Two black coverless humbuckers and one black six-polepiece pickup (in centre).
- Two controls (volume, tone) and five-way selector, all on pickguard; side-mounted output jack.
- Pickguard.
- Two-pivot locking bridge/vibrato unit.
- *** RG350DX** 1998–current As RG350 but sharktooth markers, bound neck, some with white pickups and controls.
- *** RG350EX** 2005–11 As RG350 but sharktooth markers, mirror pickguard.
- *** RG350GX** 2000–03 As RG350 but white only with pearl pickguard.
- *** RG350M** 2010–current As RG350 but maple fingerboard.
- *** RG350MDX** 2010 As RG350 but sharktooth markers, maple fingerboard.
- *** RG351DX** 2012–current As RG350 but sharktooth markers, six-saddle fixed bridge.

RG370B 1995–96, 2003–04
- Rosewood fingerboard; single-bar string-guide; locking nut.
- Various colours.
- Two black coverless humbuckers and one black six-polepiece pickup (in centre).
- Two controls (volume, tone) and five-way selector; side-mounted output jack.
- Two-pivot locking bridge/vibrato unit.
- Some with gold-plated metalwork.
- *** RG370GH** 2003–04 As RG370B but flame maple top.
- *** RG370DX** 2003–current As RG370B but sharktooth markers.

RG450 1992–95
- Maple or rosewood fingerboard; single-bar string-guide; locking nut.
- Various colours.
- Two black coverless humbuckers and one black six-polepiece pickup (in centre).
- Two controls (volume, tone) and five-way selector, all on pickguard; side-mounted output jack.
- Pickguard.
- Two-pivot locking bridge/vibrato unit.

* **RG450DX** 1994–97 *As RG450 but triangle or sharktooth markers, bound neck; some with white pickups and controls.*
* **RG450GX** 2004 *As RG450 but gold-plated metalwork.*
* **RG450LTD** 2001–04 *As RG450 but sharktooth markers, mirror pickguard.*
* **RG450LTD1** 2000 *As RG450 but blue or red only with matching pickguard.*
* **RG470** 1992–2004 *As RG450 but no pickguard; some with gold-plated metalwork.*
* **RG470A** 2011 *As RG450 but no pickguard, sharktooth markers, natural ash body.*
* **RG470DX** 1996 *As RG450 but no pickguard, sharktooth markers, bound neck.*
* **RG470FM** 1994 *As RG450 but maple fingerboard, no pickguard.*
* **RG470FX** 1994 *As RG450 but no pickguard, six-saddle fixed bridge.*
* **RG470MH** 2012–current *As RG450 but no pickguard, sharktooth markers, bound neck, figured mahogany body.*
* **RG470XL** 2001–02 *As RG450 but no pickguard, long scale 27-inch.*
* **RG471** 2012–current *As RG450 but no pickguard, sharktooth markers, six-saddle fixed bridge.*
* **RGR480** 1998 *As RG450 but reversed headstock, no pickguard, sharktooth markers, bound neck.*

RG505 1996–99
- Rosewood fingerboard; single-bar string-guide; locking nut.
- Various colours.
- Two black coverless humbuckers and one black six-polepiece pickup (in centre).
- Two controls (volume, tone) and five-way selector, all on pickguard; side-mounted output jack.
- Black pickguard.
- Two-pivot locking bridge/vibrato unit.
* **RG507** 1996–99 *As RG505 but no pickguard.*

RG547 / RG548 *See RG550.*

RG550 1987–2002
- Maple (some rosewood) fingerboard; single-bar string-guide; locking nut.
- Various colours.
- Two black coverless humbuckers and one black six-polepiece pickup (in centre).
- Two controls (volume, tone) and five-way selector, all on pickguard; side-mounted output jack.
- Pickguard.
- Two-pivot locking bridge/vibrato unit.
* **RG547** 1996 *As RG550 but natural wood finish, some gold-plated metalwork, no pickguard.*

* **RG548** 1997–99 *As RG550 but transparent colours over ash body, no pickguard.*
* **RG550DX** 1992–93 *As RG550 but mirror pickguard.*
* **RG550EX** 2000–02 *As RG550 but mirror pickguard.*
* **RG550LTD** 1994–99 *As RG550 but sharktooth markers, bound neck, mirror pickguard.*
* **RG550XX** 2007 *As RG550 but 20th anniversary model, yellow/red/black, anniversary plate on rear body.*

RG570 1989–2002
- Rosewood fingerboard; single-bar string-guide; locking nut.
- Various colours.
- Two black coverless humbuckers and one black six-polepiece pickup (in centre).
- Two controls (volume, tone) and five-way selector; side-mounted output jack.
- Two-pivot locking bridge/vibrato unit.
- Some with gold-plated metalwork.
* **RG570EX** 2000–02 *As RG570 but sharktooth markers.*
* **RGR570** 1997–99 *As RG570 but reversed headstock, sharktooth markers.*

RG670DX 1994
- Maple fingerboard; coloured sharktooth markers; single-bar string-guide; locking nut.
- Various colours.
- Two black coverless humbuckers and one black six-polepiece pickup (in centre).
- Two coloured controls (volume, tone) and coloured five-way selector; side-mounted output jack.
- Transparent pickguard.
- Two-pivot locking bridge/vibrato unit.

RG750 1989–92
- Bound rosewood fingerboard; sharktooth markers; single-bar string-guide; locking nut.
- Various colours.
- Two black coverless humbuckers and one black six-polepiece pickup (in centre).
- Two controls (volume, tone) and five-way selector, all on pickguard; side-mounted output jack.
- Pickguard.
- Two-pivot locking bridge/vibrato unit.
* **RG770** 1990–93 *As RG750 but no pickguard.*
* **RG770DX** 1990–93 *As RG750 but maple fingerboard, coloured sharktooth markers, coloured pickups, transparent pickguard.*

RG870Q 2011
- Bound rosewood fingerboard; offset dot markers; locking nut.

- Solid offset-double-cutaway bound body; various transparent colours on quilted maple.
- Two black coverless humbuckers and one black six-polepiece pickup (in centre).
- Two controls (volume, tone) and five-way selector; side-mounted output jack.
- Two-pivot locking bridge/vibrato unit.
* **RG870Z** 2011 *As RG870Q but black finish.*

RG1200 1992
- Rosewood fingerboard; small oval markers; single-bar string-guide; locking nut.
- Solid offset-double-cutaway bound body; transparent red or transparent blue on flame-maple top.
- Two white coverless humbuckers and one white six-polepiece pickup (in centre).
- Two white controls (volume, tone) and white five-way selector, all on pickguard; side-mounted output jack.
- Pearl pickguard.
- Two-pivot locking bridge/vibrato unit.

RG1451 2010–11
- Rosewood fingerboard.
- Various colours.
- Two black coverless humbuckers and one black six-polepiece pickup (in centre).
- Two controls (volume, tone) and five-way selector, all on pickguard; side-mounted output jack.
- Black or white pickguard.
- Six-saddle fixed bridge.

RG1550 2002–04
- Maple fingerboard; single-bar string-guide; locking nut.
- Solid offset-double-cutaway bound body; black or red.
- Two black coverless humbuckers and one black six-polepiece pickup (in centre).
- Two controls (volume, tone) and five-way selector, all on pickguard; side-mounted output jack.
- Black pickguard.
- Two-pivot locking bridge/vibrato unit.
* **RG1550MZ** 2010 *Reissue of RG1550.*
* **RG1570** 2003–current *As RG1550 but rosewood fingerboard, no pickguard.*

RG2120X *See RG2020X.*

RG2550E / RG2550EX / RG2550Z 2003–11
- Rosewood fingerboard; dot markers (sharktooth markers from 2007); single-bar string-guide; locking nut.
- Solid offset-double-cutaway bound body; various colours.

- Two black coverless humbuckers and one black six-polepiece pickup (in centre).
- Two controls (volume, tone) and five-way selector, all on pickguard; side-mounted output jack.
- Mirror pickguard.
- Two-pivot locking bridge/vibrato unit.
- *Known first as ...EX , from 2006 as ...E , and from 2008 as ...Z.*

* **RG2570E / RG2570EX / RG2570Z**
2003–10 *As RG2550EX but sharktooth markers, no pickguard. (Known as ...EX first, as ...E from 2007, and as ...Z from 2008.*

* **RG2570MZ** 2010–11 *As RG2550 but maple fingerboard, sharktooth markers, no pickguard.*

RG3070 1996
- Green-coloured maple fingerboard; single-bar string-guide; locking nut; pearl logo.
- Solid offset-double-cutaway bound body; green.
- Two black coverless humbuckers and one black six-polepiece pickup (in centre).
- Two gold-plated controls (volume, tone) and five-way selector; side-mounted output jack.
- Two-pivot locking bridge/vibrato unit.
- Some with gold-plated metalwork.

RG3180 1997
- Rosewood fingerboard; some early examples with 'Prestige' inlay at 24th fret; single-bar string-guide; locking nut.
- Solid offset-double-cutaway bound body; transparent purple on flame maple.
- Two black coverless humbuckers and one black six-polepiece pickup (in centre).
- Two controls (volume, tone) and five-way selector; side-mounted output jack.
- Two-pivot locking bridge/vibrato unit.

RG3250MZ 2011–current
- Maple fingerboard; sharktooth or dot markers; locking nut.
- Solid offset-double-cutaway bound body; various colours.
- Two black coverless humbuckers and one black six-polepiece pickup (in centre).
- Two controls (volume, tone) and five-way selector; side-mounted output jack.
- Two-pivot locking bridge/vibrato unit.

RG3550 2009–11
- Maple fingerboard; sharktooth markers; locking nut.
- Solid offset-double-cutaway bound body; various colours.
- Two black-and-white coverless humbuckers and one black six-polepiece pickup (in centre).

- Two controls (volume, tone) and five-way selector; side-mounted output jack.
- Two-pivot locking bridge/vibrato unit.

* **RG3550MZ** 2012–current *As RG3550 but dot markers, mirror pickguard.*

RG3570 2009–11
- Rosewood fingerboard; sharktooth markers; locking nut.
- Various colours.
- Two yellow coverless humbuckers and one yellow six-polepiece pickup (in centre).
- Two yellow controls (volume, tone) and yellow five-way selector; side-mounted output jack.
- Two-pivot locking bridge/vibrato unit.

* **RG3750Z** 2012–current *As RG3570 but black pickups.*

RG4570 2010
- Rosewood fingerboard; locking nut.
- Solid offset-double-cutaway bound body; transparent finish on flame maple.
- Two black coverless humbuckers and one black six-polepiece pickup (in centre).
- Two controls (volume, tone) and five-way selector; side-mounted output jack.
- Two-pivot locking bridge/vibrato unit.

HSS ONE HUMBUCKER (AT BRIDGE) AND TWO SINGLE-COILS

RG360 1988–90
- Rosewood fingerboard; 22 frets; single-bar string-guide; locking nut.
- Various colours.
- One black coverless humbucker (at bridge) and two black six-polepiece pickups.
- Two controls (volume, tone) and five-way selector; side-mounted output jack.
- Two-pivot locking bridge/vibrato unit.

RG560 1988–92
- Rosewood fingerboard; single-bar string-guide; locking nut.
- Various colours.
- One black coverless humbucker (at bridge) and two black six-polepiece pickups.
- Two controls (volume, tone) and five-way selector; side-mounted output jack.
- Two-pivot locking bridge/vibrato unit.

RG760 1989–92
- Bound rosewood fingerboard; sharktooth markers; single-bar string-guide; locking nut.
- Various colours.
- One black coverless humbucker (at bridge)

and two black six-polepiece pickups.
- Two controls (volume, tone) and five-way selector; side-mounted output jack.
- Two-pivot locking bridge/vibrato unit.

SEVEN-STRING AND EIGHT-STRING

RG1077XL 2001–02
- Seven-string; rosewood fingerboard; offset dot markers; long scale 27-inch; single-bar string-guide; locking nut.
- Solid offset-double-cutaway bound body; various colours.
- Two black coverless humbuckers and one black six-polepiece pickup (in centre).
- Two controls (volume, tone) and five-way selector; side-mounted output jack.
- Two-pivot locking bridge/vibrato unit.

RG2027X 1999–2001
- Seven-string; rosewood fingerboard; offset dot markers at 12th fret only; single-bar string-guide; locking nut.
- Solid offset-double-cutaway bound body; sunburst.
- Two black coverless humbuckers.
- Three controls (two volume, tone), one mini-switch, one button, and five-way selector; two side-mounted output jacks.
- Two-pivot locking bridge/vibrato unit with piezo pickup.

RG2077XL 2003
- Seven-string; bound rosewood fingerboard; offset dot markers; long scale 27-inch; single-bar string-guide; locking nut.
- Solid offset-double-cutaway bound body; various colours.
- Two black coverless humbuckers and one black six-polepiece pickup (in centre).
- Two controls (volume, tone) and five-way selector; side-mounted output jack.
- Two-pivot locking bridge/vibrato unit.

RG2228 2007–current
- Eight-string; bound rosewood fingerboard; offset dot or regular dot markers; long scale 27-inch; single-bar string-guide; locking nut.
- Black.
- Two black-cover humbuckers.
- Two controls (volume, tone) and five-way selector; side-mounted output jack.
- Locking bridge unit (not vibrato).

RG7321 2001–current
- Seven-string; rosewood fingerboard.
- Various colours.

- Two black coverless humbuckers.
- Two controls (volume, tone) and five-way selector; side-mounted output jack.
- Six-saddle fixed bridge.

RG7420 2000–02
- Seven-string; rosewood fingerboard; single-bar string-guide; locking nut.
- Various colours.
- Two black coverless humbuckers.
- Two controls (volume, tone) and five-way selector; side-mounted output jack.
- Two-pivot locking bridge/vibrato unit.
- * **RG7421** 2000–01 *As RG7420 but six-saddle fixed bridge.*
- * **RG7421XL** 2001–02 *As RG7421 but long scale 27-inch.*

RG7620 1998–2002
- Seven-string; rosewood fingerboard; single-bar string-guide; locking nut.
- Various colours.
- Two black coverless humbuckers.
- Two black controls (volume, tone) and five-way selector; side-mounted output jack.
- Two-pivot locking bridge/vibrato unit.
- * **RG7621** 1998–99 *As RG7620 but six-saddle fixed bridge.*

RGA7 2010–current
- Seven-string; rosewood fingerboard.
- Solid carved offset-double-cutaway body; black.
- Two black-cover humbuckers.
- One control (volume), mini-switch, five-way selector, all on body; side-mounted output jack.
- Seven-saddle fixed bridge.
- * **RGA7QM** 2012–current *As RGA7 but quilted maple top.*

RGA8 2010–current
- Eight-string; four-tuners-each-side headstock; rosewood fingerboard; long scale 27-inch.
- Solid carved offset-double-cutaway body; black.
- Two black-cover humbuckers.
- One control (volume), mini-switch, five-way selector, all on body; side-mounted output jack.
- Eight-saddle fixed fine-tuning bridge.
- * **RGA8QM** 2012–current *As RGA8 but quilted maple top.*

RGA427Z 2011
- Seven-string; rosewood fingerboard; locking nut.
- Solid carved offset-double-cutaway body;

flamed maple top.
- Two black-cover humbuckers.
- Two controls (volume, tone) and five-way selector; side-mounted output jack.
- Two-pivot locking bridge/vibrato unit.

RGD7320Z 2011
- Seven-string; rosewood fingerboard; fancy markers; long scale 26 1/2-inch; locking nut.
- Solid offset-double-cutaway bevel-cut body; various finishes.
- Two coverless humbuckers.
- wo controls (volume, tone) and five-way selector; side-mounted output jack.
- Two-pivot locking bridge/vibrato unit.

RGD7421 2012–current
- Seven-string; rosewood fingerboard; long scale 26 1/2-inch.
- Solid offset-double-cutaway bevel-cut body; black.
- Two coverless humbuckers.
- One control (volume) and three-way selector; side-mounted output jack.
- Seven-saddle fixed bridge.

RGD2127Z 2010–current
- Seven-string; rosewood fingerboard; long scale 26 1/2-inch; locking nut.
- Solid offset-double-cutaway bevel-cut body; metallic finish.
- Two coverless humbuckers.
- One control (volume) and three-way selector; side-mounted output jack.
- Two-pivot locking bridge/vibrato unit.

LEE RITENOUR

1981–87
LR10 semi-solid Gibson-ES-like signature model.

ROADCORE

2012–current
Debut retro-flavoured RC320 model has two humbuckers and through-body stringing.

ROADSTAR II – RG

All with "old style" stumpy non-pointy body shape, 1986–87. At first with "Roadstar II" on old-shape "curved" headstock, then with "tick" Ibanez logo on new-shape headstock. For the later pointy-body-style RGs, introduced in 1987, see RG NEW STYLE.

RG120 1987
- Rosewood fingerboard; dot inlay; 22 frets.

- Solid offset-double-cutaway body; various colours.
- Three black six-polepiece pickups (bridge pickup angled).
- Two controls (volume, tone), three-way selector, and output jack, all on pickguard.
- Black pickguard.
- One-pivot bridge/vibrato unit
- * **RG135** 1987 *As RG 120 but h-h pickup layout, five-way selector.*
- * **RG140** 1987 *As RG 120 but h-s-s pickup layout, five-way selector.*

RG240 1987
- Rosewood fingerboard; dot inlay; 22 frets; single-bar string-guide; locking nut.
- Solid offset-double-cutaway body; various colours.
- One coverless humbucker (at bridge) and two black six-polepiece pickups.
- Two controls (volume, tone), five-way selector, and output jack, all on body face.
- Two-pivot fine-tuning bridge/vibrato unit.
- * **RG250** 1987 *As RG240 but flamed maple top.*

RG410 1986–87
- Rosewood fingerboard; dot inlay; 22 frets; single-bar string-guide; locking nut.
- Solid offset-double-cutaway body; various colours.
- One black-cover or coverless humbucker (angled at bridge).
- One control (volume) on body face; side-mounted output jack.
- Two-pivot locking bridge/vibrato unit.
- * **RG420** 1986–87 *As RG410 but h-h pickup layout, two controls (volume, tone), three-way selector.*
- * **RG425** 1986 *As RG410 but h-h pickup layout (both at bridge), two controls (volume, tone), three-way selector.*
- * **RG430** 1986–87 *As RG410 but s-s-s pickup layout, two controls (volume, tone), five-way selector.*
- * **RG440** 1986–87 *As RG410 but h-s-s pickup layout, two controls (volume, tone), five-way selector.*
- * **RG450** 1986 *As RG410 but h-s-h pickup layout, two controls (volume, tone), five-way selector, mini-switch.*

RG525 1986
- Rosewood fingerboard; dot inlay; 24 frets; locking nut.
- Solid offset-double-cutaway body; various colours.
- Two black-cover humbuckers.
- Three controls (two volume, tone), three-way

selector, all on body face; side-mounted output jack.
- Two-pivot locking bridge/vibrato unit.
- * **RG530** 1986 *As RG525 but flame-maple top.*

RG600 1986
- Ebony fingerboard; dot inlay; 24 frets.
- Solid bound offset-double-cutaway body; various colours.
- Two black-cover humbuckers.
- Three controls (two volume, tone), three-way selector, all on body face; side-mounted output jack.
- Six-saddle fixed bridge.

ROADSTAR II – RS
"Roadstar II" on headstock, 1982–86.

Comet II *See RS110.*

Steve Lukather *See RS1010SL.*

RS100 1982–83
- Maple fingerboard; dot inlay; 21 frets.
- Solid offset-double-cutaway body; various colours.
- Three black plain-top pickups (bridge pickup angled).
- Two controls (volume, tone), five-way selector, mini-switch, and output jack, all on pickguard.
- Black pickguard.
- Six-saddle fixed bridge.
- * **RS125** 1982–83 *As RS100 but h-h pickup layout, six-pivot bridge/vibrato unit.*
- * **RS130** 1983–84 *As RS100 but no mini-switch, white pickguard, 22 frets.*
- * **RS135** 1983–85 *As RS100 but white, black, or coloured pickups, white pickguard, 22 frets, one-pivot bridge/vibrato unit.*

RS110 1986
- Maple fingerboard; dot inlay; 22 frets.
- Solid offset-double-cutaway body; black or white.
- One black coverless humbucker (at bridge).
- Two controls (volume, tone) and output jack on pickguard.
- Black pickguard.
- One-pivot bridge/vibrato unit.
- * **RS111** 1985 *As RS110 but body black or cream, coloured or black pickguard.*
- * **RS120** 1986 *As RS110 but h-h pickup layout, three-way selector.*
- * **RS121** 1985 *As RS110 but h-h pickup layout, three-way selector, body black, blue, cream, or orange.*
- * **RS135** 1986 *As RS110 but s-s-s pickup*

layout, five-way selector and mini-switch, body black, red, or white.
- * **RS136** 1985 *As RS110 but s-s-s pickup layout, five-way selector and mini-switch, body blue, orange, peach, or pink.*
- * **RS140** 1986 *As RS110 but h-s-s pickup layout, five-way selector.*
- * **RS141** 1985 *As RS110 but h-s-s pickup layout, five-way selector, body black, orange, pink, cream, or peach.*
- - *RS111, 121, 136, 141 known as Comet II series.*

RS205 1982–84
- Maple fingerboard; dot inlay; 21 frets.
- Solid offset-double-cutaway body; various colours.
- Three white six-polepiece pickups (bridge pickup angled).
- Two controls (volume, tone), five-way selector, mini-switch, and output jack, all on pickguard.
- White pickguard.
- Six-pivot bridge/vibrato unit

RS225 1983–84
- Maple fingerboard; dot inlay; 22 frets.
- Solid offset-double-cutaway body; various colours.
- Two black coverless humbuckers.
- Two controls (volume, tone), five-way selector, and output jack, all on body face.
- One-pivot bridge/vibrato unit

RS230 1985
- Rosewood fingerboard; dot inlay; 22 frets.
- Solid offset-double-cutaway body; various colours.
- Three black single-blade pickups (bridge pickup angled).
- Three controls (two volume, tone), three-way selector, on body face; side-mounted output jack.
- One-pivot bridge/vibrato unit.
- * **RS240** 1985 *As RS230 but h-s-s pickup layout.*

RS315 1982–84
- Maple fingerboard; dot inlay; 21 frets.
- Solid bound offset-double-cutaway body; various colours.
- One white coverless humbucker (at bridge).
- Two controls (volume, tone); output jack on body face.
- Two-pivot bridge/vibrato unit.

RS320 1985
- Rosewood fingerboard; dot inlay; 22 frets.

- Solid offset-double-cutaway body; various colours.
- Two black-cover humbuckers.
- Two controls (volume, tone), three-way selector, on body face; side-mounted output jack.
- One-pivot bridge/vibrato unit.

RS405 1982–84
- Rosewood fingerboard; dot inlay; 21 frets.
- Solid offset-double-cutaway body; various colours.
- Three white six-polepiece pickups (bridge pickup angled).
- Two controls (volume, tone), five-way selector, and output jack, all on pickguard.
- White pickguard.
- Two-pivot bridge/vibrato unit.

RS410 1985
- Maple fingerboard; dot inlay; 22 frets; locking nut.
- Solid offset-double-cutaway body; pink, cream, or black.
- One black-cover humbucker (at bridge).
- One controls (volume); side-mounted output jack.
- Two-pivot fine-tuning bridge/vibrato unit.
- * **RS420** 1985 *As RS410 but h-h pickup layout, body black or blue.*

RS430 1984–85
- Rosewood fingerboard; dot inlay; 22 frets; locking nut.
- Solid offset-double-cutaway body; various colours.
- Three black one-blade pickups (bridge pickup angled).
- Two controls (volume, tone) and five-way selector on pickguard, side-mounted output jack.
- Black pickguard.
- Two-pivot fine-tuning bridge/vibrato unit.
- * **RS440** 1984–85 *As RS430 but h-s-s pickup layout.*

RS505 1982–84
- Rosewood fingerboard; dot inlay; 21 frets.
- Solid bound offset-double-cutaway body; various colours.
- Three white six-polepiece pickups (bridge pickup angled) with body mounts.
- Two controls (volume, tone), five-way selector, and output jack, all on body face.
- Two-pivot bridge/vibrato unit.

RS520 1984
- Rosewood fingerboard; dot inlay; 24 frets; locking nut.

- Solid offset-double-cutaway body; various colours.
- Two black-cover humbuckers.
- Three controls (two volume, tone), three-way selector, all on body face; side-mounted output jack.
- Two-pivot fine-tuning bridge/vibrato unit.
- Gold-plated metalwork.
- * **RS525** 1985 *As RS520 but archtop body, black-plated metalwork.*
- * **RS530** 1984 *As RS520 but bound body, black-plated metalwork.*

RS1000 1982–84
- Rosewood fingerboard; dot inlay; 21 frets.
- Solid bound offset-double-cutaway body; various colours.
- Two metal-cover humbuckers.
- Two controls (volume, tone), three-way selector, and output jack, all on body face.
- Two-pivot bridge/vibrato unit.
- Gold-plated metalwork.
- * **RS1400** 1983–84 *As RS1000 but four controls (two volume, two tone), six-saddle fixed bridge, side-mounted output jack.*

RS1010SL 1983–85
- Ebony fingerboard; cross inlay; 21 frets.
- Solid bound offset-double-cutaway body; blue.
- Two metal-cover humbuckers.
- Two controls (volume, tone), three-way selector, and output jack, all on body face.
- Two-pivot bridge/vibrato unit.
- Gold-plated metalwork.
- *Steve Lukather model.*

RS1300 1984–85
- Rosewood fingerboard; dot inlay; 22 frets; locking nut.
- Solid bound offset-double-cutaway body; various colours.
- Two metal-cover or coverless humbuckers.
- Three controls (two volume, tone) and three-way selector, all on body face; side-mounted output jack.
- Two-pivot fine-tuning bridge/vibrato unit.
- Gold-plated or black-plated metalwork.

RS1500 1982–84
- Rosewood fingerboard; dot inlay; 21 frets.
- Solid offset-double-cutaway body; various colours.
- Three black six-polepiece pickups (bridge pickup angled) with body mounts.
- Three controls (two volume, tone) and three-way selector, all on body face; side-mounted output jack.

- Two-pivot bridge/vibrato unit.
- Gold-plated metalwork.

ROADSTER
"Roadster Series" on headstock, 1979–81.

RS100 1979–81
- Maple fingerboard; dot inlay; 21 frets.
- Solid offset-double-cutaway body; various colours.
- Three black six-polepiece pickups (bridge pickup angled) with body mounts.
- Two controls (volume, tone) and five-way selector; jack on body face.
- Six-saddle fixed bridge.
- * **RS300** 1979–80 *As RS300 but with mini-switch by controls.*

OMAR RODRIGUEZ-LOPEZ
2008–current
ORM signature model, based on Jet King with one blade pickup (at bridge).

RS
See **ROADSTAR II – RS**.

RT
1992–93
Based on RG shape but with "traditional" features, including alder body, rounder neck profile, non-locking vibrato, but locking tuners, 24 frets, HSH pickup layout.

RX
1994–97
Based on RG shape but with "traditional" features.

S
All have offset-double-cutaway S body profile, with ultra thin, curved, tapered cross-section.

GSA20 2000–03
- Rosewood fingerboard, dot markers; 22 frets.
- Various colours.
- Two black coverless humbuckers.
- Two controls (volume, tone) and five-way selector on body; side-mounted output jack.
- One- or two-pivot bridge/vibrato unit.
- * **GSA60** 2000–11 *As GSA20 but h-s-s pickup layout.*

Pro540 Saber 1987–88
- Rosewood fingerboard, dot markers; 22 frets; single-bar string-guide; locking nut.
- Various colours.
- One black coverless humbucker (at bridge) and two black six-polepiece pickups.
- Two controls (volume, tone), three mini-switches, output jack, all on body.
- Two-pivot locking bridge/vibrato unit.
- *Also known as 540S.*
- *Custom 1988, Hoshino 80th anniversary guitars.*
- * **540SHH** 1988 *As Pro540 Saber but h-h pickup layout, two mini-switches.*
- * **540SSH** 1988 *As Pro540 Saber but h-s pickup layout, two mini-switches.*

S1XXV 2012
- Rosewood fingerboard, green or yellow dot markers; 24 frets; locking nut.
- Green or yellow finish.
- Two black coverless humbuckers and one black six-polepiece pickup (in centre).
- Two controls (volume, tone), five-way selector, output jack, all on body.
- Two-pivot locking bridge/vibrato unit.
- *25th anniversary model.*

S320 2007–09
- Rosewood fingerboard, fancy markers 12th fret; 22 frets; single-bar string-guide; locking nut.
- Various colours.
- Two black coverless humbuckers.
- Two controls (volume, tone), five-way selector, output jack, all on body.
- Two-pivot locking bridge/vibrato unit.

S370 2001–02
- Rosewood fingerboard, wavy-line markers; 22 frets; single-bar string-guide; locking nut.
- Various colours.
- Two black coverless humbuckers and one black six-polepiece pickup (in centre).
- Two controls (volume, tone), five-way selector, output jack, all on body.
- Two-pivot locking bridge/vibrato unit.
- * **S370DX** 2002 *As S370 but metallic finish.*

S420 2010–current
- Rosewood fingerboard, fancy markers at 12th fret; 24 frets; locking nut.
- Various colours.
- Two black coverless humbuckers.
- Two controls (volume, tone), five-way selector, output jack, all on body.
- Two-pivot locking bridge/vibrato unit.

S470 1992–2007
- Rosewood fingerboard, dot or wavy-line

markers; 22 frets; single-bar string-guide; locking nut.
■ Various colours.
■ Two black coverless humbuckers and one black six-polepiece pickup (in centre).
■ Two controls (volume, tone), five-way selector, output jack, all on body.
■ Two-pivot locking bridge/vibrato unit.
- Also known as 470S.
* **S470DX** 1996 *As S470 but bound fingerboard with sharktooth markers.*
* **S470DX** 2003–04 *As S470 but bound fingerboard with wavy-line markers.*
* **S470DXQM** 2003–09 *As S470 but bound fingerboard with wavy-line or pearl dot markers, quilted maple top.*
* **S470FM** 1996–98 *As S470 but bound fingerboard with oval markers, flame maple top, gold-plated metalwork.*
* **S470QS** 1999–2002 *As S470 but oval or wavy-line markers, quilted sapele top.*

S520 2001
■ Rosewood fingerboard, wavy-line markers; 22 frets; single-bar string-guide; locking nut.
■ Walnut finish.
■ Two black coverless humbuckers.
■ Two controls (volume, tone), five-way selector, output jack, all on body.
■ Two-pivot locking bridge/vibrato unit.
* **S520EX** 2005–09 *As S520 but fancy markers 11th–13th frets, various colours, two black-cover humbuckers.*

S540 1988–91
■ Rosewood fingerboard, dot or oval markers; 22 frets; single-bar string-guide; locking nut.
■ Various colours.
■ One black coverless humbucker (at bridge) and two black six-polepiece pickups.
■ Two controls (volume, tone), five-way selector, output jack, all on body.
■ Two-pivot locking bridge/vibrato unit.
* **S540BM** 1992–94 *As S540 but burl mahogany body, some with maple fingerboard, h-s-h pickup layout, some with gold-plated metalwork.*
* **S540CG** 1994 *As S540 but maple fingerboard, pearl oval markers, h-s-h pickup layout, green finish.*
* **S540CT** 1988–90 *As S540 but pearl oval markers, no string-guide or locking nut, sunburst flame maple top, h-s-h pickup layout, two-pivot bridge/vibrato unit. Also known as 540SC, 540SCT5, or 540SCT6.*
* **S540FM** 1991–97 *As S540 but flame maple top, most with h-s-h pickup layout, most with gold-plated metalwork.*

* **S540HH** 1988–89 *As S540 but h-h pickup layout, three-way selector.*
* **S540JM** 1992–93 *As S540 but maple fingerboard, pearl oval markers, h-s-h pickup layout, green finish.*
* **S540LTD** 1988–98 *As S540 but sharktooth markers, h-s-h pickup layout.*
* **S540OL** 1992–93 *As S540 but maple fingerboard, pearl oval markers, h-s-h pickup layout, oil finish.*
* **S540QS** 1998 *As S540 but pearl oval markers, quilted sapele top, h-s-h pickup layout.*
* **S540TN** 1991 *As S540 but double-neck 6/12.*
* **S5407** 1991–92 *As S540 but seven-string.*
- *Some S540-series models have "Custom Made" inlay at 21st fret.*
- *S540-series models sometimes known in earlier years as 540S.*
- *See also Pro540 Saber for earlier model.*

S570B 2010–11
■ Rosewood fingerboard, fancy markers; 24 frets; locking nut.
■ Various colours.
■ Two black coverless humbuckers and one black six-polepiece pickup (in centre).
■ Two controls (volume, tone), five-way selector, output jack, all on body.
■ Two-pivot locking bridge/vibrato unit.
* **S570DXQM** 2010–current *As S570B but bound fingerboard, flame maple top.*
* **S570MQM** 2012–current *As S570B but maple fingerboard, dot markers, quilted maple top.*

S620EX 2008
■ Rosewood fingerboard, fancy markers at 12th fret; 22 frets; single-bar string-guide; locking nut.
■ Quilted maple top.
■ Two black-cover humbuckers.
■ Two controls (volume, tone), five-way selector, output jack, all on body.
■ Two-pivot locking bridge/vibrato unit with piezo pickup.

S670FM 2007
■ Rosewood fingerboard, fancy markers; 22 frets; single-bar string-guide; locking nut.
■ Flamed maple top.
■ Two black coverless humbuckers and one black six-polepiece pickup (in centre).
■ Two controls (volume, tone), five-way selector, output jack, all on body.
■ Two-pivot locking bridge/vibrato unit.
* **S670PB** 2009 *As S670FM but burl poplar top.*

S770PB 2010–current
■ Rosewood fingerboard, fancy markers; 24

frets; locking nut.
■ Burl poplar top.
■ Two black coverless humbuckers and one black six-polepiece pickup (in centre).
■ Two controls (volume, tone), five-way selector, output jack, all on body.
■ Two-pivot locking bridge/vibrato unit.

S1220 2002
■ Rosewood fingerboard, fancy marker at 12th fret; 22 frets; single-bar string-guide; locking nut.
■ Walnut finish.
■ Two black coverless humbuckers.
■ Two controls (volume, tone), five-way selector, output jack, all on body.
■ Two-pivot locking bridge/vibrato unit.

S1520 1999–2002
■ Rosewood fingerboard, fancy marker at 12th fret; 22 frets; single-bar string-guide; locking nut.
■ Regular or figured bubinga top.
■ Two black coverless humbuckers.
■ Two controls (volume, tone), five-way selector, output jack, all on body.
■ Two-pivot locking bridge/vibrato unit.

S1620FB 2003
■ Rosewood fingerboard, fancy marker at 12th fret; 22 frets; single-bar string-guide; locking nut.
■ Figured bubinga top.
■ Two black coverless humbuckers.
■ Two controls (volume, tone), five-way selector, output jack, all on body.
■ Two-pivot locking bridge/vibrato unit.
* **S1625** 2004 *As S1620 but bubinga top, vibrato with D-tuner.*
* **S1670FM** 2003 *As S1620 but flamed maple top, h-s-h pickup layout.*
* **S1675FM** 2004 *As S1620 but flamed maple top, h-s-h pickup layout, vibrato with D-tuner.*

S2020X 1999–2001
■ Rosewood fingerboard, fancy marker at 12th fret; 22 frets; single-bar string-guide; locking nut.
■ Various finishes.
■ Two black coverless humbuckers.
■ Three controls (volume, tone, magnetic/piezo selector), five-way selector, one mini-switch, one button, two output jacks, all on body.
■ Two-pivot locking bridge/vibrato unit with piezo pickup.
* **S2120X** 2002 *As S2020 but four controls (one stacked), no button.*

S2075FW 2005
- Rosewood fingerboard, fancy markers at 12th fret; 22 frets; single-bar string-guide; locking nut.
- Figured poplar top.
- Two black coverless humbuckers and one black six-polepiece pickup (in centre).
- Two controls (volume, tone), five-way selector, output jack, all on body.
- Two-pivot locking bridge/vibrato unit with D-tuner.

S2170FW 2006–08
- Rosewood fingerboard, fancy markers at 12th fret; 22 frets; single-bar string-guide; locking nut.
- Figured poplar top.
- Two black coverless humbuckers and one black six-polepiece pickup (in centre).
- Two controls (volume, tone), five-way selector, output jack, all on body.
- Two-pivot locking bridge/vibrato unit.
- *Also known as S2170FB.*
- * **S2170FB** 2007–08 *As S2170FW but figured bubinga top.*
- * **S2170FM** 2006 *As S2170FW but flame maple top.*

S2540 1999
- Rosewood fingerboard, fancy markers; 22 frets; single-bar string-guide; locking nut.
- Figured sapele top.
- Two black coverless humbuckers and one black six-polepiece pickup (in centre).
- Two controls (volume, tone), five-way selector, output jack, all on body.
- Two-pivot locking bridge/vibrato unit.
- Gold-plated metalwork.

S4170AB 2007
- Bound rosewood fingerboard, fancy markers at 12th fret; 22 frets; single-bar string-guide; locking nut.
- Burl ash top.
- Two black coverless humbuckers and one black six-polepiece pickup (in centre).
- Two controls (volume, tone), five-way selector, output jack, all on body.
- Two-pivot locking bridge/vibrato unit.

S5470 2008–current
- Rosewood fingerboard, offset dot markers with fancy markers at 12th fret; 24 frets; locking nut.
- Various colours.
- Two black coverless humbuckers (bridge unit with one blade magnet) and one black six-polepiece pickup (in centre).

- Two controls (volume, tone), five-way selector, output jack, all on body.
- Two-pivot locking bridge/vibrato unit.
- * **S5470F** 2009–current *As S5470 but flamed maple top.*
- * **S5470Q** 2011–current *As S5470 but quilted maple top.*

S7320 2007–09
- Seven-string; rosewood fingerboard, dot markers; 22 frets; single-bar string-guide; locking nut.
- Black finish.
- Two black coverless humbuckers.
- Two controls (volume, tone), five-way selector, output jack, all on body.
- Two-pivot locking bridge/vibrato unit.

S7420 1999–2000, 2012–current
- Seven-string; rosewood fingerboard, dot markers; 22 frets (24 from 2012); single-bar string-guide; locking nut.
- Black finish.
- Two black coverless humbuckers.
- Two controls (volume, tone), five-way selector, output jack, all on body.
- Two-pivot locking bridge/vibrato unit.
- * **S7420QM** 2012–current *As S7420 but 24 frets, quilted maple top.*

SA120 2004–06, 2009–10
- Rosewood fingerboard, dot markers; 22 frets.
- Various colours.
- Two black coverless humbuckers.
- Two controls (volume, tone), five-way selector, output jack, all on body.
- Two-pivot bridge/vibrato unit.

SA160 2000–03
- Rosewood fingerboard, dot markers; 22 frets.
- Various colours.
- One black coverless humbucker (at bridge) and two black six-polepiece pickups.
- Two controls (volume, tone), five-way selector, output jack, all on body.
- Two-pivot bridge/vibrato unit.
- * **SA160QM** 2001–04 *As SA160 but quilted maple top.*

SA260FM 2004–06, 2009–11
- Rosewood fingerboard, dot markers; 22 frets.
- Flamed maple top.
- One black coverless humbucker (at bridge) and two black six-polepiece pickups.
- Two controls (volume, tone), five-way selector, output jack, all on body.
- Two-pivot bridge/vibrato unit.

SA320X 2004
- Rosewood fingerboard, dot markers; 22 frets.
- Various colours.
- Two black coverless humbuckers.
- Three controls (volume, tone, magnetic/piezo selector), five-way selector, mini-switch, two output jacks, all on body.
- Two-pivot bridge/vibrato unit with piezo pickup.

SA420X 2002–03
- Rosewood fingerboard, dot markers; 22 frets.
- Various colours.
- Two black coverless humbuckers.
- Three controls (volume, tone, magnetic/piezo selector), five-way selector. mini-switch, two output jacks, all on body.
- Two-pivot bridge/vibrato unit with piezo pickup.

SA1260 2004
- Rosewood fingerboard, offset-dot markers; 22 frets.
- Sunburst finish.
- One black coverless humbucker (at bridge) and two black six-polepiece pickups.
- Two controls (volume, tone), five-way selector, output jack, all on body.
- Two-pivot bridge/vibrato unit.

SA2120FM 2006
- Rosewood fingerboard, fancy marker at 12th fret; 22 frets.
- Flame maple top.
- Two black coverless humbuckers.
- Two controls (volume, tone), five-way selector, output jack, all on body.
- Two-pivot bridge/vibrato unit.

SAS32FM 2005
- Rosewood fingerboard, dot markers; 22 frets.
- Flamed maple top.
- Two black coverless humbuckers.
- Two controls (volume, tone), five-way selector, output jack, all on body.
- Two-pivot bridge/vibrato unit.
- * **SAS32EX** 2009 *As SAS32FM but wavy-line markers, regular top, two black-cover humbuckers.*
- * **SAS32EXFM** 2009 *As SAS32FM but wavy-line markers, two black-cover humbuckers.*

SAS36FM 2006–09
- Bound rosewood fingerboard, pearl dot markers; 22 frets.
- Flamed maple top.
- One black coverless humbucker (at bridge) and two black six-polepiece pickups.

- Two controls (volume, tone), five-way selector, output jack, all on body.
- Two-pivot bridge/vibrato unit.
- * **SAS36QM** 2010 *As SAS36FM but quilted maple top.*

SAS320X 2005
- Rosewood fingerboard, dot markers; 22 frets.
- Metallic finishes.
- Two black coverless humbuckers.
- Three controls (volume, tone, magnetic/piezo selector), five-way selector, mini-switch, two output jacks, all on body.
- Two-pivot bridge/vibrato unit with piezo pickup.

SF470 1992–94
- Rosewood fingerboard, dot markers; 22 frets.
- Various colours.
- Two black coverless humbuckers and one black six-polepiece pickup (in centre).
- Two controls (volume, tone), five-way selector, output jack, all on body.
- Six-saddle bridge and separate bar tailpiece.
- * **SV470** 1992–95 *As SF470 but some with 24 2/4 scale, two-pivot bridge/vibrato unit.*

430S 1990–91
- Rosewood fingerboard, dot markers; 22 frets.
- Various colours.
- Three six-polepiece pickups (bridge pickup angled).
- Two controls (volume, tone), five-way selector, output jack, all on body.
- Two-pivot bridge/vibrato unit.
- * **440S** 1991 *As 430S but h-s-s pickup layout.*
- * **450S** 1991 *As 430S but single-bar string-guide, locking nut, h-s-h pickup layout, two-pivot locking bridge/vibrato unit.*
- * **470S** *See S470.*
- * **470STR** 1992 *As 430S but h-s-h pickup layout, six-saddle bridge and separate bar tailpiece.*
- * **473S** 1992 *As 430S but h-s-h pickup layout, gold metalwork.*

540S *See Pro540 Saber and S540.*
540SC *See S540CT under S540.*
540SCT5 *See S540CT under S540.*
540SCT6 *See S540CT under S540.*

JOE SATRIANI
All have offset-double-cutaway body with wedge-shape cross-section.

JS1 1990–93
- Rosewood fingerboard, dot markers; 22 frets; single-bar string-guide, locking nut.
- White, black, or red finish.

- Two black coverless humbuckers (two black coverless humbuckers and one black six-polepiece pickup in centre from 1992).
- Two controls (volume, tone) and three-way selector (five-way from 1992) on body; side-mounted output jack.
- Two-pivot locking bridge/vibrato unit.
- * **JS2** 1990 *As JS1 but chrome finish; soon withdrawn.*
- * **JS3** 1990–93 *As JS1 (two humbuckers) but painted custom graphic finish by Donnie Hunt.*
- * **JS4 Electric Rainbow** 1992–93 *As JS1 (two humubuckers) but painted custom graphic finish by Joan Satriani.*
- * **JS5 Rain Forest** 1992–93 *As JS1 (two humubuckers) but painted custom graphic finish by Carol Satriani.*
- * **JS6** 1992–93 *As JS1 (two humbuckers) but no string guide or locking nut, six-saddle fixed bridge, natural finish.*

JS2K Crystal Planet 2000
- Rosewood fingerboard, dot markers; 22 frets; single-bar string-guide, locking nut.
- Luminous, see-through plastic body with chrome.
- Two see-through coverless humbuckers.
- Two controls (volume, tone) and three-way selector on body; side-mounted output jack, all in see-through mount.
- Two-pivot locking bridge/vibrato unit.

JS10th 1998
- Rosewood fingerboard, dot markers; 22 frets; single-bar string-guide, locking nut.
- Chrome finish.
- Two black coverless humbuckers.
- Two controls (volume, tone) and three-way selector on body; side-mounted output jack.
- Two-pivot locking bridge/vibrato unit.

JS100 1994–current
- Rosewood fingerboard, dot markers; 22 frets, "Joe Satriani" inlay at 21st; single-bar string-guide, locking nut.
- Various colours.
- Two black coverless humbuckers.
- Two controls (volume, tone) and three-way selector on body; side-mounted output jack.
- Two-pivot locking bridge/vibrato unit.
- * **JS600** 1994 *As JS100 but no string guide or locking nut, six-saddle fixed bridge.*
- * **JS700** 1996–98 *As JS100 but no locking nut, two black soapbar pickups, six-saddle fixed bridge.*

JS1000 1994–96, 1998–current.
- Rosewood fingerboard, dot markers; 22 frets, "Joe Satriani" inlay at 21st (until 1996);

single-bar string-guide, locking nut.
- Various colours.
- Two black coverless humbuckers.
- Two controls (volume, tone) and three-way selector on body; side-mounted output jack.
- Two-pivot locking bridge/vibrato unit.
- * **JS1200** 2004–current *As JS1000 but red only.*
- * **JS1600** 2008–10 *As JS1000 but no locking nut, six-saddle fixed bridge.*
- * **JS2000** 2002–04 *As JS1000 but six-saddle fixed fine-tuning bridge.*
- * **JS6000** 1994–95 *As JS1000 but no locking nut, six-saddle fixed bridge, natural or red finish.*

JS2400 2010–current
- Rosewood fingerboard, dot markers; 24 frets, single-bar string-guide, locking nut.
- White finish.
- One white humbucker (at bridge) and one white blade pickup (at neck).
- Two controls (volume, tone) and three-way selector on body; side-mounted output jack.
- Two-pivot locking bridge/vibrato unit.

SC
1997–03
S Classic models, based on S style but with thicker body, top-mount controls, three-tuners-each side headstock.

STAGEMASTER
See **ARTIST & PRO**.

PAUL STANLEY
See **ICEMAN & PAUL STANLEY**.

JOHN SCOFIELD
2001–current
JSM signature model, based on AS200, with side-mounted output jack and "castle" headstock.

STUDIO
1978–82
ST models, set-neck takes on Musician (MC) design, some with complex electronics, and includes two double-necks.

SZ
2003–current
SC-derived models with through-body stringing.

T
Both models have single-cutaway T body profile, with R-like wedge-shape cross-section.

580B Ballback 1988
- Rosewood fingerboard, dot markers; 22 frets; single-bar string-guide; locking nut.
- Black or natural.
- Two black coverless humbuckers.
- Two controls (volume, tone) and three-way selector on body; side-mounted output jack.
- White pickguard.
- Two-pivot locking bridge/vibrato unit
- *580T Turbot* 1988 *As 580 Ballback but pink or green finish, no pickguard.*

TALMAN
1994–98
TC and TV retro models with offset body shape.

MICK THOMSON
2006–current
MTM signature models: RG-derived MTM1 and pointy 10 and 100.

ANDY TIMMONS
1999–current
AT signature models, based on RT style.

SAM TOTMAN
See **ICEMAN / PAUL STANLEY**.

UCEW, UCGR, UCMD
See **USA CUSTOM**.

UNIVERSE
To avoid repetition, we've considered a few features as common to all Universe models, and so these are not shown in every entry. Unless stated otherwise, you can always assume the following:

* Twenty-four frets.
* Single-bar string-guide and locking nut.
* Solid offset-double-cutaway body.

UV7BK 1990–96
- Seven-string; rosewood fingerboard; green dot inlay.
- Black.
- Two green coverless humbuckers and one green six-polepiece pickup (in centre).
- Two green controls (volume, tone) and green five-way selector, all on pickguard; side-mounted output jack.
- Black pickguard.
- Two-pivot locking bridge/vibrato unit with cavity.
- *UV7PWH* 1990–93 *As UV7BK but white pyramid inlay, white finish, white pickguard, white pickups and controls.*
- *UV7SBK* 1997 *As UV7BK but white dot inlay, black pickups and controls.*
- *UV77MC* 1990–93 *As UV7BK but coloured pyramid inlay, multicolour swirl finish, see-through pickguard.*
- *UV77RE* 2010 *As UV7BK but 20th anniversary model, coloured pyramid inlay, multicolour swirl finish, see-through pickguard, serial number on fingerboard below 24th fret, limited edition of 100.*
- *UV777GR* 1991–93 *As UV7BK but maple fingerboard, coloured pyramid inlay, green finish, green and yellow pickups, yellow controls, pink five-way.*
- *UV777PBK* 1998–current *As UV7BK but white pyramid inlay, metal pickguard, pyramid inlay on bound black body, black pickups and controls.*

USA CUSTOM
1990–96
Graphic (UCGR) or Metal (UCMD) models, Exotic Wood (UCEW) models, MA (American Master) models, and USRG models, largely made in USA.

USRG
See **USA CUSTOM**.

VOYAGER
See **REB BEACH**.

X
1983–current
Broad series name for various lines of mostly pointy and extreme-pointy models, including Iceman, Destroyer, Rocket Roll, and the more recent Arondite and Xiphos.

SERIAL NUMBERS
You will usually find a serial number on an Ibanez electric in one or sometimes two of the following locations: on the rear of the headstock; on the neck-plate (the small plate on the rear of the body that anchors the screws which join the body to the neck); on the label inside a hollowbody guitar.

An Ibanez serial number can come in one of several forms, but often if offers a relatively simple way to date a particular guitar. Frequently, the first digits of the serial number are all you need to provide the year of production. For many guitars, you should just ignore any initial letters and look at the first two digits in the number. If you're lucky, these indicate the last two digits of the year in which the instrument was produced.

For example: **C08XXXXXX** – ignore the initial C, and 08 indicates 2008.

(Please note that in all the examples we've shown here, an X means any irrelevant digit. So in that first example, the six Xs show that a serial number in this form has six more digits after the C08.)

Another simple possibility is that only the first digit of a serial number provides the year.

For example: **F6XXXXX** – ignore the initial F, and 6 indicates 1996.

However, you'll notice from those two examples that you'll need to have an idea of the general period in which your guitar was made in order to pinpoint the year.

What follows overleaf, therefore, is detailed information about specific systems used at different times and in different production locations. This is designed to help you narrow

things down when you have little or no idea about the general period in which your guitar was made.

First, you need to check the guitar's country of origin, which is marked somewhere on virtually all Ibanez guitars – usually near the serial number on the rear of the headstock, on the neck-plate, or on the label.

Once you've found that, go to the relevant country in the lists that follow on the next pages, and there you'll see further information that should help you date your guitar.

However, as with any system of this kind, please be aware that a serial-number interpretation does not necessarily guarantee that a particular instrument was made in a particular year. (The abbreviation "c." before a date stands for circa, which means "about".)

See information for China, Indonesia, Japan, Korea, and USA overleaf.

CHINA

Ibanez electrics made in China (1999–current) usually have a serial number with an initial (prefix) letter or letters A, GS, J, S, SS, or Z. Some have no letter prefix.

No prefix c.2005–current
Some recent Chinese-made Ibanez electrics have a nine-digit serial number with no prefix letter or letters. There is no obvious dating significance in these numbers.

A + eight digits c.2005–current
First two digits are last two digits of year.
For example: A06XXXXX indicates 2006.

GS + nine digits 2007–current
First two digits are last two digits of year; third and fourth digits are month code (01 = January to 12 = December).
For example: GS1203XXXXX indicates March 2012.

J + nine digits 2004–12
First two digits are last two digits of year; third and fourth digits are month code (01 = January to 12 = December).
For example: J1010XXXXX indicates October 2010.

S + eight digits 2002–current
First two digits are last two digits of year; third and fourth digits are month code (01 = January to 12 = December).

For example: S0402XXXX indicates February 2004.

SS + eight digits c.2010–current
First two digits are last two digits of year; third and fourth digits are month code (01 = January to 12 = December).
For example: SS1105XXXX indicates May 2011.

Z + six digits 1999–2006
ZX, ZY, ZZ + five digits 1999–2006
The first character after the initial Z is a month code, from January (1) to September (9), or October (X), November (Y), or December (Z). The next digit is the last digit of the year.
For example: Z35XXXX indicates March 2005; ZX0XXXX indicates October 2000.

INDONESIA

Ibanez electrics made in Indonesia (c.2001–current) usually have a serial number with an initial (prefix) letter or letters I or PR, and some have a final (suffix) letter as well as a prefix letter.
A or B suffix 2010–2011
Final letter is year code (A=2010; B=2011); first letter has no significance.
For example: LXXXXB indicates 2011.

C suffix 2012–current
Final letter is year code (C = 2012); first letter is

month code (A = January to L = December). Presumably this will continue beyond 2012, with D = 2013 etc.
For example: HXXXXC indicates August 2012.

I + seven digits c.2007–2009
First digit is last digit of year; third and fourth digits are month code (01 = January to 12 = December).
For example: I711XXXX indicates November 2007.

I + nine digits c.2001–current
First two digits are last two digits of year; third

and fourth digits are month code (01 = January to 12 = December).
For example: I0410XXXXX indicates October 2004.

PR + nine digits 2004–07
First two digits are last two digits of year; third and fourth digits are month code (01 = January to 12 = December).
For example: PR0503XXXXX indicates March 2005.

JAPAN

Ibanez electrics made in Japan (50s–current) at first had no serial number. Starting in late 1975 they usually have a serial number with an initial (prefix) letter. Some confusion is possible between two different systems, the first of which uses an initial letter from A to L as a month code, and the second of which always has an initial F, without relevance to the month. See the following for more information.

A, B, C, D, E, F, G, H, I, J, K, or L + five digits 1997–current
Prefix letter is month code (A = January to L = December); first two digits are last two digits of year.
For example: D07XXX indicates April 2007.

A, B, C, D, E, F, G, H, I, J, K, or L + six digits 1975–1986
Prefix letter is month code (A = January to L =

December); first two digits are last two digits of year. (Also see alternative entries below for prefix letters F, I, T, from 1987.)
For example: B83XXXX indicates February 1983.
F + six digits 1987–1996
First digit is last digit of year. Ibanez records suggest that last five digits indicate month (00001–03600 January; 03601–07200 February; 07201–10800 March; 10801–14400 April; 14401–18000 May; 18001–21600 June; 21601–25200 July; 25201–28800 August; 28801–32400 September; 32401–36000 October; 36001–39600 November; 39601–43200 December).
For example: F707231 indicates March 1987.

F + seven digits 1997–current
First two digits are last two digits of year.
For example: F09XXXXX indicates 2009.

I + six digits 1988–1989
First digit is last digit of year.

For example: I8XXXXX indicates 1988.

I + six digits 1990–current
First two digits are last two digits of year.
For example: I10XXXX indicates 2010.

T + six digits 1988–1997
First digit is last digit of year.
For example: T4XXXXX indicates 1994.

T + six digits 1998–current
First two digits are last two digits of year.
For example: T09XXXX indicates 2009.

* Many **Japanese-made George Benson GB models** have an individual four-digit number on the label, with no obvious dating significance, in addition to a regular serial number on the rear of the headstock.
* **Japanese-made Steve Vai JEM models** usually have a no-prefix six-digit serial number on the neck-plate, where the first two digits are the

last two digits of the year. *For example*: 88XXXX indicates 1988.

* Japanese-made Joe Satriani JS models usually have a no-prefix six-digit serial number on the neck-plate. This is a sequential number with no obvious dating significance. Some later JS models also have a regular serial number on the rear of the headstock.

* Some **J-Custom guitars** have "J-Custom / Reg

1,479,480 / Crafted with Advanced Technology" on front of headstock, with a regular F-prefix serial number on rear. Others have "Masterfully crafted for unparalleled sound, maximum playability and exquisite beauty" on rear of headstock, above a five-digit serial with no obvious dating significance, and "Made In Japan". Others have a "Timeless Timber / Created by Fujigen" logo to left of serial.

* Some **Japanese-made Pat Metheny PM models** have an F-prefix five-digit serial number, where the first two digits are the last two digits of the year. *For example*: F97XXX indicates 1997.

* Special or limited-edition instruments sometimes have individual sequenced numbers, usually with no obvious dating significance, or no serial number.

KOREA

Ibanez electrics made in Indonesia (1987–2008) usually have a serial number with an initial (prefix) letter or letters C, CP, KR, P, S, or W. Some have no letter prefix.

No prefix c.1988–2008
Some Korean-made Ibanez electrics, from the period noted, have a seven or eight-digit serial number with no prefix letter. These appear to follow the familiar rules where the first digit is the last digit of the year or the first two digits are the last two digits of the year.
For example: 89XXXXX indicates 1989; 02XXXXXX indicates 2002; 7XXXXXX indicates 2007.

C + six digits c.1990–95
First digit is last digit of year.
For example: C4XXXXX indicates 1994.

C + seven digits c.1995–99
First digit is last digit of year; second and third digits are month code (01 = January to 12 = December).
For example: C609XXXX indicates September 1996.

C + eight digits c.2000–08
First two digits are last two digits of year; third and fourth digits are month code (01 = January to 12 = December).
For example: C0803XXXX indicates March 2008.

CP + eight digits c.2004–08
First two digits are last two digits of year; third and fourth digits are month code (01 = January to 12 = December).
For example: CP0605XXXX indicates May 2006.

KR + nine digits 2004–06
First two digits are last two digits of year; third

and fourth digits are month code (01 = January to 12 = December).
For example: KR0602XXXXX indicates February 2006.

P prefix 1987–88
Some EX models have this prefix, and the numbers have no obvious dating significance.

S + seven digits c.1990–95
First digit is last digit of year.
For example: S4XXXXXX indicates 1994.

W + six digits c. 1999–2008
WX, WY, WZ + five digits c.1999–2007
The first character after the W is a month code, from January (1) to September (9), or October (X), November (Y), or December (Z). The next digit is the last digit of the year.
For example: W70XXXX indicates July 2000; WY4XXXX indicates November 2004.

USA

* Ibanez electrics with a US address on the neck-plate used Japanese parts for US assembly: a Bensalem address indicates a guitar made before 1991 (starting around 1988); a North Hollywood address indicates 1990 and after, up to about 1992. Sometimes there are serial numbers on these plates, which give the regular date clue,

with the first two digits indicating the last two of the relevant year, or with the *last two* digits of the serial number indicating the last two of the relevant year. Often, these guitars have a regular six-digit Japanese F serial number on the headstock, with the first digit indicating the last digit of the relevant year.
* Some guitars were largely made in the USA. These USA Custom guitars were the American

Master (c.1990–91), Exotic Wood (c.1991–93), and USRG (1993–96) models. They may have "Made in USA" of "U.S.A. Custom" somewhere on the instrument. Some have serial numbers: we've seen an H, LA, or M prefix with six digits on American Master models, and five-digit serials on Exotic Wood models.

INDEX

A page number in italic type indicates an illustration. A page number in the range 130–153 indicates an entry in the Reference Listing.

ACKNOWLEDGEMENTS

INSTRUMENT PICTURES
OWNERS KEY
The guitars photographed came from the collections of the following individuals and organisations, and we are most grateful for their help. The owners are listed here in the alphabetical order of the code that is used to identify their instruments in the Instruments Key below. **CH** Christie's. **DD** Doug Doppler. **GB** Guitar & Bass. **HA** Heritage Auctions. **HG** Hoshino Gakki Co Ltd & Hoshino USA Inc. **KN** Kosaku Nakamura. **MW** Michael Wright. **OW** Olaf Windgassen. **PD** Paul Day. **TB** Tony Bacon.

INSTRUMENTS KEY
This key identifies who owned which guitars at the time they were photographed. After the relevant **bold-type** page number(s) there is a model identifier, followed by the owner's initials (see the alphabetical list in the Owners Key above). **14–15** 2103, PD. **15** Salvador Ibáñez, CH. **18** 2370, HA. **18–19** 2350, KN. **22** 2377, DD. **22–23** 2387, KN. **26–27** 2402, HA. **27** 2348, MW. **30–31** All three, DD. **34–35** 2351, KN; 2351M, MW. **38** Artist 2662, DD. **38–39** 2405 Agent, KN; Artist 2613, KN. **39** 2408 Orient, DD. **42–43** Iceman IC210, PD; PS10 Stanley, HA. **46–47** Twin 2670, OW; GB10 Benson, TB. **50–51** All three, OW. **54–55** Performer PF400, OW. **55** Artist 2617, KN. **58** Studio ST3000, OW. **58–59** Musician MC500, OW. **59** Studio ST1200, HA. **62–63** Roadster RS100, MW. **63** Both, OW. **66–67** Both, OW. **67** Rocket Roll II RR400, OW. **70–71** Pro Line PL2550, OW. **71** XV500, MW. **74–75** S540, MW; Maxxas MX3, PD. **75** GB30 Benson, HG. **78–79** Roadster RR, MW. **79** RS1010 Lukather, HG; VM1 Moore, KN. **86–87** JEM777LG, HG. **90** Roadstar II RG420, MW. **90–91** RG550, HG. **91** JEM777VDY HG. **94–95** Both, KN. **95** RG760, HG. **98** Metal Leopard, OW. **98–99** Trick Or Treat, KN. **99** All three bodies, KN; EX140, HG. **102** Exotic Wood, HG. **102–103** Both, HG. **106–107** Both, KN. **110–111** JS2, HG. **111** All three, HG. **114** Iceman ICJ100, KN. **114–115** Both, HG. **115** PM100 Metheny, HG. **118–119** Talman TC530, GB; Apex100 Munky HG. **119** GRX150, HG. **122** RGA8, HG; JEM20TH, KN. **122–123** Artcore AF125, GB. **123** FRM1 Gilbert, KN. **126–127** Both, HG. **127** Roadcore RC320, HG.

Guitar photography was by Robert Acocella (DIGImmortal Photo), Garth Blore, Sam Crayne, Miki Slingsby, Mirko Waltermann (Waltermann-Fotografie), and Michael Wright.

ARTIST PICTURES
Images are identified by bold-type page number, subject, and photographer and/or collection and agency. **2–3** Vai, Frans Schellekens/Redferns/Getty. **31** Van Halen, Fin Costello/Redferns/Getty. **43** Stanley, Richard E Aaron/Redferns/Getty. **54** Partridge, Michael Putland/Hulton Archive/Getty. **62** Abba, Denis O'Regan/Hulton Archive/Getty.

MEMORABILIA
Other items illustrated in this book – including advertisements, brochures, catalogues, and photographs (in fact anything that isn't a guitar or an artist shot) – are from the collections of Tony Bacon, Mace Bailey, Balafon Image Bank, Rainer Daeschler, Paul Day, Hoshino Gakki Co Ltd, Hoshino USA Inc, Dave Humphreys, *Japan Music Trades*, Rich Lasner, Roy Miyahara, *The Music Trades*, Nick Sugimoto, Maurice Summerfield, U.S. Patent Office, Vintage Vault Fine Guitars, and vintaxe.com.

INTERVIEWS
Original interviews for this book were conducted by Tony Bacon as follows: Mace Bailey (January 2013); George Benson (October 2012); Ronald Bienstock (December 2012); Jim Donahue (October 2012); Elwood Francis (January 2013); Jeff Hasselberger (October 2012); Fritz Katoh (November 2012); Chris Kelly (January 2013); Rich Lasner (October 2012, January 2013); Al Marinaro (January 2013); Roy Miyahara (May 2012); Andy Partridge (December 2012); Bill Reim (July 2012); Harry Rosenbloom (July 2012); Joe Satriani (May 2012, October 2012); Nick Sugimoto (October 2102, November 2012); Maurice Summerfield (May 2012); Nick Suyama (October 2012); Tom Tanaka (June 2012); Mick Thomson (December 2012); Steve Vai (June 2012).

THANKS
For help above-and-beyond: Paul Day, Jim Donahue, Jeff Hasselberger, Fritz Katoh, Rich Lasner, Roy Miyahara, Bill Reim, Nick Sugimoto, Maurice Summerfield, Mick Suyama, Tom Tanaka, and Michael Wright. **In addition** to those already named in these acknowledgements, I'd also like to thank: Tony Arambarri (NAMM); Mace Bailey; Ronald Bienstock;

Bruce Bolen; Julie Bowie; Mick Brigden; Steve Brown (Vintaxe.com); Dave Bunker (Bunker Guitars); Walter Carter (Carter Vintage Guitars); Gary Cooper; Jamie Dickson (*Guitarist*); Doug Doppler; Orval Engling; Jim Fisher; Stephanie Gonzalez (Apropos Management); Alan Greenwood (*Vintage Guitar Magazine*); Mike Gutierrez (Heritage Auctions); Joel Hoffner (Vector Management); Tak Hosono (Hoshino USA Inc); David Humphreys; Blair Jackson; Kerry Keane (Christie's); Chris Kelly (Peavey Electronics); Masako Koyama (*Japan Music Trades*); Rob Laing (*Total Guitar*); Al Marinaro; Joe Marinic (Shadow Electronics); Reinhold Meinl; John Morrish; Kosaku Nakumura; Hasy Neuenschwander; Hiroyuki Noguchi (Rittor Music); Hannes Oelfke; Paul Oldfield (Headstock Distribution); Kevin Parsons; Phil (Vintage Vault Fine Guitars); Oliver Pfaender; Heinz Rebellius; Thierry Reynaud; John Reynolds; Harry Rosenbloom; Hugo Ryan (Hoshino USA Inc); Chuck Schneider; Thomas Jerome Seabrook; Diony Sepulveda (5B Artist Management); Achim Sommer; Mike Taft (Hoshino USA Inc); Kazuma Tanabe (Fujigen Gakki); Mick Taylor (*Guitarist*); Rob Terstall (Meinl); Katie Wheeler (NAMM); Olaf Windgassen.

BOOKS

Tony Bacon *Flying V, Explorer, Firebird* (Backbeat 2011); *The Les Paul Guitar Book* (Backbeat 2009); *Squier Electrics* (Backbeat 2012); *The Ultimate Guitar Book* (Dorling Kindersley 1991).
Tony Bacon (ed) *Echo & Twang* (Backbeat 2001); *Electric Guitars: The Illustrated Encyclopedia* (Balafon 2000); *Fuzz & Feedback* (Backbeat 2000).
Bizarre Guitars (Rittor 1993).
Walter Carter *The Gibson Electric Guitar Book* (Backbeat 2007); *Gruhn's Guide To Vintage Guitars* (Backbeat 2010).
Gitarre & Bass Special *Ibanez: Instrumente Musiker Geschichte Kult* (MM Musik-Media-Verlag 2009)
The Guitars Friend (Quick Fox 1977).
Paul Specht with Michael Wright & Jim Donahue *Ibanez: The Untold Story* (Hoshino USA 2005).
René Vannes *Dictionnaire Universel Des Luthiers* (Les Amis de la Musique 1988).
Michael Wright *Guitar Stories Volume One* (Vintage Guitar 1995).

WEBSITES

arnesibanez.com; ibanez.co.jp; ibanez.com; ibanezcollectors.com; ibanezmc.com; ibanezrules.com; ibanezwiki.com; ibanez.wikia.com; jemsite.com; kosakuworld.com; mr-ibanez.com; noahjames.com; vintageibanez.tripod.com; vintage-ibanez-museum.de; vintaxe.com.

TRADEMARKS

Throughout this book we have mentioned a number of registered trademark names. Rather than put a trademark or registered symbol next to every occurrence of a trademarked name, we state here that we are using the names only in an editorial fashion and that we do not intend to infringe any trademarks.

UPDATES?

The author and publisher welcome any new information for future editions. Write to: Ibanez, Backbeat & Jawbone, 2A Union Court, 20–22 Union Road, London SW4 6JP, England. Or you can email: ibanez@jawbonepress.com.

"We need more tools, we need newer tools, we need updated tools. Some days we may want to go back, to reflect on the older tools. But eventually we have to use the modern ones." Joe Satriani, 2012